ALSO BY DENIS DONOGHUE

The Third Voice (1959)

Connoisseurs of Chaos (1965)

The Ordinary Universe (1968)

Jonathan Swift (1969)

Emily Dickinson (1969)

Yeats (1971)

Thieves of Fire (1973)

The Sovereign Ghost (1976)

Ferocious Alphabets (1981)

The Arts Without Mystery (1984)

(EDITOR)

(*with J. R. Mulryne*) An Honoured Guest: New
Essays on W. B. Yeats (1965)

Swift Revisited (1968)

Jonathan Swift: A Critical Anthology (1971)

Memoirs: by W. B. Yeats (1973)

Selected Essays of R. P. Blackmur (1986)

WE IRISH

WE IRISH

Essays on Irish Literature and Society

DENIS DONOGHUE

University of California Press
Berkeley • Los Angeles • London

For Frances

University of California Press
Berkeley and Los Angeles
University of California Press, Ltd.
London, England

Copyright © 1986 by Denis Donoghue

Owing to limitations of space, acknowledgments for
permission to reprint previously published material
can be found on page 276.

Library of Congress Cataloging-in-Publication Data
Donoghue, Denis. We Irish.
1. English literature -- Irish authors -- History and criticism. 2. English
literature -- 20th century -- History and criticism. 3. Ireland in literature.
4. Ireland -- Intellectual life -- 20th century. I. Title.
{PR8754.D66 1988}   820'.9'89162   88-20477
ISBN 0-520-06425-9

Manufactured in the United States of America
First California Paperback Printing 1988

Composed by Superior Type, Champaign, Illinois.
Printed and bound by
The Maple-Vail Book Manufacturing Group, Binghamton, New York.
Typography and binding design by Tasha Hall.

CONTENTS

THREE: *CONTEXTS*

FOUR: *OCCASIONS*

INTRODUCTION

Most of these essays and reviews have been published in Irish, English, and American periodicals over the past several years. Some of them were written as chapters of books. A few of them started as lectures or broadcast talks. Three items are published for the first time: these are "Yeats, Ancestral Houses, and Anglo-Ireland," "Bakhtin and *Finnegans Wake*," and "Maud Gonne."

I have excluded essays on some political issues which have been resolved by time. There seemed little merit in bringing forward an essay on Long Kesh and the Hunger-Strikes, which appeared in *The New York Review of Books* in October 1981; the issues raised by that event were immediate and intense, but it would be tendentious to bring them up again. For a different reason, I have excluded a more general essay on the political situation in Northern Ireland, which I published in *The Atlantic* in May 1972. Not that the situation has greatly changed in the meantime, despite the Anglo-Irish Agreement (1985). The constitutional position of the North remains as it was: the British Government is still committed to "the Unionist guarantee"—that Northern Ireland will remain part of the United Kingdom unless and until a majority of the people in the North want a change. Indeed, the only change I can detect is that the Dublin Government under Dr. Fitzgerald seems to have accepted in practise, though not in principle, that Partition is a permanent feature of life in Ireland. His Government still acknowledges the Constitution of 1937 and the aspiration it expresses toward the unity of Ireland, but the acknowledgement is silently made. Discussion between the Irish and the British Governments is predicated upon the indefinite continuance of Northern Ireland as part of the U.K. Dr. Fitzgerald wants to improve the conditions of daily life in the North, and to remove or mitigate the features of government which are most persistently resented by Northern nationalists, but he has given up even the appearance of working toward the unity of Ireland as described in the *Report of the New Ireland Forum.* In effect, his policy is the one long and insistently advocated by his former colleague in government, Dr. Conor Cruise O'Brien: to abandon, in practise, the traditional demand for an united Ireland.

The political essays I have published from time to time in *The Atlantic, The Listener,* and other periodicals don't seem to me any more naive than essays by other people on these subjects; but I find it hard to maintain an appropriate voice when political issues are in question. In retrospect, my few political interventions now strike me as respectable, but erratic in tone. But in any case my concern is with literature. I don't disavow an occasional inclination to set statesmen right; their being so regularly wrong is a sufficient excuse. Professionally, I am concerned with politics only when it invades literature and prescribes the gross conditions under which poems, plays, stories, and novels are written. The fact that the same conditions impede the general work of intelligence hardly needs to be emphasised.

I have also excluded a few essays—on Swift and Goldsmith, for instance—which would only confound the issue implicit in the title of the book, and disturb such unity of theme as the essays have.

The periodicals in which many of these essays and reviews appeared include *The Times Literary Supplement, The London Review of Books, The New York Review of Books, The New York Times Book Review, The New Republic, The New Review, Sewanee Review, Magill, Hibernia, The Spectator,* and *The Listener.* The readers of these periodicals are, I suppose, more diverse than any description of them would suggest. The common reader, the educated public, the professional reader: these phrases imply a certain range of interests and sentiments, easy enough to assume in practise but difficult to specify. The ideal reader I envisage is one who moves with winning flexibility between these categories without committing himself to any of them.

I have not brought any of the material "up to date," but I have changed the phrasing, here and there, out of respect for decent observances in the matter of style. An adjective which seemed acceptably spirited at the time may look brash a few years later: reasons for retaining it are quickly set aside by the urge to get rid of it. But I don't think I've altered the pieces to an unacceptable extent. Some excisions have been made in the cause of removing repetitions; but I am aware that minor instances of repetition have had to be retained.

WE IRISH

WE IRISH

"We Irish, born into that ancient sect"—a line from Yeats's "The Statues," a poem he started in April and finished in June 1938, seven months before his death. The poetry he wrote during those months was nearly as strident as the prose of *On the Boiler,* exorbitant even to the situation that provoked it. Rage kept him going when reasonableness would have brought him down. But the argument of "The Statues" is outlandish even by Yeats's standards. *On the Boiler* gives it in ostensibly high-minded prose. "There are moments," he wrote, "when I am certain that art must once again accept those Greek proportions which carry into plastic art the Pythagorean numbers, those faces which are divine because all there is empty and measured. Europe was not born when Greek galleys defeated the Persian hordes at Salamis; but when the Doric studios sent out those broad-backed marble statues against the multiform, vague, expressive Asiatic sea, they gave to the sexual instinct of Europe its goal, its fixed type."[1]

No historian of art has commented on this notion, so far as I am aware. In a comparable passage in the revised version of *A Vision,* Yeats refers to Furtwaengler, presumably to his *Masterpieces of Greek Sculpture,* a book which doesn't seem to me to yield a Yeatsian conclusion. There are other passages in Yeats's prose which make it clear that he was thinking of various matters which he brought together for no objective reason but presumably for a subjective one that appeased him. These matters included Maud Gonne's beauty as the decisively European type, Pythagoras' doctrine of numbers which made possible the Greek sculpture of the fifth century B.C., the work of Phidias in which Ionic and Doric modes were supposedly united, and the analogy of sculpture and the exertion of power.

The specific argument of "The Statues" is that it was not mere banks of oars but Greek intellect, under Pythagorean auspices and reaching fulfilment in a Phidian conception of form, that defeated the Persians at Salamis. What the Greeks "put down"—the verb is significant, in view of Yeats's sentiments on the theme of race and stock—was the mess of formlessness, "All Asiatic vague immensities." In Greek sculpture, intellect deduced not from nature but from its sense of itself the formal perfection which has given to the sexual instinct of Europe its fixed type.

It is clear from *On the Boiler* that Yeats associated the vague immensities and the "many-headed foam at Salamis" with the vulgarity of the democratic spirit. In the same passage from which I've quoted some sentences, he referred to the "flesh-tints that Greek painters loved as have all the greatest since," and said that "nowhere upon any beautiful body, whether of man or woman" did Greek painters allow "those red patches whereby our democratic painters prove that they have really studied from the life."[2]

The moral of Yeats's story is clear:

> *We Irish, born into that ancient sect*
> *But thrown upon this filthy modern tide*
> *And by its formless, spawning, fury wrecked,*
> *Climb to our proper dark, that we may trace*
> *The lineaments of a plummet-measured face.*

Filthy, formless, spawning: only a democratic society provokes Yeats to such terms. "Since about 1900," he said in another passage from *On the Boiler*, "the better stocks have not been replacing their numbers, while the stupider and less healthy have been more than replacing theirs."[3] "Climb to our proper dark": the mood is imperative rather than indicative. The dark proper to Irishmen is that of subjective or antithetic consciousness, Parnell's as a fine example: we are to climb, as by a winding stair, to the lonely tower of symbolic vision. "Lineaments" is Blake's word, we are to trace in the Yeatsian sense of divining or construing, and the plummet-measured face is Phidian.

What precisely we Irish are exhorted to do is not clear. We are not to do what the English do, who are positivist, scientist, pragmatic in everything, dreary products of the Industrial Revolution, the spinning jenny their emblem. We are to imagine a nation presided over by Oisin and not by St. Patrick; Celtic paganism expressing itself in nature-poetry; the spiritual union of Gaelic Ireland and Anglo-Ireland. We are presumably to live in the spirit of Kevin O'Higgins and undo the disaster of his murder. What else? Nearly any social organization, so long as it is not democratic: government by those few who are best capable of governing. Not necessarily a dictatorship: it could be an oligarchy, finding its type and form in the idea of a military class, the kinship of a few great families. Beyond that, there is no knowing what Yeats wanted or how close he was willing to come to the rough stuff. Very close, according to Conor Cruise O'Brien; but he reads the evidence literally and can't imagine what it would mean for a poet near the end of his tether to recite such promises and threats.

But my theme is the phrase "We Irish." Just as bizarre as the argument of "The Statues" is Yeats's notion that to be Irish was indeed to share a special mentality. In several contexts he asserted that while English thought in the eighteenth century was given over to mechanism, to Locke and Hobbes and the positivism they sponsored, Irish thought—from about 1690—was in every respect the reverse. To arrive at such an idea, Yeats had to regard Molyneux, Archbishop King, Berkeley, Swift, Burke, Goldsmith, and Grattan as defining, each of them, a particular type of consciousness. The intellectual problem of bringing these figures together in a single image didn't perturb him. It was enough that they were born in Ireland and therefore members of that ancient sect.

On November 30, 1925, in a lecture to the Irish Literary Society, Yeats was more specific in separating Irish from English mentality:

In Gaelic literature we have something that the English-speaking countries have never possessed—a great folk literature. We have in Berkeley and in Burke a philosophy on which it is possible to base the whole life of a nation. That, too, is something which England, great as she is in modern scientific thought and every kind of literature, has not, I think. The modern Irish intellect was born more than two hundred years ago when Berkeley defined in three or four sentences the mechanical philosophy of Newton, Locke and Hobbes, the philosophy of England in his day, and I think of England up to our day, and wrote after each: "We Irish do not hold with this," or some like sentence.[4]

Berkeley proved, to Yeats's satisfaction, "that the world was a vision," Burke "that the State was a tree, no mechanism to be pulled in pieces and put up again, but an oak tree that had grown through centuries."

In his Introduction to J. M. Hone and M. M. Rossi's *Bishop Berkeley* (1931), Yeats returned to the same assertions, and added a further consideration, the conflict between Irish mentality and English conditions. "Born in such a community"—that is, a community where solitaries flourish—"Berkeley with his belief in perception, that abstract ideas are mere words, Swift with his love of perfect nature, of the Houyhnhnms, his disbelief in Newton's system and every sort of machine, Goldsmith and his delight in the particulars of common life that shocked his contemporaries, Burke with his conviction that all States not grown slowly like a forest tree are tyrannies, found in England the opposite that stung their own thought into expression and made it lucid."[5] In his Diary for 1930, Yeats said that Berkeley's comment—"We Irish do not hold with this"—was "the birth of the national intellect and it caused the defeat in Berkeley's philosophical secret society of English materialism, the Irish Salamis."[6]

Berkeley's secret society was merely a debating society he revived at Trinity College, Dublin, where he brought together a number of like-minded friends who were willing to be persuaded that Locke, great philosopher as he was allowed to be, bewildered himself with abstract ideas. But it is clear that Berkeley, like Yeats, believed in something called the Irish intellect. The source of the "We Irish" sentence is Berkeley's journal, which remained unpublished till 1871:

There are men who say there are insensible extensions. There are others who say the wall is not white, the fire is not hot, etc. We Irishmen cannot attain to these truths.

The mathematicians think there are insensible lines. About these they harangue—these cut in a point at all angles—these are divisible ad infinitum. We Irishmen can conceive no such lines.

The mathematicians talk of what they call a point. This, they say, is not altogether nothing, nor is it downright something. Now we Irishmen are apt to think something & nothing are next neighbours.[7]

Hone and Rossi drew attention to these remarks in their book on Berkeley, and asked the natural question: what on earth could he have meant? I quote the answer they propose, since it is the one that Yeats resorted to:

> Now so far as can be ascertained, Berkeley himself had no trace of pure Irish blood, and he belonged by association and religious sympathies to a comparatively recent English colonisation. Therefore, without getting any certain answer, we ask what he meant when he wrote, like Mr. Bernard Shaw two hundred years later, though with quite other instances, of "we Irish" as the fact-realising people *par excellence,* out of whom should come a genuine philosophy of common-sense? Did he think only of a tendency noted by him to exist in his own ambient, peopled chiefly by members of the later English (sixteenth and seventeenth century) influx into Ireland, who were separated from the mass of the old Irish people, as also in some degree from the old Anglo-Irish civilisation, by the great religious quarrel? Or was he supposing a sentiment of Irish nationality—over and above the religious difference—such a sentiment as is generally believed to have come into being only after Swift's publication of the *Drapier's Letters?*

To this, Hone and Rossi added an interesting footnote:

> But many of the old Anglo-Irish families conformed to Reformation principles, and consequently the eighteenth-century Protestant ascendancy was not purely English in race. A writer in the *Dial* (May 1927) declares: "The true roots of culture in Ireland (except for the real Gaelic in the west) are to be found after the Norman conquest. Writers like Berkeley, Swift and even Congreve were all moulded by a nationality which has only now political recognition."[8]

The writer in the *Dial* probably meant political recognition of such people as Yeats in Seanad Éireann. Of the two possibilities outlined by Hone and Rossi, the second seems the more plausible: that Berkeley is projecting as a characteristic of Irish intellect the resistance to English materialism he feels in himself.

For Yeats's purpose, it was enough. He could then associate Berkeley and Swift with Blake's rejection of the English thought of Bacon, Newton, and Locke—the denial of imagination for which Blake hated them—and

he could maintain the conflict into his own day by thinking of Bertrand
Russell as an English materialist and, to oppose him, of the spiritual or
idealist tradition in philosophy as variously propounded by Croce, Gentile,
McTaggart, and Whitehead. In his Introduction to the Hone and Rossi
book, he refers to "the Pure Act of Italian philosophy"—meaning Gentile—
and says:

> Only where the mind partakes of a pure activity can art or life attain
> swiftness, volume, unity; that contemplation lost we picture some
> slow-moving event, turn the mind's eye from everything else that
> we may experience to the full our own passivity, our personal
> tragedy.[9]

Indeed, Yeats thought of Pound and Joyce as failing by this criterion;
they represent "a new naturalism that leaves man helpless before the
contents of his own mind." Think of "Joyce's *Anna Livia Plurabelle,*
Pound's *Cantos,* works of an heroic sincerity, the man, his active faculties
in suspense, one finger beating time to a bell sounding and echoing in the
depths of his own mind."[10]

II

In the past few years, Yeats's dealings in the rhetoric of "We Irish"
have been much resented. Seamus Deane is not alone in arguing—I'm
thinking of his *Field Day* pamphlets and other essays—that the wretched
state of the North is at least partly due to the fact that its two communities have inherited stereotyped images of themselves which, subconsciously,
they live and die to resemble. These images, in turn, are based upon a
presumed spirit or essence which is to be identified with the very soul of
Ireland, the special privilege of being Irish. Yeats, according to Deane's
argument, did much to present the question of Irishness as a moral
criterion.

But there are several other considerations. Yeats did not invent the
interest with which writers have attended to the Celtic spirit or the Irish
intellect. Renan, Matthew Arnold, and several other writers preceded
him—leaving Berkeley entirely aside—in thinking the complex fate of
being Irish a matter of extreme concern. Nor did he bring it to an end:
think of Corkery, O'Faolain, and virtually every modern Irish writer.

Besides, the infatuation—if it is that—is not confined to the Irish. What it means to be a Jew is endlessly examined, even in the attenuated form of considering what it means to be Jewish. President Reagan's dealings with El Salvador and Nicaragua are not merely essays in foreign policy but responses to the tradition of self-consciousness by which America still sees itself as the "Redeemer Nation." When Mrs. Thatcher speaks "for Britain," we know what she means, and the ground of the claim she makes. It should also be pointed out that while Yeats was preoccupied with the destiny of Irishness, the particular description he gave of it could not be invoked by either of the communities in conflict in the North today. No one in the North thinks of himself as fulfilling the spiritual kinship of Gaelic Ireland, pre-Christian, pagan, inspired by Oisin rather than St. Patrick, and Anglo-Ireland in the tradition of Berkeley and Swift.

But even in philosophic terms, the question is not vain. If you say that essence precedes existence, you propose a quasi-historical relation which you are free to ignore or not. If you say that existence is predicated upon essence, you are proposing a logical rather than an historical relation. Either way, a mind does not show itself to be dizzy merely by assuming that the meaning of a particular historical existence issues from a situation which may be beyond the reach of historical scholarship. Nothing is gained, and only the satisfaction of ridicule is acquired, by scorning "essence" as an object of interest and concern. Anyone is free to pursue the object or not.

Indeed, I am not sure that Deane or anyone else could indicate the point at which an acceptable degree of self-consciousness can be distinguished from a vain "essentialism." The attempt to correlate essentialism with myth, and to urge that the sentiment that accommodates them should be rebuked by the more astringent sentiment that respects existence and history, is fruitless. It only requires a further degree of irony to drive the second sentiment after the first.

III

Seamus Heaney's recent poetry includes a nuanced version of the "We Irish" motif. The poem "Traditions," in *Wintering Out,* begins with rueful, quizzical reflection on the forces that make an Irishman assimilate his speech to the decencies of "the British Isles," which in effect give privilege to the received standard English of London and the South of England. By an easy concession, people in the North of Ireland are to be proud of their bits of Elizabethan English. The poem ends by reciting two literary episodes. In Act 3, Scene 2, of Shakespeare's *Henry V,* when Fluellen addresses Macmorris and refers to "many of your nation," Macmorris answers:

> Of my nation? What ish my nation? Ish a villain, and a basterd, and a knave, and a rascal. What ish my nation? Who talks of my nation?

In the "Cyclops" chapter of *Ulysses* (Gabler's text), Bloom gets into an argument with John Wyse and the Citizen about nationality:

> —Persecution, says he, all the history of the world is full of it. Perpetuating national hatred among nations.
> —But do you know what a nation means? says John Wyse.
> —Yes, says Bloom.
> —What is it? says John Wyse.
> —A nation? says Bloom. A nation is the same people living in the same place.
> —By God, then, says Ned, laughing, if that's so I'm a nation for I'm living in the same place for the past five years.
> So of course everyone had the laugh at Bloom and says he, trying to muck out of it:
> —Or also living in different places.
> —That covers my case, says Joe.
> —What is your nation if I may ask? says the citizen.
> —Ireland, says Bloom. I was born here. Ireland.
> The citizen said nothing only cleared the spit out of his gullet and, gob, he spat a Red bank oyster out of him right in the corner.

Heaney's poem produces both episodes:

> *MacMorris, gallivanting*
> *round the Globe, whinged*
> *to courtier and groundling*
> *who had heard tell of us*
>
> *as going very bare*
> *of learning, as wild hares,*

> *as anatomies of death:*
> *"What ish my nation?"*
>
> *And sensibly, though so much*
> *later, the wandering Bloom*
> *replied, "Ireland," said Bloom,*
> *"I was born here. Ireland."*

Maybe it is the sensible way: to be born here, and take the consequences, without whinging. But Heaney's poems, some of them in *North* especially, show that he has accepted that he has particular responsibilities as a poet of the North. He has evidently felt uneasy not about his feelings but about their not being the right ones, adequate to their occasion. In 1975, he said of poets who were expected to write of the North that "in the end they will only be worth listening to if they are saying something about and to themselves." Which applies to every poet, of course. "The truest poetry may be the most feigning," Heaney continued, "but there are contexts, and Northern Ireland is one of them, where to feign a passion is as reprehensible as to feign its absence."[11] But surely it shouldn't be necessary to feign a passion about the North: if you don't feel it, well and good, let it go, write something else.

Heaney has indeed written many other poems, but he has not dropped the subject of being Irish.

The title-poem of *Station Island* includes, in section XII, a passage in which the poet imagines that on a pilgrimage to Lough Derg he has met James Joyce. The immediate source of the passage is clearly enough the episode in *Little Gidding* in which Eliot imagines meeting a "familiar compound ghost," compounded—it appears—of Yeats, Swift, Dante, and other masters. The ultimate source of both passages is Dante's imagined meeting, in Canto 15 of *Inferno,* with his dead master Brunetto Latini. Formally, Heaney's poem alludes to Dante's, with the qualification that in his terza rima off-rhymes do the work of rhymes. The burden of the scene is that the shade of the old master gives his pupil shrewd if hard advice.

It is not one of Heaney's best poems. Eliot was wiser in making his master a compound figure, the edges blurred between several notations, rather than an individual: no challenge is required to arise. Heaney's invocation to Joyce can't escape being brash, as if vanity were inscribed in it from the start. In any case, Joyce is supposed to urge Heaney to strike out on his own, write for the exhilaration of it, and let others wear the sackcloth and ashes. It is not clear what sacrifices Heaney has made for the sake of being an Irish poet: nothing particularly painful seems to present itself, but I suppose one never knows such things. At this point in the encounter Heaney speaks to Joyce of the passage in Stephen Dedalus's diary at the end of *A Portrait of the Artist as a Young Man*, where he recalls the edged discussion he had with the English Dean of Studies about the words "tundish" and "funnel":

> April 13. That tundish has been on my mind for a long time. I looked it up and find it English and good old blunt English too. Damn the dean of studies and his funnel! What did he come here for to teach us his own language or to learn it from us? Damn him one way or the other!

The passage has been on Heaney's mind, it appears, for a long time too, "a revelation / set among my stars . . ." Joyce's impatience breaks out:

> *"Who cares,"*
> *he jeered, "any more? The English language*
> *belongs to us. You are raking at dead fires,*
>
> *a waste of time for somebody your age.*
> *That subject people stuff is a cod's game,*
> *infantile, like your peasant pilgrimage.*
>
> *You lose more of yourself than you redeem*
> *doing the decent thing. Keep at a tangent.*
> *When they make the circle wide, it's time to swim*
>
> *out on your own and fill the element*
> *with signatures on your own frequency,*
> *echo soundings, searches, probes, allurements,*
>
> *elver-gleams in the dark of the whole sea."*

The English language belongs to us, but it doesn't follow that we belong to it, or that Heaney dwells in it as comfortably as Philip Larkin or Charles Tomlinson. "That subject people stuff" is not the problem: it has long been possible to regard the periphery as animating the centre.

Virtually none of the major writers of the early twentieth century was English in Larkin's sense or Tomlinson's: Yeats, Eliot, James, Pound, Joyce. The problem is the imputation of bad faith toward the Irish language, not the English; and toward the experience the Irish language alone takes responsibility for.

It is significant, too, that while Joyce tells Heaney to strike out at a tangent, especially when they make the circle wide—which means, I suppose, when they keep adding to a poet's responsibilities—he prescribes his own idiom—"signatures"—rather than leave Heaney's choice wide open. The poetry of *Station Island* is, according to Seamus Deane, a subtle performance "in which a decent person laments his inability to perform heroic actions while making that inability itself into a heroic refusal."[12] That used to be called having one's cake and eating it too: it was thought to be a sign of spiritual pride, sometimes called vanity. But in any case it locates the episode within the interrogated condition of being Irish.

Another poem in *Station Island* raises the issue in more modest terms. In "Making Strange" the poet is looking after a visiting friend— the West Indian poet Louis Simpson, I gather—and they meet Heaney's father, "unshorn and bewildered / in the tubs of his wellingtons." Embarrassed, the elder Heaney looks to his son for help. A cunning middle voice speaks to Heaney from across the road, the shade of old wisdom, telling him to:

> *"Be adept and be dialect,*
> *tell of this wind coming past the zinc hut,*
>
> *call me sweetbriar after the rain*
> *or snowberries cooled in the fog.*
> *But love the cut of this travelled one*
> *and call me also the cornfield of Boaz."*

As if to say: trust in what you know, but go beyond it, make your poetry a pastoral above the indefeasible divisions which in any case you can't avoid. Let your poetry encompass both your father's bewilderment and Louis Simpson's travelled sophistication. Dialect is what you've grown up knowing and not needing to learn. Adept as an adjective means proficient, well-versed: as a noun it retains a good deal of adeptus, Latin for those alchemists who have attained the great secret, and it means one who is skilled in his craft or mystery. The poem ends with Heaney driving the poet Simpson

> *through my own country, adept*
> *at dialect, reciting my pride*
> *in all that I knew, that began to make strange*
> *at that same recitation.*[13]

The lines are cluttered with "that," but no matter. Making strange is a complicated idiom. My father used to say that the right way to act toward people was to be "civil and strange" to them. He was suspicious of intimacy. But a less vigilant man would regard making strange as unnecessarily distancing, withdrawing from a reasonable degree of friendship. But in Heaney's lines the phrase is, I think, more literary. There is a theory of literary language, first developed by some of the Russian Formalists, which says that the purpose of such language is to make one's experience brilliantly strange, removing from it the haze of familiarity which normally prevents us from engaging with it at all. Literary language should enliven its object by making us see it afresh, as if for the first time. What Heaney knows, according to the quoted lines, starts familiar but becomes strange as soon as he recites it to a stranger. This is the right kind of making strange: be adept in and beyond your dialect.

Heaney's is one way of being an Irish poet, seeking "both/and" rather than "either/or." His procedure is Stephen Dedalus's, who started with his name, acknowledged that he was in Class of Elements at Clongowes Wood College, in Sallins, County Kildare, which was in Ireland, which was in Europe, which was in the World, which was in the Universe. That's enough to be going on with. But it entails the risk of wanting to give oneself "the history that sets one free of history." I take that phrase from Hans Blumenberg's *The Legitimacy of the Modern Age,* in which the historian deals sharply with "a kind of thinking that removes problems by specifying the conditions under which they no longer arise." As if one could assimilate every consideration to the role of being an adept: a risk, indeed.

The stereotypes remain. One of the conditions under which Irish writers learn their trade is that the stereotype of an Irish writer is overbearingly in place. Irishwomen are expected to look like Edna O'Brien and, if they write fiction, to write like her. Irish poets are expected to write like Yeats in his equestrian mode—an expectation they go a long way round to circumvent. Dramatists are expected to write the kind of plays the Abbey Theatre made famous. So there are resistances to be overcome. But they can be overcome, as Derek Mahon's poetry is not alone in showing. Nobody is obliged to coincide with a stereotype.

It is not my business to tell poets what they should do. They should proceed as they wish, provided the result is a good poem. It is probably wise for some poets to brood as little as possible upon their being Irish and to let the constituents of their poetry settle down without fuss. But a thoughtful sense of the conditions and possibilities is not a disability. T. S. Eliot's "Tradition and the Individual Talent" offered itself as a programme for young poets, a word of advice on the particular way in which their seriousness might be employed. The essay has been much impugned in recent years, but it still seems to me to be helpful. For one thing, it indicates that what a poet needs is material embodying feelings other than his own and, ideally, better than his own. There should be a wooing both ways between an individual talent and tradition, however the poet construes the tradition and identifies its constituents. The value of acknowledging a tradition is mostly disciplinary: it warns a poet that his feelings are not valid merely because they are his.

How self-consciously a poet should attend to these considerations is a difficult question. In a recent issue of *The New Republic,* Leon Wieseltier, commenting on Harold Brodkey's *Women and Angels,* complained: "why must everything that a Jew does be Jewish?" And he urged Brodkey to deal with the question of what is Jewish and what is not by leaving it alone. But he went on to show that there is, indeed, a distinctive Jewish experience:

> Moreover, messianic disappointment is the Christian problem, not the Jewish problem. The Jewish problem, rather, is the deferral of salvation, and the postponement of the immediate experience of the divine. The history of Jewish messianism has been the history of the more or less consistent refusal of the Jews to accept a messiah. The Jews prefer to wait. . . . Firm in its conviction that the world is already a sufficient theatre of meaning . . . traditional Judaism has sought, rather successfully, to contain the hunger for transformation.[14]

Now if this is true, I don't see why a Jewish writer should not be aware of it, and ponder his relation to the typical experience it describes; if for no other reason than that the feelings arising from his sense of it are likely to be rich rather than poor, serious rather than trivial. A writer who is not a Jew could imagine such an experience, but hardly with the intimacy, the sense of history and apocalypse a Jewish writer seems to come to as if by nature. (Though Jewish writers can be very different from one another.)

If there is a distinctive Irish experience, it is one of division, exacerbated by the fact that division in a country so small seems perverse. But the scale doesn't matter. At various times, the division has taken these forms: Catholic and Protestant, Nationalist and Unionist, Ireland and England, North and South, the country and the one bloated city of Dublin, Gaelic Ireland and Anglo-Ireland, the comfortable and the poor, farmers and P.A.Y.E. workers, pro-Treaty and anti-Treaty, child and parents, the Irish and the English languages, the visible Ireland and the hidden Ireland, landlord and tenant, the Big House and the hovel. To which it is now necessary to add: a defensive Church and an increasingly secular State, Irish law and European law.

Among the poets who have engaged such division, Thomas Kinsella is the one who has turned the experience into the most formidable poetry. At the beginning of his career he tried to circumvent Yeats's high-horse rhetoric by recourse to Auden. More recently he has taken possession of virtually the whole available range of Irish literary, religious, and historical experience and, in his translation of the *Táin*, found for himself an unYeatsian resonance. There are more accessible poets; Kinsella has set his chisel to some very hard stone. But he has become an Irish poet by taking full responsibility for everything that phrase entails. *The Messenger* (1978) is only one—but that one superb—of many consequences.

IV

We can now take a second and better shot at saying what Berkeley had in view. We should note that in the first half of the eighteenth century there were three discernible social classes in Ireland. The class that held such power as was available was the Protestant Ascendancy: these were the people who commanded the professions and government, owned the great houses and estates. Then there were the Protestants who engaged in trade and the subletting of land: a far more numerous class than the first. They had their own problems, many of them constraints imposed by England upon Irish trade in the export of wool, glass, and other products.

Finally, the Catholic peasants, tenants if they could afford to rent some land, farm-labourers if they could not.

To Berkeley, "We Irish" meant, I think, those men, upper-class Protestants, who had no power and only whatever prestige accrued to them from their talents in philosophy, divinity, law, and natural science. Such men—Molyneux, Archbishop King, Swift, and Berkeley himself— were often provoked into sentiments that could be mistaken for those of modern nationalism. They resented, in one degree or another, the mercantilist restrictions imposed by English Parliaments from Poynings's Act of 1495 to the Wool Acts of 1660 and 1699. But they resented them on behalf of the Protestants who felt the imposition at once; not on behalf of the Catholic peasants whose condition of life was far more completely abject. Indeed, the Catholic peasants were so low in the scale of civic life that they could be ignored, as slaves were ignored by Greek philosophers. It is doubtful if any sentiment, even Swift's in his Irish pamphlets and "A Modest Proposal," encompassed the whole people of Ireland; though I agree that Swift let his anger so round out the rhetoric of his pamphlets that nothing less than the whole people seemed to be included.

In Berkeley's social class, there were several variations of attitude. Molyneux, taking up an argument made by Sir William Domville in 1660, insisted that Ireland, though united through the Crown, was independent of the English Parliament. The argument was animated mainly by considerations of natural justice and the right of freedom. King's position depended more upon the conditions at hand. He did not rest his case upon principle, but upon intelligence and policy. "If the English in Ireland be treated as Englishmen," he argued, "they will be Englishmen still in their hearts and inclinations, but if they be oppressed, they will turn Irish, for fellowship in suffering begets love and unites interests."[15] On the question of a political union of Ireland and England, or later of Ireland and Great Britain, he wavered. Henry Maxwell, Arthur Dobbs, Robert Molesworth, and Samuel Madden argued for union, not with any intention of marking spiritual kinship between the two cultures but on the pragmatic consideration that English restrictions on Irish trade would then be withdrawn as a matter of course. But King was not convinced. Sometimes he was openly scathing: it could not be believed that England would do anything to help Ireland. Sometimes he thought Irish representatives at Westminster would at least be able to keep the miserable condition of Ireland before the minds of the English. After the Act of Union between Scotland and England in 1707, King came to the view that union, all things measured, would be the best recourse for Ireland. But the matter was resolved on March 8, 1720, when the notorious 6 George I, the Declaratory Act, came into force, asserting that the King on the advice of the Parliament of Great Britain had the right "to make laws and statutes of sufficient force and validity to bind the Kingdom and people of Ireland." King attacked the bill, and denounced the Whig administration that enacted it.

Berkeley had moments of truculence, but in general he urged that Ireland should make the best of things and take care not to cause England any displeasure. He asked, in *The Querist,* "whether our hankering after our woollen trade be not the true and only reason which hath created a jealousy in England towards Ireland: and whether anything can hurt us more than such jealousy?" Indeed, Berkeley seems to have gone out of his way to distance himself from Swift's ferocity, as if higher considerations of civility must be respected.

In *The Querist,* there is no talk of "We Irish." By 1735, Berkeley had lost interest in defining an Irish mentality or a distinctively Irish stance in philosophy, politics, and economics. He was disgusted with "the common Irish," and asked "whether the bulk of our Irish natives are not kept from thriving by that cynical content in dirt and beggary which they possess to a degree beyond any other people in Christendom?"; and "whether our old native Irish are not the most indolent and supine people in Christendom?" He could still feel sympathy for the natives, or at least pity them: "Whether there be upon earth any Christian or civilized people so beggarly, wretched, and destitute as the common Irish?" he asked. But the ambiguity of "We Irish" is silently removed.

Indeed, Berkeley now insists on regarding himself as English. The formula of "English blood and Irish birth" was persuasive. In *The Querist,* again, he asked "whether the upper part of this people are not truly English, by blood, language, religion, manners, inclination, and interest?" Further: "Whether we are not as much Englishmen as the children of old Romans, born in Britain, were still Romans?" A child may have reason to find his mother from time to time unloving, perhaps cruel, but the tie of nature persists: "Whether England doth not really love us and wish well to us, as bone of her bone, and flesh of her flesh: and whether it be not our part to cultivate this love and affection all manner of ways?" he rather desperately asked.[16] The only way he had in view was that of being unfailingly biddable.

ONE

Yeats

ROMANTIC IRELAND

The phrase "Romantic Ireland" denotes an idea or a sentiment, and mostly the sentiment of desire and loss. The meaning of the phrase is the desire it appeases or, if the spirit of the phrasing is rueful, fails to appease. Similarly with such phrases as "Merrie England" and "The Golden Age": the chief character of these phrases is that they are uttered when England is felt to be no longer merry, the age no longer golden, Ireland no longer romantic. Thoreau wrote in his journal: "The lament for a golden age is only a lament for golden men"; or, as we would say, a lament uttered at a time when men are seen to be no longer golden but iron, leaden, brazen, or otherwise inferior in their mettle. But there is a distinction to be made, or an old one to be recited. If such phrases as "Romantic Ireland," "Merrie England," and "The Golden Age" express our desires, the desires can't be particular or highly individual, they must be desires that have already been felt by other people. We share these desires, but we have not invented them. If we are willing to express our desires in these standard phrases, it is because they denote the general category of the desires rather than the particular or intimate form in which you or I feel them. The old distinction we need is between myth and fiction. We say that a consciously invented form or structure is a fiction: we do not claim for it any practical or applicable truth, we produce it solely upon our own authority; we do not live by it or act upon it; we value it because it helps us to be more conscious. Fiction is a means of being conscious without further responsibility. A myth may be equally fictive, but it has these quite different qualities: we have not invented it; we have received it from its use by other people: in many cases it may already be a force in the world at large. We say, to take the examples Frank Kermode has given in *The Sense of an Ending,* that a poem is a fiction but that anti-Semitism is a myth; and we mean that people act upon anti-Semitism but not upon poems. If people act upon a poem, that is, carry it into a corresponding form of action, it means that the poem has become a myth. For the moment it is enough to say that "Romantic Ireland" is a myth rather than a fiction, a distinction that may be verified by thinking of modern Irish history as a drama at once romantic and revolutionary. I do not need to prove that people have acted upon the genre or category of desires which we call Romantic Ireland.

Partly to annotate these remarks and partly to carry them further, I shall refer to some of Yeats's poems which use the vocabulary of Romance. The word itself turns up in the poem "King and No King," where the No King is allowed to become King at last because, as Yeats has it,

> . . . *Old Romance being kind, let him prevail*
> *Somewhere or somehow that I have forgot.*

Romance is given the character of being old, presumably to say that it has seen a lot of human life and many deaths, and that it is correspondingly patient. If the poet's mood were religious rather than pagan, he would call Romance Providence, meaning to emphasise its lenient character. When we refer to the ostensible force embodied in human life as such, we call it Destiny if our thought is neutral, Fate if it is melancholy, Providence if it is buoyant in faith, and Romance if we think it somehow responsive to our desire. Indeed, we can say that Romance is a function of our desire, so far as it is felt as a power in the land. Yeats says that the power is kind, meaning that it likes to give us happy rather than miserable endings. In a story, the happy ending is the native form of our desire, unless it has sophisticated itself to the point of disowning the naivete of its native character. If you say that our desires are more elaborate than those which are appeased by happy endings, I answer that the genre of literary Romance has always recognised that they are elaborate, and has ministered to their character also in that respect. In Yeats's poem,

Romance is the force in the world which eventually appeases our desire, after delays and frustrations which make our satisfaction, when it comes, more complete.

When the phrase "Romantic Ireland" appears in the poem "September 1913," it comes with the additional force of being, in three of the four stanzas, a refrain:

> *Romantic Ireland's dead and gone,*
> *It's with O'Leary in the grave.*

If what I have been saying is valid, to say that Romantic Ireland's dead and gone is to commit a redundancy; its character of being dead and gone is already given in its being Romantic Ireland. The line about John O'Leary is an attempt to rescue the first line from tautology; it is not Romance in general but the particular version of it which takes O'Leary for its tragic or romantic hero. If the first line of the refrain invokes a myth, the second gives it a specifying force that concentrates the desire and makes it personal; it directs the feeling toward the personal invention of fiction.

A more elaborate account of the lines would involve something like the theory of the "concrete universal." The first line recites the universal, the general idea or sentiment, but lest it remain too remote, the second gives it a concrete accompaniment, a personal image to elect one of the many possible kinds of Romance and give it a particular form. Romantic Ireland is declared to be everything that modern Ireland is not: it is not Catholic, bourgeois, or otherwise circumspect.

Having named O'Leary in the first stanza, Yeats goes on to speak of "the names that stilled your childish play," without yet naming them. They were the objects of the hangman's rope, they had no time to pray or save: "and what, God help us, could they save?" The phrase "God help us" is both Irish and Catholic, so I assume that Yeats is using it to shame Irish Catholics out of the mean-spiritedness ascribed to them in the first stanza. The refrain comes now as if with the force of truth as familiar as it is inescapable; which is mostly how refrains come.

The third stanza is full of names: the Wild Geese, Fitzgerald, Robert Emmet, Wolfe Tone, enclosed in a phrase that nearly floats free from its syntax, "All that delirium of the brave." I once tried to persuade Conor Cruise O'Brien that the reference to delirium makes Yeats's sense of revolutionary courage more complex than it would otherwise be; that it qualifies what otherwise seems full endorsement of revolutionary fervour. But he would not be persuaded, and I suppose he was right: delirium, in Yeats's context, is a word of praise, as in saying that someone was driven crazed for something he loved. In the last stanza a different source of delirium is indicated, another kind of desire, but the moral judgment, "they weighed so lightly what they gave," applies to each about equally. The poem ends with the refrain displaced:

> But let them be, they're dead and gone,
> They're with O'Leary in the grave.

The cadence is not as Yeatsian as I have sometimes thought: or it is Yeatsian in a sense that marks its continuity with Moore's Melodies, songs that invoke Romantic Ireland so memorably that it is impossible to distinguish between the songs and their burden of reference. "But let them be" exchanges for Romantic Ireland the funereal decency of silence as we stand at the graves of those heroes whose names, except for O'Leary's, we are admonished not even to breathe. Romantic Ireland becomes a place or a scene of tragic heroes, opposing to the limit of their deaths the casual comedy that has displaced them.

I have hesitated between saying "place" and "scene." Ireland is indeed a place, but it does not follow that Yeats's Ireland is a place: it could be a scene as in a theatre, a scene of romance and tragedy in which the locale scarcely matters, or matters only because it is the point of conjunction between our desires and their symbolic form. Even if we leave Yeats aside for a while, we find little reason to think of Ireland as place and only place. I recall, some years ago, bringing Frank Kermode to see some of the portraits in the National Gallery of Ireland which Yeats described in the *Autobiographies,* including Sargent's portrait of President Wilson. Kermode remarked that Ireland, more than most countries, is seen through a haze of allusion, mainly literary, musical, and pictorial: it seems perverse to try to see it more directly than its received forms allow. Kermode did not remark something equally true, that to see Ireland through its received artistic forms is mostly to see it as a lost cause. Richard Blackmur once said of Ford Madox Ford that his special concern is with lost causes known to be lost. The phrasing makes a difference. Lost causes are often known by others to be lost, but not by ourselves: we may think there is still time. But when we give ourselves to a lost cause which we know to be lost, we do so from a different structure of desires and needs; perhaps because we dwell in impossibility and would not live elsewhere even if we could. Even when we have accepted the loss, we have not released ourselves from it; or not necessarily. In an essay called "Two or Three Ideas," Wallace Stevens wrote of these desires as a secularist on principle if not entirely at heart, and he said that "to speak of the origin and end of gods is not a light matter":

> It is to speak of the origin and end of eras of human belief. And while it is easy to look back on those that have disappeared as if they were the playthings of cosmic make-believe, and on those that made petitions to them and honored them and received their benefits as legendary innocents, we are bound, nevertheless, to concede that the gods were personae of a peremptory elevation and glory. It would be wrong to look back to them as if they had existed in some indigence of the spirit. They were in fact, as we see them now, the clear giants of a vivid time, who in the style of their beings made the style of the gods and the gods themselves one.

Stevens prefers to speak of giants than of gods, because it eases somewhat the question of believing in them. But it makes little difference, in Yeats's context, whether we speak of gods, giants, heroes, fighting men, or golden men: under any sign it is to speak of a peremptory glory and elevation. And if there is any question of indigence of spirit, the indigence is now and in Ireland rather than then and in the other Ireland, the country sustained by the desire and need of it. Where Stevens speaks of gods and giants of a vivid time, Yeats speaks of Romantic Ireland, but the speech is continuous; it issues from the desire to be more and better than ourselves. It is only natural, or if not natural then cultural, to express such desires and to propose as their fitting object such men as gods and giants, and to set such gods and giants in a landscape fit to receive them. Doing so, we draw the attendant feelings toward ourselves and hope to claim something of their elevation and glory.

We are moving toward Romance in a different sense, the sense we think of as having much to do with Romanticism. Yeats referred to it in a swift account of literary history called "Three Movements":

> *Shakespearean fish swam the sea, far away from land;*
> *Romantic fish swam in nets coming to the hand;*
> *What are all those fish that lie gasping on the strand?*

Presumably these lines ask us to think that the freedom of Shakespearean fish was real, true to the element that sustained it: the freedom of Romantic fish was a delusion, they were already a lost cause though ignorant of their state: they merely felt and thought themselves free. The modern fish know that they are lost, and feel it through sand and the loss of their element. That page in the *Collected Poems* is fixed upon loss and diminution, the thinning out of "Spilt Milk," the loss of the great song and the rueful accounting of what we still have in "The Nineteenth Century and After," God's fire upon the wane in the poem "Statistics." I have said that Romance and Romanticism are different, but there are continuities between them: in both cases the gods and giants act as though they were immortal, which they are in one special sense: they live as long as there are enough people to desire that they live. But when the people lapse from that desire, the giants and gods die; and the people dwindle with them.

In some such mood, Yeats wrote "Coole Park and Ballylee, 1931," where after five stanzas of nostalgia and hauteur he took up the adjective "romantic" and made a noun of it:

> *We were the last romantics—chose for theme*
> *Traditional sanctity and loveliness;*
> *Whatever's written in what poets name*
> *The book of the people; whatever most can bless*
> *The mind of man or elevate a rhyme;*
> *But all is changed, that high horse riderless,*
> *Though mounted in that saddle Homer rode*
> *Where the swan drifts upon a darkening flood.*

I would read these lines somewhat narrowly. The "we" to whom Yeats refers are probably best taken as Lady Gregory, Synge, and Yeats, to begin with, and then such of their associates at Coole and the Abbey Theatre as maintained the true Irish themes. They were the last romantics in the sense that they attended upon Romantic Ireland, kept the sense of it alive by sustaining in themselves and a few others the desire for such glory and elevation. According to that sense, traditional sanctity and loveliness are the property of gods, giants, and fighting men, the book of the people, some chapters of which Yeats and Lady Gregory collected by talking to the few people left in the neighbourhood who still had memories and fidelities. Homer is Yeats's example partly because his unchristened heart had a place for gods, giants, and beautiful women. The stanza can be interpreted otherwise if we think of Yeats's friends not only in Coole Park but in London and make a context of predicament and loss to include them all. But I choose the narrower reading, mainly because the poem looks back to "Meditations in Time of Civil War" and other poems local in provenance however wide in reverberation.

I have been maintaining that we come upon Romantic Ireland more tellingly if we feel the desires its syllables appease rather than if we enumerate its constituents. Indeed, our notion of Romantic Ireland is all the better if it is boundless and without contour, because such vagueness testifies the better to the limitlessness of desire. Somewhere in *Per Amica Silentia Lunae* Yeats says that the desire that is satisfied is not a great desire: and to this we may add that the desire that is strictly defined is compromised by the definition. What Yeats meant by Romantic Ireland is indicated well enough by thinking of *The Celtic Twilight* and *The Secret Rose,* the *Stories of Red Hanrahan,* many of the early poems, Lady Gregory's *Cuchulain of Muirthemne* and *Gods and Fighting Men,* the first volume of Standish O'Grady's *History of Ireland,* and nearly anything we remember of Davis, Mangan, and Ferguson. The distinctions of theme and quality between these works are of no account in the present context: it is all the better if they merge or even fade into one another to make a pervasive blur of loss. But if we insist on keeping the constituents of Romantic Ireland as clear as the endlessness of desire allows, we may choose to represent them in a passage from the introduction to O'Grady's account of "the heroic period" in Irish history:

> Now it is not to be supposed that the heroes and events of this won-
> derful period are to be lightly passed over — a period which, like the
> visible firmament, was bowed with all its glory above the spirit of
> a whole nation. Those heroes and heroines were the ideals of our
> ancestors, their conduct and character were to them a religion, the
> bardic literature was their Bible. It was a poor substitute, one may
> say, for that which found its way into the island in the fifth century.
> That is so, yet such as it was under its nurture, the imagination and
> spiritual susceptibilities of our ancestors were made capable of that
> tremendous outburst of religious fervour and exaltation which char-
> acterised the centuries that succeeded the fifth, and whose effect was
> felt throughout a great portion of Europe. It was the Irish bards and
> that heroic age of theirs which nourished the imagination, intellect,

and idealism of the country to such an issue. Patrick did not create these qualities. They may not be created. He found them, and directed them into a new channel.

O'Grady took the same occasion to distinguish his treatment of the early Irish sagas from Keating's in the *History of Ireland*. Keating could not love a story unless he thought it was true. O'Grady was indifferent to the question of true or false: what mattered in a story was its epic and dramatic force, the nature of the feelings it expressed. So he was not troubled by the obligation of saying where fact ended and epic invention began. Yeats was of O'Grady's party in this dispute, as he was of Oisin's party in every dispute with Patrick. In each case, Yeats speaks up for what he called, in an early letter, "the revolt of the soul against the intellect."

O'Grady used the words "bardic" and "heroic" almost interchangeably, and I think Yeats meant much the same thing or things in using the phrase "Romantic Ireland." The values he found in the early Irish legends, or ascribed to them from a mixture of ignorance, knowledge, and desire, were those he later called "antithetical" as opposed to the punier values he called "primary." Northrop Frye's essay on *A Vision* gives a fairly considerable list of terms under each heading, but the list is incomplete. It rightly includes personality as opposed to character, tragedy superior to comedy, discord superior to concord, lunar to solar, Michael Robartes opposed to Owen Aherne; but it does not include Parnell's superiority to O'Connell, or conflict between Irish voice and English print. Nor does it include the most heart-breaking conflict between Romantic Ireland and the modern Ireland that achieved shoddy victory by a conspiracy of precaution and forgetfulness. Was it for this the wild geese spread the grey wing upon every tide?

Even if we argue that Romantic Ireland existed for Yeats only in his need of it and his desire for it, his quarrel with modern Ireland persists unchanged. The difference it makes is that in one version Yeats's contemporaries in Ireland are accused of ignoring their history, the values and sacrifices undertaken by heroic ancestors, so that magnanimity would not die. In another version they are accused of repudiating the noblest forms of desire in favour of the shoddiest. Instead of the bardic poems, we hear only "money's rant." But this is to look toward Yeats's middle and later poems, in which the defeat of heroic Ireland is taken for granted—at least till 1916—and the poetic mood is correspondingly bitter. In the early years, Yeats assumed, or hoped against hope, that the values of

Romantic Ireland might still prevail. The Irish Literary Revival is predicated upon that hope: in poetry, the scholarship of translation, the Gaelic League, in the gathering of Irish stories and songs, the teaching of Irish dancing, the fostering of Irish games, we find the same hope, that the broken tradition of Ireland may still be mended, that past and present may still be brought into league. O'Grady's phrase comes again to mind: the heroic period which, "like the visible firmament, was bowed with all its glory above the spirit of a whole nation." In political terms, it is a vision of "a nation once again," freedom from Britain. In aesthetic or spiritual terms, it is a sense of nationhood which depends upon memory; or rather, upon being mindful of the responsibility of the present to the past and future. Remember that I have remembered, Ezra Pound said, with a sense of responsibility different from Yeats's in its circumstance but not in its essential character. Yeats's desire was to stir people into a sense of their participation in an Ireland that had expressed itself long before Patrick directed the Irish imagination into one channel.

What can we say of this predicate upon which the Irish Literary Revival was sustained? It is easy to say that the attempt to arouse a sense of national unity by appealing to a common origin was childish; that it was based upon the absurd assumption that several hundred years of dissension can be transcended by stimulating the "emotion of multitude." It is just as easy to say that the three Yeatsian unities make only a dream, and then a frustration: unity of race, unity of culture, unity of being. But the question is far more difficult than these sentences suggest. I propose to come upon them by making a little detour. We are still annotating Yeats's sense of Romantic Ireland and the values proposed by the phrase, but the harder question turns upon Yeats's own relation to those values, not as themes of propaganda but as the motifs of his own early experience.

The detour I propose to make is by way of Schiller's essay on naive and sentimental poetry. The difficulty in reading the essay arises mainly from the necessity of clearing from our minds the normal meaning of these words, "naive" and "sentimental." The gist of the distinction is that, as Schiller says, the poet either *is* nature or he will *seek* her. If he is nature, he is of the naive mode of poetry: if, lacking nature, he seeks her, he is of the sentimental mode:

So long as man is pure nature, he functions as an undivided sensuous unity and as a unifying whole. Sense and reason, passive and active faculties, are not separated in their activities, still less do they stand in conflict with one another. . . . [But] once he has passed into the state of civilization and art has laid her hand upon him, that *sensuous* harmony in him is withdrawn, and he can now express himself only as a *moral* unity, that is, as striving after unity. The correspondence between his feeling and thought which in his first condition *actually* took place, exists now only *ideally;* it is no longer within him, but outside him, as an idea still to be realized, no longer as a fact in his life.

I shall interrupt Schiller's sentences only to say that the naive and the sentimental modes of poetry correspond to these two conditions, respectively. In the naive mode the poet has a simple, direct relation to nature, and his only task in poetry is to imitate or transcribe it. In the sentimental mode, the harmonious cooperation of the poet with nature is only an ideal, not an actuality, and poetry can only be the representation of that ideal. As Schiller says:

> Since the naive poet only follows simple nature and feeling, and limits himself solely to imitation of actuality, he can have only a single relationship to his subject and in this respect there is for him no choice in his treatment. [The sentimental poet, on the other hand] *reflects* upon the impression that objects make upon him, and only in that reflection is the emotion grounded which he himself experiences. . . . [He] is thus always involved with two conflicting representations and perceptions—with actuality as a limit and with his idea as infinitude; and the mixed feelings that he excites will always testify to this dual source.

Schiller's example of the naive mode in poetry is Homer, and his example of the sentimental mode is Horace; but the names do not matter to us. What matters is the distinction between two ways of being present in the world. In the naive way, the poet is possessed by the object of experience; there is no gap between them, no ambiguity, no shadow or guilt. In the sentimental way there is every form of shadow, because the poet is of necessity more directly related to the idea than to the object. Self-consciousness obtrudes: no object can be seen free of the shadow of reflection.

What then do we find in Yeats, if not a sentimental poet trying to persuade himself, to begin with, and his readers thereafter, that a naive relation to nature is possible? For what else is Romantic Ireland but the assertion that a naive relation to an original or aboriginal Ireland is indeed possible? If many of Yeats's early poems are sickly, it is because they are trying and failing to maintain the pretence that a sentimental poetry can at the same time achieve naivete. Matthew Arnold produced as one of the distinctive marks of the modern element in literature "the dialogue of the mind with itself." Yeats tried to convince himself, by recourse to Irish legends and myths, that a dialogue of the mind with objects, unperturbed by self-consciousness, was possible, and that many favours would drop from practising it. He may have been encouraged in this belief by the diverse examples of Blake and other Romantic poets who insisted that nothing was impossible to the human imagination. As we know, he retained his concern with Romantic Ireland all his life: from the early plays and poems to *The Death of Cuchulain,* he continues to recite these themes. But I think it could be shown that he gave up the ambition of naivete and settled for the fate of being in the sentimental mode of poetry by historical determination as much as by a poetic temper self-reflective through and through. He continued to invoke Romantic Ireland for occasions of praise and blame; that is, he continued to use it for its ideological force, and to direct that force against his timid compatriots. But he did not continue to practise the repellent art of *faux-naïveté.* I put in evidence for this view such poems as "The Man and the Echo" and "The Circus Animals' Desertion," which take full responsibility for self-consciousness, and practise it upon certain masterful images from Oisin and Cuchulain to Maud Gonne. In those poems, Yeats stands in judgment not only upon his soul but upon its rhetoric. The effect is not to repudiate the old themes or to dispose of them as compounded of vanity and dreams, but to confess that one's relation to them must register the lateness of the hour. At the end, everyone feels himself native of a dwindled sphere, and acts upon this feeling with patience or with hysteria; in Yeats, often with hysteria and its violence. But I have found no evidence that Yeats turned against the values of Romantic Ireland, or indeed expressed any attitude in regard to them except regret that in modern practise they are likely to fail.

We are considering naivete in both the ordinary sense and the technical sense prescribed by Schiller. I shall not go beyond a general reference to the relation between naivete, the desire for a naive relation to the world, and the various forms they have taken in pastoral literature. Jacques Derrida has remarked, in his meditation on Nietzsche, that all great noise makes one imagine happiness in calm and in distance. Noise and the desire to escape from it may have as much to do with Yeats's early poems as the other constituents we have ascribed to them. In any case, so long as we think of the spiritualising of passion, and of silence as the necessary condition of spirit, we are in Yeats's world, so far as the early poems invoke them.

But it would be ingenuous on my part to leave the subject in a terminology of desire, calm, and distance. So far as naivete is present, there is always a corresponding desire to rebuke its folly out of existence. In contemporary criticism we refer to this activity as deconstruction, which proposes to show that our motives are mainly pathetic and childish. But there is no need for us to deconstruct the ideology of Romantic Ireland; the work of irony and scepticism has already been done by Joyce. Answering in "The Holy Office" not only Yeats but the entire tradition of Romantic Ireland, he wrote:

> But I must not accounted be
> One of that mumming company.

A few lines later he associated himself with the poet in his role as victim and scapegoat:

> But all these men of whom I speak
> Make me the sewer of their clique.
> That they may dream their dreamy dreams
> I carry off their filthy streams.

In "Gas from a Burner" the mockery is more specific:

> O Ireland my first and only love
> Where Christ and Caesar are hand and glove!

and one of the last romantics becomes "Gregory of the Golden Mouth."

A full account of Joyce's work in the deconstruction of Romantic Ireland would go from these poems to the little tetchiness between Gabriel Conroy and Miss Ivors on the subject of Ireland and the Irish language in "The Dead," and from there to many passages in the *Portrait,* *Ulysses,* and *Finnegans Wake.* Such an account would eventually begin to deconstruct itself, and would find Joyce baptised by desire, as deeply as by revulsion, in the naivete he would officially expose. It is a conclusion almost foregone and foretold: that Romantic Ireland is a set of values espoused, promoted, bought and sold in the market-place, subjected to an adversary rhetoric from Joyce to Austin Clarke, endlessly deconstructed, and yet, even now, not entirely annulled. Sequestered, rather. In law, the state may order a property to be sequestered, removed for a time from the dispute of the parties concerned, so that it may be preserved for a quieter time, a future more hospitable to justice.

Yeats, Sligo and Ireland, edited by A. Norman Jeffares
(Gerrards Cross: Colin Smythe, 1980).

YEATS: THE QUESTION
OF SYMBOLISM

From the Autumn of 1895 to the following Spring, Yeats shared with Arthur Symons a flat at No. 2 Fountain Court in the Middle Temple, London. Their conversations have not been recorded, except in snatches. We know they discussed Maud Gonne, and the relation between passion and poetry. We assume they talked of the trial of Oscar Wilde, and the difference it would make to the already difficult relation between artists and their audience. Yeats found in Symons an ideal conversationalist, meaning an impassioned listener. "He had the sympathetic intelligence of a woman," he reported many years later, "and was the best listener I have ever met."[1] Symons returned this handsome compliment in dedicating to Yeats *The Symbolist Movement in Literature,* first published in 1899 but already forming itself in Symons's mind in 1895. It was a Parisian book, not only because Paris was, as Walter Benjamin called it, the capital of the nineteenth century, but because Symons's mind was animated by the impressions of the city, its music halls, the anecdotes of Verhaeren and Maeterlinck which he brought back from Paris as gifts for Yeats.[2] "Whatever I came to know of Continental literature I learned of him," Yeats acknowledged;[3] another compliment returned when Symons in his dedication, speaking of the French Symbolists, described Yeats as "the chief representation of that movement in our country."[4]

It is generally agreed that what Yeats learned of Continental literature, from either Symons or anyone else, was slight: he was a poor linguist. But it could be argued that he had very little to learn; he was already half-way toward Symbolist procedures by instinct, as the early poems show. He was writing, from desire, poems not very different from those the Symbolists were writing to a programme. Conversations with Symons confirmed him in his feeling that those early poems, however fragile they might eventually appear, were notations in the spirit of the age, so far as that spirit was Parisian. Symons described Symbolism as "a literature in which the visible world is no longer a reality, and the unseen world no longer a dream."[5] The poets were attempting "to spiritualise literature, to evade the old bondage of rhetoric, the old bondage of exteriority."[6] Mallarmé's principle, according to Symons, was: "to name is to destroy, to suggest is to create."[7] And the most subtle instrument of suggestion was rhythm, "which is the executive soul."[8] Bringing Yeats through the translation of Mallarmé, therefore, Symons sustained him in the belief that he was not alone in the world, that he, too, would witness the trembling of the veil. For the moment, then, it was enough. When Yeats spoke of symbols, he had French authority to associate them with the condition of trance, the ultimate liberation of mind from the pressure of will, a sense of timelessness, and the corresponding rhythms. In "The Symbolism of Poetry," asking "what change should one look for in the manner of our poetry" if readers were to accept the theory "that poetry moves us because of its symbolism," Yeats answered that in such a change the new poetry would cast out "descriptions of nature for the sake of nature," as well as vehemence, opinion, the moral law, and "energetic rhythms." "We would seek out," he said, "those wavering, meditative, organic rhythms, which are the embodiment of the imagination, that neither desires nor hates, because it has done with time, and only wishes to gaze upon some reality, some beauty."[9] It is permissible to think that the poet in this spirit is more concerned with the sensation of gazing than with the beauty or the reality upon which he gazes. Reality and beauty, in that formulation, are but the occasions of the gaze; or if that is too severe, alternative names for the condition of trance to which the gazing soul aspires. At any rate, the gazing is not for the sake of anything gazed upon; the act is internal, its value is measured by internal consequences, the concentration of consciousness as a value in itself. Reality is likely to be compromised by the attention it ostensibly attracts: the mind is not really directed upon its official object.

Sartre has argued in his Preface to Mallarmé's *Poésies* that Mallarmé's devotion to the imaginary arises from his resentment against reality, and the poems written in that mood are symbolic acts of revenge: the poet's words are designed to undo the work of the first Creation, the poem being a second and higher version. Yeats's early poems do not propose to destroy reality, unless we find such a desire in their determination to escape from the given world to islands of elsewhere. Their happiness is always sought in another country, where the Muse's law is the only writ that runs. Hugh Kenner has remarked of Yeats's early poem "He Remembers Forgotten Beauty" that the language proceeds, like Mallarmé's in many poems, by systematic digression from the poem's formal structure.[10] The formal structure, the sentence upon which the poem appears to depend, can indeed be disentangled from its net of subordinate clauses, but only by an effort alien to the spirit of the poem. The poem asks to be read in a more accommodating fashion. We are discouraged from enquiring how the grammar works, or what verb goes with what noun; we are to allow ourselves to be entangled and to submit to a language in which the digressions are richer than the formal business, the sentence. I draw from this the conclusion that the sentence stands for the reality principle, and that to Yeats it is at best a necessary evil, a ball-and-chain, tolerable only to the extent to which its force is thwarted. The digressions, the subordinate clauses, are insubordinate, and they have the effect of depriving language of the nominative power in which empiricists delight; they turn the poem into a place of shadow and suggestion. The empirical world, sustained in its exorbitance by the naming power of language, the strict application of name to thing, is now made to appear blurred, rich only in the atmosphere which qualifies it: it is not allowed to assert itself. The result of reading the poem as it asks to be read is that beguiling phrases stay in one's mind, but the sentence is forgotten; the pleasure principle is dominant in the form of reverie, and reality must do the best it can for itself, with little acknowledgement from the poet.

I have laboured this theme only to emphasize Yeats's first notion of Symbolism, that it effects a blessed release from time, from the malady of the quotidian, that it enables a poet to emigrate to happier lands, fictive places responsive to desire and imagination. Reality exists, like sentences and names, only to be circumvented. A symbol may be a noun, but it imposes little or no restriction upon the suggestible mind which receives it. "Rose of all Roses, Rose of all the World!" is mostly a line of nouns, but the nouns are valued only for the latitude of their associations: the one privilege they are not allowed to claim is that of setting up strict categories or demarcations to which the reader's mind is forced to confine its attention. So even if we continue to think of symbols as nouns, we think of Symbolism as a verb, a rival act of creation which subverts the original one. That is, we think of Symbolism, for the moment, in the terms in which Symons and Yeats recited it.

Left to ourselves, we would hardly approach Symbolism in this way. It is more congenial to us to think of symbols as natural forms or events which have acquired special significance, a special aura, from the ancestral feelings gathered around them. We are happy to recognise in symbols certain unconscious commonplaces, significances to which one recurs because of long association or because of kinship of feeling between one situation and another. We like to think that the symbolic aura is the result of many generations, consanguinities of feeling which enact themselves by law entirely natural. We hope to share in those ancestral feelings, but we do not presume to invent them. It is only by courtesy and somewhat unwillingly that we allow the poet to engage in a similar enterprise from his own resources, and we are inclined to accuse him of pretentiousness, as Eliot accused Blake and Yeats, if his efforts have an air of calculation or insistence. Still, we admit that a poet may do some of the work by himself, he may resort to certain words which begin as images but which acquire a certain radiance from the largesse with which the poet uses them; as Yeats resorted to Sato's sword in "Meditations in Time of Civil War," and to the tower in several poems. With luck, these images become symbols, and we read them on the page as if they were written in italics. Perhaps I can describe the process, except for its luck, by saying that an image becomes a symbol on being touched by value or significance not attributable to its own set. For example: think of an event in narrative as a moment or a position along a line, straight or crooked, and then think of it as being crossed by another line of value from another source. Each line is a set, a paradigm. But the event which occurs at the point of intersection between two sets is an image in both; its duplicity constitutes its symbolic force. Interpreted in one set, it declares itself unrestrained by that interpretation; it is part of the other set as well. When we find an image becoming a symbol, we feel in it this double potency; its allegiance expands, as if answerable to both idioms, ready to participate in both sets of relations. This marks its freedom and its suggestiveness; we have a sense in attending to it that there is no point at which we can say for sure that its force has come to an end. We have something like this in mind on other occasions, too; when we think of chance or contingency, and then sense the participation of a seemingly arbitrary event in a pattern or rhythm of recurrence, so that it reverberates in time and appears fateful in its character: or when we advert to what seems a purely natural event, and then notice in it traces of human intervention in the form of consciousness. In these instances we mark a point of intersection where the individual event expands to fulfil several obligations of meaning, far beyond the call of a single duty.

This makes again something like the old-fashioned distinction between allegory and symbolism, where we say of allegory that it proceeds by parallel lines which never meet and can only be translated from one idiom into another; while we say of the symbolic event that it enfolds its meaning and cannot be translated into any other terms. Whitehead's account of Symbolism is for this reason not entirely satisfactory. "The human mind is functioning symbolically," he says, "when some components of its experience elicit consciousness, beliefs, emotions, and usages, respecting other components of its experience. The former set of components are the 'symbols,' and the latter set constitute the 'meaning' of the symbols. The organic functioning whereby there is transition from the symbol to the meaning [is] called 'symbolic reference.' "[11] To make this a more satisfactory account, one should interpret the eliciting process in such a way as to blur the otherwise too sharp distinction between a symbol and its meaning; if, for instance, one spoke of the symbol not as a thing followed by its meaning, but as an act barely separable from its consequence. The symbolic act is unitary, it does not divide itself or set limits to its force; only by a retrospective and somewhat mechanical process can we presume to say where the act ends and its consequence begins, and even in saying so much one knows that the act is injured by the imposition of alien categories.

I would prefer to speak of Symbolism in terms of action, because the concept of meaning can be considered as dissociated from time, but action is helplessly temporal; and this is as it should be. We should not conspire too readily with a literary theory which has purity in mind. I have remarked that Symbolism plans to evade reality, and most particularly the reality of time, the inescapable Mondays and Tuesdays, but the plan acknowledges time as the governing dimension and seeks only to elude it. Indeed, thinking of Symbolism, we must hold in mind simultaneously two desires which, if taken bluntly, may appear to contradict each other. When we register the presence or the activity of a symbol, we mark a moment in time in which the world of objects is reconciled to the desires of the spirit: object and subject are folded in a single party, and this is happiness. It is true that in such a moment the subject is first among two forces only ostensibly equal, but this does not destroy the happiness of the reconciliation. The second desire must also be registered, however, the desire that such reconciliations be prolonged, that they never end, though we know they are merely momentary and cannot be prolonged. There is no structure, according to the Symbolist aesthetic, within which they could be retained. If Symbolism appears to us today a peculiarly vulnerable form of art, and beautiful for that reason, I think the main consideration is that it exhibits a radical disaffection from time as from an alien element or an alien action. Reconciliation with time, according to such a prescription, can only be a momentary release, a stolen kiss, because such moments are surrounded by a void on each side. The Symbolist finds nothing but void in the latitude of time; it is as much as he can do to catch an instant in which an event in his imaginary set is touched by an event in the historical set, and the two events coalesce, becoming one. The "dissociation of sensibility" described by Eliot upon a hint by Remy de Gourmont is a condition in which the mind's reconciliation with time cannot be looked for or counted on, except in glimpses: as a general felicity, it has become impossible, according to Eliot's thesis. Hence the moral justification of living according to the imagination for all it is worth: if imagination and reality happen to join hands from time to time, that is good fortune beyond the reach of prediction.

But we must take the matter somewhat more strictly, to consider what we mean by saying, as we do, that Yeats started out as a Symbolist and ended as something else. Specifically, I want to describe the scruple which prevented him from making his entire art with Symons and the Symbolists, because I find the scruple present from the start, even though it was suppressed, in the early years, more often than not. So we ought to proceed more consecutively and see what happened. In "The Symbolism of Poetry" Yeats says that "all sounds, all colours, all forms, either because of their preordained energies or because of long association, evoke indefinable and yet precise emotions, or, as I prefer to think, call down among us certain disembodied powers, whose footsteps over our hearts we call emotions."[12] And in "The Philosophy of Shelley's Poetry" he speaks of the Great Memory as "a dwelling-house of symbols, of images that are living souls."[13] The aura we feel in the symbol marks for Yeats the presence of the supernatural in the natural: if he believed in anything, he believed in reincarnation. The souls of the dead were understood as inhabiting places sacred because of that residence, mountains "along whose sides the peasant still sees enchanted fires."[14] Yeats's evidence for these fancies is not a theory of the occult: it is the fact that certain images and places have long been "steeped in emotion," and sacred for that reason. In "Magic" he writes that "whatever the passions of men have gathered about becomes a symbol in the Great Memory, and in the hands of him who has the secret it is a worker of wonders, a caller-up of angels or of devils."[15] The poet is therefore a mage, adept in secret but traditional knowledge. Yeats is hoping to establish between subjectivity and inherited symbols the kind of relation which Eliot proposed between the poet's talent and tradition, a relation of discipline in the sense that if you want tradition you must work for it, if you want symbols you must attend to them. The poet must become an alchemist of the word, if he is to escape from the tautology of himself. Symbols, inherited rather than invented, mediate between the individual consciousness, which would otherwise be solipsist, and the given world, which would otherwise be, for all time, alien. Symbols are at once given and created: given, but given by creative souls not unlike our own. A race is a communion of such souls. Yeats speaks of the Symbolist poet as we might more naturally speak of the mage: "the poet of essences and pure ideas," he says, "must seek in the half-lights that glimmer from symbol to symbol as if to the ends of the earth all that the epic and dramatic poet finds of mystery and shadow in the accidental circumstances of life."[16] The Symbolist fills our minds "with the essences of things, and not with things": his instrument is rhythm, presumably because human feeling, which seeks release in words and is outraged by the poor release it finds, sways to rhythm as to music. "In art, rhythm is everything," Symons wrote in 1898, a pardonable exaggeration in a critic of Mallarméan persuasion.

With Yeats in mind, therefore, and especially the early Yeats under Symons's rhetoric, it is well for us to understand that Symbolism is the poet's form of magic, except that what the mage does consciously the poet does half consciously and half by instinct. The ancient secret is common to both disciplines. A mage believes he can do what a Symbolist does, but deliberately. Their activities are so congenial, one to the other, that their double presence in the poets of "the tragic generation" is not surprising; two forms of the same impulse, to command a spiritual power, like an ancient art not quite lost. Cornelius Agrippa's *De Occulta Philosophia* was one of Yeats's sacred books, Shelley's *Prometheus Unbound* another:

their joint presence in his mind was a choice, not an aberration. Magic was congenial to Yeats's mind for many reasons, but especially because it exerted the heuristic power of language, the common grammar of mage and poet. There is a passage in *The Philosophy of Symbolic Forms* where Cassirer says that "all word-magic and name-magic are based on the assumption that the world of things and the world of names form a single undifferentiated chain of causality and hence a single reality."[17] But the names are evocations, not labels affixed to objects. This goes some way to account for the incantatory note in Yeats's hieratic style, where his lines are more readily acceptable if we take them as rituals, prescriptions, or interdictions than as secular utterances delivered from a high horse. The basic assumption is that souls do not die and therefore may be evoked: "the dead living in their memories are, I am persuaded," Yeats says, "the source of all that we call instinct, and it is their love and their desire, all unknowing, that make us drive beyond our reason, or in defiance of our interest, it may be."[18] Correspondingly, the *anima mundi* is not merely a store of images and symbols, it is what a race dreams and remembers. The great soul may be evoked by symbols, but spirits are not mere functions of ourselves, they have their own native personalities, or so Yeats thought. The natives of the rain are rainy men. So the best reading of the *anima mundi* is that it is the subjective correlative of history, a nation's life in symbols; it is not our invention, but it may respond to our call, if like the mage we speak the right words. Yeats found in Blake's *Milton* a figure or an action to represent the process by which these symbols are engendered:

> *When on the highest lift of his light pinions he arrives*
> *At that bright Gate, another Lark meets him and back to back*
> *They touch their pinions, tip tip, and each descend*
> *To their respective Earths and there all night consult with Angels*
> *Of Providence and with the Eyes of God all night in slumbers*
> *Inspired, and at the dawn of day send out another Lark*
> *Into another Heaven to carry news upon his wings.*[19]

This figure Yeats interpreted as meaning that man gains spiritual influence in like fashion: "He must go on perfecting earthly power and perception until they are so subtilized that divine power and divine perception descend to meet them, and the song of earth and the song of heaven mingle together."[20]

I suppose one ought to say that these songs are agreeably vague, and perhaps that they are both Songs of Myself. In the Symbolist tradition, as in the Idealist tradition for similar reasons, the exemplary act is the contemplation of one's mind; like Mallarmé watching himself in a mirror in order to think. In Yeats, contemplation registers the mind moving within its own circle, gathering its strength in a symbolic act, purged of every impurity. Dance is its embodiment, its truce with earth and time. The subtle language within a language corresponds to the self-delighting, self-appeasing gestures of the dancer, a sensuous metaphysic within the physical body. The emblem for this is Mallarmé's Hérodiade, gathering everything into the artifice of the dance, annihilating the world for the sake of her own image. To quote it in Symons's version, which Yeats recited and praised in "The Tragic Generation":

> And all about me lives but in mine own
> Image, the idolatrous mirror of my pride,
> Mirroring this Hérodiade diamond-eyed.

Mallarmé's virgin is crucial in the mythology of Yeats's dance-plays and especially his Salomé-play, *A Full Moon in March*. Quoting Symons's translation, Yeats said, "Yet I am certain that there was something in myself compelling me to attempt creation of an art as separate from everything heterogeneous and casual, from all character and circumstance as some Hérodiade of our theatre, dancing seemingly alone in her narrow moving luminous circle."[21] We have here an almost complete aesthetic for a Symbolist theatre: the dancer, like the mind, moves by her own sweet will, and in the climax of the play disengages her force from character and circumstance; the stage becomes a luminous circle answerable to the mind, and everything is transfigured in the dance. Yeats gave another version of this condition in *A Vision*, the perfection of subjectivity:

> The being has selected, moulded and remoulded, narrowed its circle of living, been more and more the artist, grown more and more "distinguished" in all preference. Now contemplation and desire, united into one, inhabit a world where every beloved image has bodily form, and every bodily form is loved.[22]

But Yeats has moved surreptitiously here from Mallarmé to Dante, remembering the "perfectly proportioned human body," and the admission of body and bodily motives qualifies the otherwise pure Symbolism of his theatre.

The qualification is extreme in *The Death of Cuchulain.* But for the moment it is enough if we recognise that Yeats's Symbolism, which owes much to Shelley, is turned toward the theatre by Mallarmé. Mallarmé's theatre is not Nietzsche's, and the Japanese Noh theatre differs from each, but for the moment Mallarmé is enough. The programme outlined in *Crise de vers* established the procedures of Symbolism, so far as we need them in reading the early Yeats. Mallarmé is describing the modern motive, to retain nothing but suggestion, and he tells how this may be done:

> Instituer une relation entre les images exacte, et que s'en détache un tiers aspect fusible et clair présenté à la divination. (To set up an exact relation between the images, and let there stand out from it a third aspect, bright and easily absorbed, offered to divination.)[23]

In this context, the chief characteristic of a Symbolist poem is that the third aspect disables interpretation except insofar as the interpreter aspires to divination: since the images live by action rather than by knowledge, they refuse to be translated. This refusal gives them their esoteric aura, as of a secret life they live: they attract the attention of the interpreter while repelling any attempt he might make to explicate them. The poet's imagination establishes these images and the relation between them, then keeps its secret, casting out everything that is not itself. The process is described in the elegy "In Memory of Major Robert Gregory" as "our secret discipline / Wherein the gazing heart doubles her might." That is to say, the Symbolist sees not with the eye but with the mind's eye, narrowing the luminous circle for greater intensity. At a late stage in this process, the imagination is ready to transfigure the world in its own image. "Gazing" is therefore a technical term in Yeats because its force is internal and subjective. Yeats distinguishes between the gaze and the glance; the glance is objective, administrative, as when the eyes of a civil servant look upon a world to be controlled, a world in which subject and object are sharply distinguished and names are attached, with undue confidence, to things: the gaze is internal and secret, as in Yeats's reference to "vague Grecian eyes gazing at nothing." To gaze is to set one's mind dancing in its own circle, until reverie passes into trance.

When we speak of Yeats as a Symbolist, then, we speak of him in association with Symons, Mallarmé, Shelley, Pater, and other writers for whom the mind, in its exemplary moment, hovers on the outer edge of consciousness, swaying to a rhythm which leads it toward the condition of trance. But Yeats retained a certain scruple and much misgiving even while he worked, by instinct or design, to a Symbolist aesthetic. I think he was discontented with an aesthetic which had no hope of prolonging the reconciliation between symbol and time, consciousness and experience. He wanted the latitude of allegory, with the radiance of symbol; or that is a way of putting it. The symbol was valued for its depth, its ancient lore, its endlessness as if both above and below the finite condition. But it was not enough: one still had to live in the ordinary world among confusions of time and feeling. What Yeats sought was a dynamic relation between time and feeling, and it is generally agreed that the majesty of such poems as "Sailing to Byzantium" and "Among School Children" depends upon the achievement of a just relation between those values; between "the young in one another's arms" and the "artifice of eternity." The imagination mediates between the two worlds because it has the rights of a citizen in each: this is not strictly in the Symbolist programme, but it is crucial to Yeats's art; he could not transcend the limitations of Symbolism until he had registered, with full commitment, the extent of the imagination's reach, its self-possession in both worlds. Still, the accommodation of time and eternity was not achieved in a day. I would maintain that there is a middle term between the Symbolist Yeats, at one extreme, and at the other, the Yeats who made his art from the roughage of daily experience, chance, choice, and history. The middle term I propose is legend, which Yeats sometimes called myth, and we may think of it as situated between the unseen world of Symbolism and the indisputable world of fact and time.

The text we need for this middle term is a passage in *The Trembling of the Veil* where Yeats explains that he was not content with "an international art, picking stories and symbols where it pleased." "If Chaucer's personages," he says,

> had disengaged themselves from Chaucer's crowd, forgot their common goal and shrine, and after sundry magnifications became each in turn the centre of some Elizabethan play, and had after split into their elements and so given birth to romantic poetry, must I reverse the cinematograph? I thought that the general movement of literature must be such a reversal, men being there displayed in casual,

temporary contact as at the Tabard door. I had lately read Tolstoy's *Anna Karenina* and thought that where his theoretical capacity had not awakened there was such a turning back: but a nation or an individual with great emotional intensity might follow the pilgrims, as it were, to some unknown shrine, and give to all those separated elements, and to all that abstract love and melancholy, a symbolical, a mythological coherence.

"Might I not," Yeats asks, "create some new *Prometheus Unbound;* Patrick or Columcille, Oisin or Finn, in Prometheus' stead; and, instead of Caucasus, Cro-Patrick or Ben Bulben? Have not all races had their first unity from a mythology that marries them to rock and hill?" Finally, he says that "nations, races, and individual men are unified by an image, or bundle of related images, symbolical or evocative of the state of mind which is, of all states of mind not impossible, the most difficult to that man, race, or nation; because only the greatest obstacle that can be contemplated without despair rouses the will to full intensity."[24] I have quoted these sentences to show that before Yeats could incorporate in his art the rough worlds of O'Connell, Parnell, Kevin O'Higgins, "theatre business, management of men," he had to start at the beginning, with a sense of those images upon which mythological coherence is based, even if most of the images were only half-remembered if remembered at all. He could not go in a rush from the imaginary to the real; he needed a mediating term. The Celtic legends which he recited and dramatized were invoked to enforce an elaborate net of associations and fidelities corresponding to what Burke called "prejudice," the instinctual responses of a race; what Whitehead called "our vast systems of inherited symbolism."

The trouble is that it is not vast enough, and that it is falling away. It is probably true that we can never have enough symbols if what we want in our lives is density and range of feeling. W. H. Auden has reflected upon the impoverishment of our symbols as one of the chief forms of our penury. Yeats's recourse to Celtic symbols and legends as the matter of his early art may have been misguided, an indulgence of nostalgia and dream, since most of his audience had forgotten those legendary figures if they had ever received them, but there is no way of knowing for sure that a symbol is dead or that someone's spirit cannot be roused to a sense of what it shares with others by a passing cadence or a dimly remembered name. Yeats proposed to set before Irishmen not an international art but "an Irish literature which, though made by many minds, would seem the work of a single mind, and turn our places of beauty or legendary association into holy symbols."[25] In poems, plays, and stories, he put his circus animals on show: Conchubar, Cuchulain, Fergus, Caoilte, Oisin, the Fool, and the Blind Man. Such figures were congenial to him for many reasons, congenial especially to his Symbolist affiliation, because their legends were suggestive but not overbearing. Legends present themselves for an interest largely intrinsic, but they do not claim to compel the reader, as fact and time compel him: they offer themselves to his feeling, but they do not make demands upon his beliefs; no one has ever felt himself intimidated by a legend, as he has felt himself intimidated by a fact. The stories which Yeats recited, partly received from Standish O'Grady and the nineteenth-century translators, were therefore easy on his spirit, they let his mind dance while he attended to them, they did not browbeat him. They beguiled his mind as the lore of neo-Platonism and Swedenborg beguiled it, but they did not press hard upon it. In fact, the legends allowed him to apply them to his own poor case, so that when he wrote of Oisin "led by the nose through three enchanted islands," he wrote of himself and his own enslavement. In "The Circus Animals' Desertion" he confesses as much, saying of Oisin:

> But what cared I that set him on to ride,
> I, starved for the bosom of his faery bride?[26]

And in the next stanza the experience of writing *The Countess Cathleen* is intertwined with Yeats's longing for Maud Gonne, as he watched her tearing herself apart in fanaticism and hate. I am saying, then, that the legends which allowed Yeats's mind to move freely and suggestively along their margins allowed him also to find their analogies in his own life; they gave him a terminology which he was free to apply and, applying it, to move from legend into history, his own history but history nonetheless. In that sense, a mythology reflects not only its region, as Stevens said, but the experience of the mind that receives it.

This is consistent with the beliefs Yeats expressed when Magic was his theme. "I believe in three doctrines," he says:

1) That the borders of our mind are ever shifting, and that many minds can flow into one another, as it were, and create or reveal a single mind, a single energy.

2) That the borders of our memories are as shifting, and that our memories are a part of one great memory, the memory of Nature herself.

3) That this great mind and great memory can be evoked by symbols.[27]

Clearly, the great mind and the great memory are subjective equivalents of history; they are loyal to individual feeling as history is loyal to the calendar. So Edmund Wilson was right when he said in *Axel's Castle* that Yeats was intent upon discovering symbols which would stand for "the elements of his own nature" or which would seem to possess "some universal significance."[28] I would say *and* rather than *or*, because the symbols which appealed to Yeats were those that issued from a sense of his own experience and, after much wandering, flowed back there. The difference between symbol and a fact is that the symbol is willing to be surrounded by an aura of personal feeling, different for each mind that contemplates it; the fact tries to insist that it be taken on its own severe terms, and remains impervious to any but the most fictive act of the mind that receives it.

There is a famous passage in Pater's *Studies in the History of the Renaissance* which appears to tell against this distinction, where he says that external objects dissolve in our reflection and analysis until they become nothing more than "impressions unstable, flickering, inconsistent, which burn and are extinguished with our consciousness of them."[29] But even if this were true, it would require the force of reflection and analysis, the gem-like flame, to make those sensations possible, and the external objects would resist the flame and wait for it to die. In a certain mood, the plum survives its poems, as Stevens said. But symbols do not resist the mind, they are willing to be dispersed and re-formed, they are hospitable to our feeling, they know that they have had many lives and are not yet exhausted. They die only when there is no longer a personal feeling to receive them. This explains why Yeats hoped, as he said, to find everything in the symbol. I think he hoped also to lose himself there, committing his feelings to their verbal fate.

I have quoted from "The Circus Animals' Desertion" and will do so again, because it is the poem in which Yeats confesses to a vulnerable relation between symbol and his own experience. We are to suppose that he begins with his own feeling—where else could he begin?—and that he sought to resolve its conflicts by recourse to some of the classic legends of

Irish mythology; and in doing so he devised certain "masterful images" which, he says, "grew in pure mind." Their origin makes little difference; he comes back to that question in the last stanza. But before reaching that point, Yeats confesses that he was enchanted by the dream itself. I assume that the dream means desire, so far as that has established itself in the symbolic world to which it aspires. Or perhaps Yeats means that desire has been transformed, given permanence and inexhaustibility, in the form of art:

> And when the Fool and Blind Man stole the bread
> Cuchulain fought the ungovernable sea;
> Heart mysteries there, and yet when all is said
> It was the dream itself enchanted me:
> Character isolated by a deed
> To engross the present and dominate memory.
> Players and painted stage took all my love
> And not those things that they were emblems of.[30]

We need not take this as final. I associate its sentiment with the "secret discipline" of "In Memory of Major Robert Gregory" where the gazing heart doubles her might by bringing to bear upon her experience such concentration, purely internal, that the external object is indeed virtually dissolved, and feeling is exhilarated by a sense of its own power. Subjectivity is always the chosen form of power.

It is well known that this indulgence is a scandal to writers of a different persuasion; it is the character of Symbolism which even now constitutes an outrage, especially for writers who feel that life is tolerable only if we live, with whatever difficulty, among facts deemed indissoluble. This is what Ezra Pound had in view in *Canto* 83 when he asserted against Baudelaire and Yeats that Paradise is not artificial, that Baudelaire's hymn to the hieroglyphics of dream and symbol is perverse. If Paradise exists, Pound appears to say, it exists in fragments of fact, such as excellent sausage, the smell of mint, and Ladro the night cat. Pound would not deny that it exists in our sense of these facts, but he would insist that the facts come first and stay indisputable to the end. And then he teases Yeats:

> and Uncle William dawdling around Notre Dame
> in search of whatever

paused to admire the symbol
with Notre Dame standing inside it. [31]

The point is well taken, so far as it smiles upon Yeats's tendency to dissolve the external object in favour of his Symbolist imagination, the enchanting dream: "in search of whatever," since this effect is possible only by vacancy, gazing, taking one's eye off the object or looking through it. Pound is asserting that the given world, such as it appears even to common and un-Symbolist imaginations, is more durable than artificial bronzes: it stands forth in its own right, bodied against the golden bird and the hieroglyphic dream of "Byzantium." Pound's position is clear; we should lay aside our dreaming and try to make sense, preferably historical sense, of the given world; we should put our house in order rather than replace it by a castle in the Symbolist air. Perhaps this explains why Pound, hostile to Symbolism because of its collusion with subjectivity, endorsed in its stead Imagism, grateful for its ostensible objectivity: the image is newly invented, while the Symbol, being old, is too tired to resist. The image, in Imagism, represents the poet's self-denial, his refusal of ancestral resonance: the image is hard, the symbol soft. This is substantially the critique which D. H. Lawrence, too, directed upon Yeats. "We are such egoistic fools," he wrote. "We see only the *symbol* as a *subjective expression:* as an expression of ourselves. That makes us so sickly when we deal with the old symbols: like Yeats." [32]

Lawrence's position is given even more specifically near the end of *Women in Love,* when Ursula intervenes in the obnoxious discussion of art between Gudrun and the sculptor Loerke, denouncing their assumption that the world of art is independent of the real world. "The world of art is only the truth about the real world, that's all—but you are too far gone to see it." [33] The same aesthetic is implicit in the Lincoln Cathedral chapter of *The Rainbow;* that the Cathedral, however intensely it is seen and registered, is not to be dissolved into a sequence of impressions, or treated as a mere expression of ourselves. Cathedrals which have weathered so much ought to be able to withstand Walter Pater's attention. Stephen Dedalus knew as much, reading the "signatures of all things." "Then he was aware of them bodies before of them coloured. How? By knocking his sconce against them . . . Open your eyes now. I will. One moment. Has all vanished since? . . . See now. There all the time without you: and ever shall be, world without end." [34] Finally, I quote a few lines from

Charles Tomlinson's sequence "Antecedents," his meditation upon the joys and sorrows of Symbolism:

> The white mind holds
> An insufficiency, a style
> To contain a solitude
> And nothing more.[35]

I quote these diverse passages to register variant readings of experience, in one degree or another hostile to Yeats's reading so far as his may be described as Symbolist. Hostility to Symbolism often takes a benign form, regret that it could not succeed, reality being there all the time without you, waiting for you to tire of your excess. To Tomlinson and other poets, Symbolism in its French forms was a *cul de sac,* and the only way out was back. It is a familiar argument. But it would be wrong to present Yeats as if he were Mallarmé's pupil in all things, or merely a more robust Symons. Very few of Yeats's poems are written from a purely Symbolist mind, that mind which sets consciousness to devour the world, filling the void with itself. There are very few poems, I mean, in which Yeats is willing to let mere life die so that consciousness may reincarnate itself in the poems. We come back to his double motive: on the one hand, to give consciousness every privilege; on the other, to respect every value in life which is not attributable to consciousness. The Symbolist cannot forever escape the fear that life for him is an epistemological circle, that the seer merely sees himself in everything he sees, that everything dissolves in the flow of his consciousness. The true Symbolist is content to live in a world purer, more spiritual, than the common one, but Yeats is not. There are moments in which he is satisfied with whatever the subjective will chooses to do, however destructive the result; but there are other moments in which he is satisfied with nothing short of the truth, even if it asserts itself as independent of his will. These rival allegiances are brought into a dynamic relation by the theatrical force of his imagination, its delight in conflict for the energy it creates, and there is good reason to think his poetry was saved by that pleasure.

Against symbol, therefore, we should place history, meaning by this ambiguous term, for the moment, whatever the imagination recognises as distinct from itself and finally indissoluble. History in that old-fashioned sense means not only the past as more or less successfully resisting our sense of it, but the usual, whatever comes from the chance of things and not from the imagination's choice. In "A Dialogue of Self and Soul" Yeats calls it simply "life," and the rhetoric of that poem favours it, at the end. It may be thought that at this stage he has reneged on Symbolism entirely, forgotten his French. In 1937 he wrote to Dorothy Wellesley of these matters, saying of Mallarmé that he "escapes from history," while "you and I are in history," though he means "the history of the mind." Roger Fry's translation of Mallarmé, Yeats said, "shows me the road I and others of my time went for certain furlongs . . . It is not the road I go now, but one of the legitimate roads."[36] But even this is not the whole story. Yeats was never willing to allow history to press upon him as a dead weight: his mind would wrestle with fact, as the dialogues and plays show, but only with live fact, still open to change and greater life. I quote again the great sentence from the Diary of 1930: "History is necessity until it takes fire in someone's head and becomes freedom or virtue."[37] In what sense can history be established or stabilised: that is a perennial embarrassment. We argue the question relentlessly. But this seems the right note on which to leave the question; nothing of the poet's old allegiance is disavowed, but old motives are incorporated in a stronger aesthetic, animated by the idiom of conflict and theatre. Yeats is attending to time, "the cracked tune that Chronos sings," as well as to the ethereal music of consciousness.

Myth and Reality, edited by Joseph Ronsley (Waterloo, Ontario: Wilfred Laurier University Press, 1977).

Yeats, Ancestral Houses, and Anglo-Ireland

On August 7, 1909, Yeats wrote in his Journal:

> Subject for poem. "A Shaken House." How should the world gain if this house failed, even though a hundred little houses were the better for it, for here power [has] gone forth or lingered, giving energy, precision; it gave to a far people beneficent rule, and still under its roof living intellect is sweetened by old memories of its descent from far off? How should the world be better if the wren's nest flourish and the eagle's house is scattered?

On the same day, Yeats turned these sentiments into verse, a draft of the poem "Upon a House Shaken by the Land Agitation." Immediately under the verses he added: "I wrote this on hearing the results of reductions of rent made by the court." Then he entered a few more sentences in the spirit of the verses:

> One feels always that where all must make their living they will live not for life's sake but the work's, and all will be the poorer. My work is very near to life itself, and my father's very near to life itself, but I am always feeling a lack of life's own values behind my thought.

They should have been there before the strain began, before it became necessary to let the work create its values. This house has enriched my soul out of measure, because here life moves without restraint through spacious forms. Here there has been no compelled labour, no poverty-thwarted impulse.[1]

The house was Coole Park, Lady Gregory's home, where Yeats was spending the summer months. The reduction of rents, which provoked the poem, was secured on July 30, 1909. Fifteen tenants of the Gregory estate at Coole Park applied to the Land Court to have their rents reduced. The Land Commissioner, the Hon. Gerald Fitzgerald, granted their application, and reduced the rents by approximately twenty per cent. Yeats interpreted the judgment, quite reasonably, as yet another sign of the Government's determination to transfer the ownership of lands in Ireland from landlords to tenants.

Two pieces of legislation were particularly significant. On November 24, 1908, Augustine Birrell introduced his Irish Land Bill to expedite the purchase of land. The Bill was designed to press further the terms of the Wyndham Act of 1903, by which landlords were encouraged to sell their estates to their tenants: the money would be provided by the State and repaid over a period of sixty-eight-and-a-half years by annuities at three-and-a-quarter per cent. In order to stimulate sales, the Wyndham Act gave landlords a bonus, which was to be paid from Irish revenues. Nationalists resented this arrangement, and thought the price of the land too generous to the landlords. In the event, the Wyndham Act didn't work well; the bonuses proved too expensive, and it cost the State too much to provide the tenants with the full purchase price. Birrell's Land Act reduced the bonuses and provided for compulsory purchase in certain cases.

The second piece of legislation was Lloyd George's Finance Act—the Budget—of 1909, which he introduced on April 29. To pay for Old Age Pensions, he imposed a series of land taxes, including a tax of twenty per cent on any unearned increment in land values, payable either when the land was sold or when it changed hands on the owner's death; a capital tax of a halfpenny in the pound on the value of undeveloped land and minerals; and a reversion duty of ten per cent on any benefit that accrued to a lessor at the end of a lease. The Finance Act was resisted by the House of Lords; their refusal to pass it precipitated a general election, so the Budget didn't go through till April 28, 1910; but its provisions couldn't be successfully challenged.

I should remark, in passing, that many of the landlords in Ireland saw the Wyndham Act as a blessing: they were finding the upkeep of their estates a burden, and welcomed the opportunity to sell, especially as they could buy back any part of their estates they wanted, on favourable terms. The only landlords who resented the Wyndham Act and, even more bitterly, the provisions of the Acts of 1909 and 1910, were those, like Lady Gregory, who wanted to retain their estates, and to be free of Government interference. So it was not surprising that Yeats saw the reduction of her rents as a conspiracy of the British Government and the Irish members of Parliament—especially John Redmond and John Dillon—to placate the tenants and destroy the landlords at one stroke.

Later in the summer—on September 16, 1909—Yeats developed his sentiments on the matter into larger considerations of culture and its seemingly inevitable decline. "Is it not always the tragedy of the great and the strong that they see before the end the small and the weak, in friendship or in enmity, pushing them from their place and marring what they have built, and doing one or the other in mere lightness of mind?"[2] The poem "These Are the Clouds" corresponds to that fear.

In the earlier poem, "Upon a House Shaken by the Land Agitation," Yeats has Blake's authority for the privilege of eagle over wren—the eagle, which is proverbially supposed to be able to look directly at the sun without blinking—and for the fear that wrens will win in the end. Blake's King Edward the Third has Sir Thomas Dagworth saying

> The Wolf is hunted down by causeless fear;
> The Lion flees, and fear usurps his heart,
> Startled, astonish'd at the clam'rous Cock;
> The Eagle, that doth gaze upon the sun,
> Fears the small fire that plays about the fen.

The eagle thoughts that grow

> Where wings have memory of wings, and all
> That comes of the best knit to the best

amount to Yeats's most succinct description of a tradition, the consanguinities of memory and lore retained through generations. In the poem, they are deemed to issue in a noble style, "a written speech / Wrought of high laughter, loveliness and ease," which I construe as issuing mostly from the culture of Urbino—Yeats visited Urbino in 1907—Castiglione's *Book of the Courtier,* and the Duchess Elisabetta giving the theme.

Many of Yeats's early references to the Anglo-Irish tradition—the Ascendancy—were bitter; as if he blamed those men of power and wealth for failing to live up to their vision. When he referred to Trinity College, Dublin, and to Provost Mahaffy and Professor Dowden, he was invariably dispirited: such men, in such a place, should have maintained intelligence, passion, and style commensurate with the tradition in their keeping. The tradition itself he revered. Indeed, he invented a century and called it the eighteenth, so that he could invoke at least one period in Irish history that had, as he said, "escaped from darkness and confusion."[3] Molyneux, Swift, Berkeley, Archbishop King, Goldsmith, Burke, Grattan, Lord Edward Fitzgerald: surely those men denoted a culture, and made intelligence, at least for a time, prevail.

Yeats believed that Ireland had two traditions worth maintaining. The Anglo-Irish tradition, mainly Protestant and aristocratic, was capacious enough to include the "old fathers" Yeats celebrated in the prefatory poem to *Responsibilities*—his own family, and the Pollexfens, named in the same breath with Butlers and Armstrongs. There was also the Gaelic tradition, to which Yeats had only indirect access by way of translations of the Celtic sagas, and the stories Lady Gregory and other enthusiasts collected in Sligo and Galway. Yeats well knew that the constituents of the Gaelic tradition had been suppressed if not destroyed—the Irish language, Irish music, the literature of Daniel Corkery's "Hidden Ireland" —but he joined with Douglas Hyde and the translators in hoping that much of Gaelic culture could be revived in poetry, song, and drama. The translators—John O'Daly, Charlotte Brooke, Ferguson, O'Curry, Sigerson, as well as Hyde—opened the right doors. Yeats was easily persuaded that this culture was as noble as any, and that its values were those of freedom, fantasy, imaginative excess. If these two traditions could be brought together, they would provide a moral basis for the development of an independent Ireland. In 1930 he wrote in his Diary:

> Preserve that which is living and help the two Irelands, Gaelic Ireland and Anglo-Ireland, so to unite that neither shall shed its pride.[4]

Not at all incidentally, such a union would suppress—or at least intimidate— the new, petit-bourgeois class, the small shopkeepers "fumbling in a greasy till," which Yeats despised and feared. These were the people to whom Daniel O'Connell gave voice; Catholic, but not at all emancipated from the penury of their daily interests. O'Connell was "the Great Comedian," image of every force that Yeats despised and feared in modern Ireland. Against O'Connell, he thought of Parnell, the proud, lonely figure, man of intellect and vision.

In the few years before and after the composition of "Upon a House Shaken by the Land Agitation," Yeats was outraged by several episodes in which he saw the defeat of aristocratic values. The episodes are well known: the attacks on Synge for *In the Shadow of the Glen* and again on the Abbey production of *The Playboy of the Western World* in January 1907; the destruction of the landlord-class—though Yeats didn't foresee the neglect of Coole Park, after Lady Gregory's death, and the Government's vandalism in selling it, in 1941, to a local builder for the price of its stone: George Moore's sneers at Yeats and Lady Gregory in *Vale;* and the controversy over Hugh Lane's proposal for a municipal art gallery in Dublin. The poem "To a Wealthy Man who Promised a Second Subscription to the Dublin Municipal Gallery if it were proved the People wanted Pictures" brought many of Yeats's sentiments together on these issues; the wealthy man was Lord Ardilaun, who should have had the spirit of a Renaissance prince, or something close enough to it to make him do the right thing, whatever the citizens of Dublin—the "blind and ignorant town"—chose to do:

> Let Paudeens play at pitch and toss,
> Look up in the sun's eye and give
> What the exultant heart calls good
> That some new day may breed the best
> Because you gave, not what they would,
> But the right twigs for an eagle's nest!

Pitch and toss is a street-game: you put two or three pennies on the flat of a stick, throw them up, and see how they fall—heads or tails. It is what urchins do who couldn't even imagine what it means to look without blinking in the sun's eye, or how an eagle differs from a wren.

The effect of these and other episodes was that Yeats gave up thinking of "the Big House" as an emblem of intelligence in active relation to power. He saw it now as an aesthetic image of defeat, the enslavement of the strong to the weak.

"Ancestral Houses," the first poem in "Meditations in Time of Civil War," was written in England before the War began. Yeats, his wife, and their daughter Anne spent much of 1921 in England, mainly in Oxford and in Thame, the village in Oxfordshire where their son Michael was born on August 22. When the Treaty was ratified by the Dail on January 7, 1922, it was clear that the Republicans would not accept the decision. Yeats and his family moved to Dublin at the end of March 1922, and to Thoor Ballylee almost immediately thereafter. Within a month, the Civil War began.

I propose to look at "Ancestral Houses" as indicating one moment in the flux or quarrel of Yeats's feelings about civilization, peace and war, gentleness and violence. I leave aside the complicated and complicating development of those feelings in the remaining poems of the sequence.

As it happens, I don't find "Ancestral Houses" as translucent as other readers evidently do. The grammar of the fourth stanza seems difficult, so I will attempt a paraphrase, to make the progression of the argument a little clearer. Then I will make a few comments on the poem itself. The first stanza says that in a rich man's garden, beauty issues as if directly from nature; or that art is the sweet completion of what nature has begun. As in Blake, the fountain overflows, taking whatever shape it chooses. But a sentence that begins with "surely" indicates that Yeats isn't sure at all, he is persuading himself that the sentiment is valid. The second stanza seems to give up the attempt: "Mere dreams, mere dreams!" But dreams have high repute in Yeats, as in his father, who once told him that "A people who do not dream never attain to inner sincerity, for only in his dreams is a man really himself. Only for his dreams is a man responsible — his actions are what he must do."[5] Besides, Homer is Yeats's example to show that the true source of beauty is the conviction of life's own self-delight; though now the most fitting symbol for the inherited glory of the rich is the sea-shell (beautiful, intricately formed over many years, but vulnerable to every rascal's boot) rather than the effortlessly abounding jet or fountain. Like the sea-shell, the rich are now elegant but without power. Donald Torchiana has quoted, in his *W. B. Yeats and Georgian Ireland,* a passage in which Yeats says that when the rule of educated and able men is gone, the order they once maintained "lies an empty shell for the passing fool to kick in pieces."[6] That the symbol "shadows" the inherited glory of the rich is odd: the verb is only barely available for such a purpose, unless Yeats means — as he may well — that the glory is at once shadowed or depicted and shadowed or darkened, its darkness registered, by the symbol which denotes its decline. The third stanza implies that beauty doesn't, indeed, issue "naturally" from nature, but from man; and not from man, but from men, bitter and violent because Yeats construes consciousness as conflict. The lion and the honeycomb, what has Scripture said? The Book of Judges, Chapter 14, has Samson say that "out of the strong came forth sweetness." But Yeats, a father, worries about generations, loss, decline. Two generations may see a great family peter out, the heroic note gone timid—Yeats is one of the few poets who have turned "violent" and "bitter" into words of praise. The syntax of the fourth stanza is hard: the gist of the lines is that there is a kind of beauty which makes us passive in its presence, and takes away our strength with our bitterness. Maybe we lose our greatness when we yield ourselves to such elegances as these: gardens where peacocks stray; all the things that Juno displays from an urn to indifferent garden deities; levelled lawns and gravelled ways. In these settings Juno and the peacocks are separate, we don't hear the scream which, according to *A Vision,* announces the next turn of the gyre:

> A civilisation is a struggle to keep self-control, and in this it is like some great tragic person, some Niobe who must display an almost superhuman will or the cry will not touch our sympathy. The loss of control over thought comes towards the end; first a sinking in upon the moral being, then the last surrender, the irrational cry, revelation— the scream of Juno's peacock.[7]

Quite a different thing from the straying peacocks on the lawns of Garsington Manor or whatever great house Yeats had in view. No new civilization is announced; more likely, the decline of an old one. The last stanza continues in much the same vein. "Haughtier" indicates that Yeats is thinking of the eighteenth century, the age of "haughtier-headed Burke," as in "Blood and the Moon"—another adjective turned from its common course to do the work of praise.

Parnell is never far from Yeats's mind in this mood. Nietzsche, too, when Yeats is trying to convert pathos into the gestures of tragedy and defiance. "Ancestral Houses" had to be the first poem in a sequence, because otherwise Yeats would have had to remain locked in the sentiment which regards the Big House as the sign of defeat. The remaining poems in the sequence try to escape from "Ancestral Houses" by Nietzschean devices and tones.

It is well understood that Yeats in his later years gave up hoping that Gaelic Ireland and Anglo-Ireland could be united to curb the vulgarity of petit-bourgeois Catholic Ireland. Or rather, he abandoned that hope in any of its agreeably civic forms. The assassination of Kevin O'Higgins, Minister of Justice in the Free State Government, on July 10, 1927, brought that dream to an end. I have always thought that Yeats's last poems embody, with two or three exceptions, a certain hysteria of the imagination, and display a Nietzschean will at the end of its tether. The stridency of "Under Ben Bulben" and "The Statues" gives the terrible show away. But what it means is that the dream has turned not only into nightmare but into rage and vituperation.

Much of that sentiment went into *Purgatory,* the play which is closest to the feelings that also went into the pamphlet *On the Boiler.* It is possible to interpret *Purgatory* in high-minded terms involving Yeats's notion, in *A Vision,* of "dreaming back," and to make the play enact a psychic action. But there is something ingenious and willed in that sense of it. The real source of the play is Yeats's disgust with an Ascendancy Ireland which lost courage and corrupted its blood. The Big House of the play may be Castle Dargan, but the account the Old Man gives of it brings together the history of Coole Park and, more generally, that of several houses of like kind:

> *Great people lived and died in this house;*
> *Magistrates, colonels, members of Parliament,*
> *Captains and Governors, and long ago*
> *Men that had fought at Aughrim and the Boyne.*
> *Some that had gone on Government work*
> *To London or to India came home to die,*
> *Or came from London every spring*
> *To look at the may-blossom in the park.*[8]

—which last is something Sir William Gregory did, according to his wife; and indeed the Government work is a generalised allusion to Sir William's years as Governor of Ceylon. But in any case the force of Yeats's feeling is turned upon a social class that failed to defend itself, entered into debauched relation with the worst of drunkards, gamblers, and lechers, and "killed the house":

> *to kill a house*
> *Where great men grew up, married, died,*
> *I here declare a capital offence.*

The crime, in the play, takes a double form. The marriage of the fine lady to the drunken groom in a training stable is a crime against her kind, and a crime against herself, a corruption of nature and of history. The Boy is the degraded consequence of generations gone rotten. The Old Man who killed his father now kills his son in an endless cycle of retribution and remorse.

It is only in the context of Yeats's feeling for Ascendancy Ireland that the play becomes tolerable: otherwise, it must appear merely a demand for practical eugenics. In a good production, the values of the Big House, of ancestral houses in general, would be shown as continuous with those of individual integrity, courage, and intelligence. In *A Vision* and elsewhere, Yeats alludes to Vico's idea of a struggle of classes and the regeneration of society by a return to a primitive state of mind and a new barbarism. But in the immediate setting of the last years of his life, he could think of the destiny of ancestral houses only in violent terms. Indeed, *On the Boiler* is an attempt to justify violence while seeming merely to express a sentiment in its favour. "If human violence is not embodied in our institutions," Yeats wrote, "the young will not give them their affection, nor the young and old their loyalty." He had in mind military families and a strong government, but in the next paragraph his sense of the improbability of his programme turns to rage. "Desire some just war, that big house and hovel, college and public-house, civil servant—his Gaelic certificate in his pocket—and international bridge-playing woman, may know that they belong to one nation."9

This is the hysterical version of Yeats's dream of kinship between peasant and nobleman, predicated upon the great estates in rural Ireland. It is a dreadful mood to have come to, but it is also touching in its appalling way. The sentiment of belonging to one nation is supposedly so vital that the mere characters of those it unites cease to matter. The gibe at the Irish-speaking civil servant is not in poorer taste than the one mocking the bridge-playing woman. In the next paragraph Yeats steadies himself to say that while "the Irish masses," as he calls them, meaning the Catholic middle-and-lower-middle class, "are vague and excitable because they have not yet been moulded and cast, we have as good blood as there is in Europe. Berkeley, Swift, Burke, Grattan, Parnell, Augusta Gregory, Synge, Kevin O'Higgins are the true Irish people, and there is nothing too hard for such as these." If the Catholic names in that list are few, he says, "history will soon fill the gap. My imagination goes back to those Catholic exiled gentlemen of whom Swift said that their bravery exceeded that of all nations." But of course Yeats found it easier to praise Catholics if they were gentlemen, to begin with, and exiles after that, than if they opened a small shop in Sligo and made enough money to send their children to university.

But we must take decent account of the fact that Yeats lived to see the Irish Free State become, on the whole, a middle-class Catholic state, and the Big House fall mostly—though not totally—into neglect. The symbols of Ascendancy Ireland are retained for show and adornment: they are no longer in any relation to power. The political leaders of Ireland have gone O'Connell's way, not Parnell's: there is no place for proud, lonely men in a Dail of gross vulgarity and a rhetorical system dominated by television. Yeats played a certain part in the social and political life of the Free State, but he never accepted the character it sought for itself. It is difficult to warm to his last poems, plays, and essays, but there is grim propriety in his refusal to comport himself to the observances of an Ireland he mostly despised.

But suppose we ask: what exactly was this Ascendancy Ireland which caught Yeats's imagination? Was it accurately embodied in Gandon's Custom House, Powerscourt, Charlemont House, and such?

On June 20, 1776, Arthur Young arrived at Dunleary at the beginning of an extended visit to study the social condition of Ireland. His *A Tour in Ireland* (1780) offered "general observations on the present state of that kingdom, made in the years 1776, 1777, and 1778, and brought down to the end of 1779." Young's procedure was to visit the Big House in each district, lodge with the most prominent landlords, and move about from those lodgings to study the development of Irish agriculture. His interests were entirely taken up with the land: he regarded trade and commerce as social necessities, but he denounced a trading spirit in government. In the first chapters of his book he praised Lord Charlemont's house and the Duke of Leinster's house, but he said that walking in the streets of Dublin, "from the narrowness and populousness of the principal thoroughfares, as well as from the dirt and wretchedness of the canaille, is a most uneasy and disgusting exercise."

So he made his way through the country, praising Luttrelstown Castle, Mr. Conolly's Castletown, Lord Conyngham's Slane Castle, Lord Bective's Headfort, Lord Longford's Packenhan Hall, Lord Altamont's Westport House, Powerscourt House, and many other splendours. He found many estates well kept up, the land well drained, the houses in good repair. But he thought the landlords, on the whole, intolerably arrogant. "The landlord of an Irish estate, inhabited by Roman Catholics," he said, "is a sort of despot who yields obedience, in whatever concerns the poor, to no law but that of his will."[10] More explicitly: "The domineering aristocracy of five hundred thousand Protestants feel the sweets of having two millions of slaves."[11] Young then named 195 absentee landlords, whose rents amounted to 732,200 pounds a year. As for the condition of the peasants: he reported that "generally speaking the Irish poor have a fair belly full of potatoes, and they have milk the greatest part of the year."[12] But Young's description of their houses may be quoted without comment:

> The cottages of the Irish, which are all called cabins, are the most miserable looking hovels that can well be conceived; they generally consist of only one room: mud kneaded with straw is the common material of the walls; these are rarely above seven feet high, and not always above five or six: they are about two feet thick, and have only a door, which lets in light instead of a window, and should let the smoke out instead of a chimney, but they had rather keep it in: these two conveniences they hold so cheap, that I have seen them both stopped up in stone cottages, built by improving landlords; the smoke warms them, but certainly is as injurious to their eyes as it is to the complexion of the women, which in general in the cabins of Ireland has a near resemblance to that of a smoked ham. The number of the blind poor I think greater there than in England, which is probably owing to this cause.[13]

Seventy years later, when Carlyle made a tour of several weeks through Ireland, the account of it he jotted down in his diary didn't differ much from Young's; except that Carlyle was weary of the people—"this brawling unreasonable people," as he called them—before he set foot on the country. Where Young reported that the Irish peasants would steal anything that wasn't nailed down, Carlyle saw mostly the beggars: "Beggars, beggars; only industry really followed by the Irish people," he noted.[14] Carlyle's disciple James Anthony Froude didn't need to make a tour of the country to decide that the Irish peasants were congenitally indolent. Besides, the terms on which they were supposed to work the land had only one consequence. "They grew up," he said, "in compulsory idleness, encouraged once more in their inherited dislike of labour, and enured to wretchedness and hunger." Froude's conclusion was that Gladstone should move quickly and go far beyond his declared intention in the matter of Home Rule. The British should clear out of Ireland. "We cannot govern India: we cannot govern Ireland":[15] this was Froude's last word in his book *The English in Ireland in the Eighteenth Century.*

Even among the Anglo-Irish themselves, there were some who saw the tradition of Ascendancy Ireland as a failure of nerve. Standish O'Grady in "Toryism and Tory Democracy" and again in "The Great Enchantment" said of his own kind:

> They might have been so much to this afflicted nation; half-ruined as they are, they might be so much to-morrow; but the curse that has fallen on the whole land seems to have fallen on them with double power—the understanding paralysed, the will gone all to water, and for consequence a sure destruction.[16]

O'Grady was willing to be rueful about the decline, but not to enquire further into the merit of a society which did little to rescue millions of Irish peasants from poverty and hunger.

II

What I have been saying about Yeats and his sense of ancestral houses has been based upon certain theoretical axioms. Or rather, it has issued from an intermittent and sometimes heretical relation to those axioms. I have to refer to them now, if only because they are so often set aside.

When I first read Yeats, Eliot, Pound, and the other major modern poets, I was admonished to respect what was called "the autonomy of the poem." It was not clear to me what precisely I was to respect, except in the rudimentary sense that a poem is not the same as the arguments it appears to advance. I was also aware of Henry James's assertion that the reader must concede to the artist his *donnée*; and even if James merely meant that the novelist should be free to take up any theme or subject he chooses, I took him to mean, in addition, that he should be free to adopt toward his theme or subject pretty much whatever attitude suited him. Put these sentiments together and you quickly find that they insist on giving the artist whatever latitude he seems to ask for.

Yeats's poetry, in that context, caused a difficulty at two points. The political attitudes implicit or explicit in his last poems seemed so outlandish that it was hard to extend to them the hospitality I readily extended to attitudes in Eliot or Stevens. The second problem arose from Yeats's dealings with magic and occult interests generally, from what Auden called the Southern Californian element in a number of Yeats's poems.

Readers who wanted to give poets all the latitude in the world tended to make up justifications good enough for the case at hand. Richard Blackmur spoke for many in maintaining that the poet who announces a doctrine in his essays is likely to take up an informal or ad libbing relation to the doctrine in his poems; or an opportunistic relation, which amounts to much the same thing. Or it could be argued, as Blackmur did, that while any one of Yeats's interests might be thought to be bizarre or exorbitant, the work as a whole somehow cohered as "a felt unity of disproportions." Somewhat more strenuously, Blackmur maintained that a poet in the twentieth century, a time in which there is no accredited structure of values by which meanings are identified and authenticated, must be free to make his own system. The metaphor regularly used to explain this procedure was that of scaffolding, which may be of any shape or kind so long as it does the job, at which point it may be dispensed with. The criterion in such cases was given in one of Blackmur's formulae: "not emotion put into doctrine from outside, but doctrine presented as emotion." It was by an assertion in that spirit that Blackmur could then say that Yeats's magic, "like every other feature of his experience, is rational as it reaches words; otherwise it is his privation, and ours, because it was the rational defect of our society that drove him to it."[17]

I should not give the impression that Blackmur's concessions went unchallenged. John Crowe Ransom was only one of those who complained that in Blackmur's essays on Yeats "there is no ideological emphasis; the social or religious ideas are looked at shrewdly, but they are appraised for their function within the work; even though they may be ideas from which, at the very moment, out in the world of action, the issues of life and death are hung." Blackmur, that is to say, "is repudiating the ideas as ideas, and reckoning their usefulness for the poem."[18] But generally in those years it was felt that the poet needed whatever he said he needed, and that he should be given nearly every concession. Readers were willing to postpone their decision on the material of a poem and wait to see how it transpired in the words. If at that point they recognised a force of conviction among the words, and the irrefutable character of the poem's idiom and rhythm, they were likely to take the ideas on trust, or even to forget that in a sullen mood they would make a fuss.

I mention this context of theory mainly because it is now mostly set aside. Readers are no longer willing to give poets the latitude they ask for, especially when political attitudes are in question. We seem to be at the end of the period in which the theory of literature was construed in philosophical terms. Our setting is now much more overtly political. Issues are named as ideological as soon as they are recognised as issues at all.

Raymond Williams's *The Country and the City* has been highly influential in this development. Like Fredric Jameson's *The Political Unconscious,* it has done much to make readers feel that the political issue, the nature of political attitudes, takes priority over every other consideration, and especially over those which would be represented as formal or aesthetic. But I assume these books have merely articulated and given a rhetorical edge to attitudes more pervasively held.

One of the consequences of this critical setting is that Yeats's poems are now given little or no latitude; especially in Ireland, for local reasons I'll try to explain. But also for reasons more widely asserted.

But I shall give my sense of the critical situation rather than quote chapter and verse for each item. In Ireland, a revisionist reading of Yeats is offered by Seamus Deane, Declan Kiberd, and other critics: abroad, by critics otherwise so diverse that it would be misleading even to name them. Most of them are affronted, in Ireland and elsewhere, by Yeats's sense of history as the deeds of great men; and of culture as, in this respect, indistinguishable from history. An age is known by the names of those men who dominated it: a culture by the forms their domination took. History is the will of a few people, so far as it impressed itself upon the conditions at large. Discriminations of social class are replaced by those of caste, a spiritual attribute. Hugh Kenner, sensitive to the acts of great men, gives the gist of a corresponding philosophy of history in a Yeatsian chapter of *A Colder Eye*: "Ruined castles, ruined houses, ruined towers round or square, mark achievement that flared briefly and flamed out, whereupon a few more stragglers shifted their ground."[19] A famous stanza from "In Memory of Major Robert Gregory" distinguishes those lives which flare and flame from timid ones that burn like damp faggots. It is not surprising that Yeats, in his later zeal for Ascendancy Ireland, thought only of six or seven great men and not at all of those millions who starved in their presence. Nor is it surprising that the rhetoric of his poems, the Yeatsian music, depends upon the poet's will, which draws experience to a distinctly personal centre and takes possession of it there.

But there is a further exacerbation. In Yeats's rhetoric the deeds of great men are not allowed to be understood only in their context, or as responses to their conditions. They are reconstituted as an "essential" diagram of human life: that is, history is understood as myth, a timeless structure of meaning and value. Yeats paid the same tribute to his own life. When he complained, or feared, in "Ancestral Houses," that civilization defeats the forces that created its emblems, by accommodating their violence to an aesthetic image, as in houses or paintings, he allowed no barrier to stand between what he had seen or thought or divined or suffered. His own life was sufficient evidence. Indeed, he identified that life with the only destiny Ireland should want, and wrote as if the forms of culture he favoured had the salience of natural law. When he saw that the destiny he espoused was likely to be rejected by those for whom he invoked it, he resorted to the figures of tragedy to turn loss into aesthetic gain, defeat into the triumph of a tragic gesture. The heroes of Ascendancy Ireland, from Swift to its defeat in Kevin O'Higgins, became tragic heroes in a theatre overwhelmed in the end by groundlings and stragglers.

In Ireland, it is fair to say, Yeats is resented; not for his snobbery, his outlandish claim to the possession of Norman blood, or even for his evasion of history by appeal to two classes of people who existed only as shades—Gaelic Irish and Anglo-Irish—but because he claimed to speak in the name of "the indomitable Irishry." De Valera claimed to speak for Ireland, and the claim was tenable: he has had, in that capacity, no successor. In the present confusions, readers of Yeats resent his appeal to Irishness, and his assertion that he knows the quality of Irishness when he meets it. That resentment is so inclusive that little or nothing survives in its presence.

I am describing a political judgment imposed upon poetry, and glancing at some of its consequences. My own stance is that of a latitudinarian, and I would hold to its concessiveness until a particularly extreme outrage makes me ashamed of it.

ON
THE WINDING STAIR

In one of his loftiest moments in *A Vision*, Yeats says:

The ultimate reality because neither one nor many, concord nor discord, is symbolised as a phaseless sphere, but as all things fall into a series of antinomies in human experience it becomes, the moment it is thought of, what I shall presently describe as the thirteenth cone.

And in "Vacillation":

> *A brand, or flaming breath,*
> *Comes to destroy*
> *All those antinomies*
> *Of day and night.*

Between extremities Yeats runs his course. In *The Winding Stair* one extreme is the poem "Chosen" in which the Zodiac is changed, under learned auspices, into a sphere; another is the "frog-spawn of a blind man's ditch," in "A Dialogue of Self and Soul." Sometimes the poet yearns for the brand or flaming breath; often the resultant simplicity, "the fire that makes all simple," is too severe, too remote to satisfy his blood-sodden heart. Hence *The Winding Stair,* a book misleadingly titled, is a storm of antinomies, the cry of their occasions.

The book begins with a memorial poem to Eva Gore-Booth and Con Markiewicz, the first of many Mutabilitie-Cantos in which we see the storm and hear the cry. The mood is caught from such poems as "Nineteen Hundred and Nineteen" and "Meditations in Time of Civil War." Yeats offers to resolve it, as Robert Gregory did, in a conflagration of self-begotten splendour: "Bid me strike a match and blow." Later, in such poems as "Spilt Milk" and "The Nineteenth Century and After," it will be too late for arson. Sometimes the fact of mutability is given with a show of urbanity ("the toil has left its mark"), but more often the tone is unyielding ("a raving autumn shears / Blossom from the summer wreath"; "that high horse riderless"; "by that inhuman bitter glory wrecked"; "Time's filthy load"). From an earlier poem, "Man is in love and loves what vanishes, / What more is there to say?" There is, in fact, much more to say, and Yeats says most of it in *The Winding Stair,* but he begins with "what vanishes." Hence the first two poems are all mutability; great dead houses, a beautiful woman now "withered old and skeleton-gaunt," life declined into politics, the assassination of Kevin O'Higgins.

And hence the question that storms and cries through the entire book: in a world of mutability, what remains, what is possible, where does value reside?

The answer, but not the whole story, is: in the imagination of Man. In the memorial poem Yeats offers his own imagination as the appropriate reply to Time, the only enemy of the innocent and the beautiful:

> Arise and bid me strike a match
> And strike another till time catch

—so the work can finish in that flare. In the second poem, "Death," the great man who

> Casts derision upon
> Supersession of breath

knows death to the bone, and in that sense "Man has created death." Reality and the Imagination, to use Wallace Stevens's terms and a little of his idiom, are equal and inseparable. This is a consolation, in its way, but the antinomies persist, and Yeats recites an elaborate version of them in the next poem, the crucial "Dialogue of Self and Soul."

Self is man committed to his mortality, assenting to time, place, history, the earth, "this and that and t'other thing," death and birth, grateful for all affections, but ready, in extremity, to live—to go on—without them. Soul is man on the high road, climbing the winding stair, aspiring to a condition in which the antinomies of day and night are transcended. Blake said, "The cistern contains: the fountain overflows," and the Soul aspires to a Heaven which features, among its pleasures, an irrefutable unity of mind:

> *For intellect no longer knows*
> Is *from the* Ought, *or* Knower *from the* Known—
> *That is to say, ascends to Heaven;*

—a formulation already given in *A Vision,* incidentally, as a description of the relation between Will, Mask, Creative Mind, and Body of Fate. The speech of Soul, in the "Dialogue," has freed itself from the hysterical intensity of its earlier version in "All Souls' Night," the last poem in *The Tower,* indicating that the condition of being "wound in mind's wandering / As mummies in the mummy-cloth are wound" was not final. For the rest of the poem Yeats gives his casting vote to the Self; the voice claims all the victories for "Life," the low road, the crime of death and birth, the ignominy of flesh and bone, accepted without remorse. Blake is still there:

> *When such as I cast out remorse*
> *So great a sweetness flows into the breast*
> *We must laugh and we must sing,*
> *We are blest by everything,*
> *Everything we look upon is blest.*

—a condition later designated, quite simply, as the "happiness" of "Vacillation."

The "Dialogue" is not, indeed, an outstanding example of free democratic speech; the casting vote is delivered before the poor Soul has well begun. Yeats has moved away from the allegiances of *The Tower,* and he is anxious to speak up on behalf of the new cause; now, at least, whatever one may say about the other occasions in the book on which the dispute is carried out more rigorously. But the argument of Self and Soul is the structural figure of the entire book; the text annotated with footnotes like "Veronica's Napkin," where the Heavenly Circuit, Berenice's Hair, and other emblems of Soul are "answered" by Self, "a pattern on a napkin dipped in blood." Self is occasionally called the heart, as in the seventh section of "Vacillation," but the voice is the same, and when the Soul invokes once again the fire that makes all simple, Heart answers: "What theme had Homer but original sin?"

The dispute of Self and Soul takes many forms in *The Winding Stair,* including very simple ones, like—from "Her Vision in the Wood"— "Why should they think that are for ever young?" or the enforced choice between perfection of the life or of the work; emblems of day, set off against those of night; and so on. In "Byzantium" the fury and the mire of human veins are scorned by the moonlit dome; the complexities of mire or blood, by the golden bird "in glory of changeless metal"; the fury of blood-begotten spirits, by the "flames begotten of flame." (But the allegiance of "Byzantium" is a difficult story.) The claims of soul are advanced by many terms and symbols. Some are easy, like the miraculous oil of "Oil and Blood," darkness, night, Heaven, Moon, salvation, hermit, Plato, water as the generated soul of "Coole Park and Ballylee, 1931," the God in whom all things remain, and even—in parody—Crazy Jane's Bishop. Some of the devotees of Self are also easy: Sato's ancient blade, the silken embroidery of the "Dialogue," earth, day, flowers, ditches, frog-spawn, blood—in several poems—power, original sin, the Fool, milk spilt on a stone, the rattle of pebbles on the shore, swallows, dolphins, gongs, Homer, and the body itself—very frequently—in the Crazy Jane poems. But the crucial symbols of the book exhibit many a sea-change and imply a much more elaborate argument than the simple dispute of Self and Soul which I have sketched. The dispute persists, but the leading terms are forced to bear new burdens, ground is lost and won, and the dividing lines are never as true as the leaders hope. To be specific: in the early poems of *The Winding Stair* Yeats sets up a strict dispute between Self and Soul; as the dispute continues, he volunteers for Self and tries to take possession of the Soul's attributes, those values which he will reject, if they threaten the Self, but which he would much more willingly commandeer. What follows is an examination of the leading terms of the book; what they are, what they suffer, what they survive.

The tower itself for instance: one of three declared possessions in the poem "Symbols"; very much the place of Soul, in the "Dialogue":

> *—and all these I set*
> *For emblems of the day against the tower*
> *Emblematical of the night . . .*

But in "Blood and the Moon" it is not the lonely tower of Milton's Platonist scholar, the contemplative man. When Yeats says, "I declare this tower is my symbol," the footnotes pointing to Alexandria, Babylon, and Shelley are imperious notations, but Yeats's tower is committed now to time, event, and history; a tower in particular time and place, broken at the top. *The Winding Stair* is a misleading title because it conceals the mockery with which Yeats invoked it:

> *In mockery I have set*
> *A powerful emblem up,*
> *And sing it rhyme upon rhyme*
> *In mockery of a time*
> *Half dead at the top.*

Yeats's Norman Thoor Ballylee becomes his symbol now only when he has managed, by a flick of historical fancy, to associate it with Swift, Goldsmith, Burke, and Berkeley. Not Stevens's "ultimate Plato." But the conjunction of these four men is still curious. What have they in common, apart from genius and an Anglo-Irish inheritance? Some of the descriptions in "Blood and the Moon" are implausible, notably "Goldsmith deliberately sipping at the honey-pot of his mind"—which (even with the complication of "deliberately") sounds more like the Keatsian decadent featured in *A Vision*. In the essay on Berkeley, Yeats brings his four together again in a prose version which clarifies the issue:

> . . . Berkeley with his belief in perception, that abstract ideas are mere words, Swift with his love of perfect nature, of the Houyhnhnms, his disbelief in Newton's system and every sort of machine, Goldsmith and his delight in the particulars of common life that shocked his contemporaries, Burke with his conviction that all States not grown slowly like a forest tree are tyrannies, found in

England the opposite that stung their own thought into expression and made it lucid.

Perception, love, delight, conviction; every possible value, in fact; only a tower hospitable alike to all these commitments will be "my symbol." If it appears that by these conjunctions Self has virtually taken possession of Soul, well and good.

Not that the battle is over. In the third and fourth sections of the poem —"Blood and the Moon"—the dispute continues as the antinomy of Power and Wisdom. The scene is still the tower, built on blood-saturated ground, and the unclouded moon has flung its shaft across the floor. Just as in "The Crazed Moon" "we grope, and grope in vain, / For children born of her pain," here we "clamour in drunken frenzy for the moon." Watching the butterflies (in Dante, symbolising the souls of the dead), Yeats says:

> Is every modern nation like the tower,
> Half dead at the top? No matter what I said,
> For wisdom is the property of the dead,
> A something incompatible with life; and power,
> Like everything that has the stain of blood,
> A property of the living; but no stain
> Can come upon the visage of the moon
> When it has looked in glory from a cloud. (C.P., 269)

These lines would have found a more congenial home in the poem "Vacillation." Wisdom is of Soul, and if a choice is inescapable, Yeats in the spirit of the "Dialogue" will choose Power. But—another way out—he will try to construe Wisdom in subversive terms. In "The Seven Sages" he returns to Swift, Goldsmith, Burke, and Berkeley and writes a tedious poem to assert that "wisdom comes of beggary"; and in "After Long Silence" he sets up an equation which suggests that what we gain by climbing the winding stair may not be worth the effort:

> Bodily decrepitude is wisdom; young
> We loved each other and were ignorant.

After this, the "fathomless wisdom" of "Her Dream" seems a tenuous boon.

Again, the self-begotten flame is one of Yeats's most persistent symbols for the unities of Soul which he invokes; but sometimes he will claim
a corresponding blaze for the Self. In the "Happiness" part of "Vacillation"
he takes care to place the experience, the immutable "moment,"

> *My fiftieth year had come and gone,*
> *I sat, a solitary man,*
> *In a crowded London shop . . .*

and then a Swedenborgian moment:

> *While on the shop and street I gazed*
> *My body of a sudden blazed;*

as if the body, in animation, were to certify an undissociated condition,
final, beyond dispute; and Yeats several times recalls that in Dante it was
so. A similar moment occurs in "Stream and Sun at Glendalough":

> *What motion of the sun or stream*
> *Or eyelid shot the gleam*
> *That pierced my body through?*
> *What made me live like these that seem*
> *Self-born, born anew?*

—clearly a moment in which the antinomies of day and night, Self and Soul,
are resolved, and the only unity is the supreme form of it, unity of being.

But even when Yeats is still mired in the antinomies, and—especially
in the love songs of this book—when Soul appears as soul and Self as
body; even then, he challenges Soul on its own ground. In "A Last
Confession" the woman promises:

> *But when this soul, its body off,*
> *Naked to naked goes,*
> *He it has found shall find therein*
> *What none other knows,*

> *And give his own and take his own*
> *And rule in his own right;*

And though it loved in misery
Close and cling so tight,
There's not a bird of day that dare
Extinguish that delight.

Perhaps so: but in these poems generally a very small margin of possibility is held out for such soul-love; normally the soul is the luminous halo surrounding a tangible body and not otherwise verifiable. The only satisfying unity is "All":

"Love is all
Unsatisfied
That cannot take the whole
Body and soul";
And that is what Jane said.

The basic pattern of the book, then, is to acknowledge the antinomies of day and night, Self and Soul, only to subvert them—as far as possible; and it will be possible only rarely. If we want a motto for this, we think of the corresponding antinomies of Time and Eternity—a common version in Yeats—and then recall Blake's aphorism "Eternity is in love with the productions of Time." Yeats gloried in this assertion and took every imaginable stock in its truth. If Soul spoke through the starlit air and invoked "the star that marks the hidden pole," the admonition was not definitive; there would be another moment in which the star is humanised with the idiom of Self, as in "The Mother of God" Mary asks of the Christ-child:

What is this flesh I purchased with my pains,
This fallen star my milk sustains.

II

But the main pressure of the book will be to resolve the antinomies of day and night. In the second stanza of "Vacillation" such a resolution is implied in the image of the tree that is "half all glittering flame and half all green / Abounding foliage moistened with the dew." Joy, as in "Michael Robartes," is the double vision:

And he that Attis' image hangs between
That staring fury and the blind lush leaf
May know not what he knows, but knows not grief.

Later in the same poem the resolution is given through the ecstasy of the tragic hero, the man who, because he has conceived life as tragedy, comes "proud, open-eyed and laughing to the tomb"; the tragic ecstasy of Lear, Hamlet, Timon, which Yeats invokes so often in prose and verse. There is a resolution also in the answer to mutability which Yeats gives in the sixth part of "Vacillation," " 'Let all things pass away.' " because this is a dignified stance in what Stevens called "the element of antagonisms." It is also something, another resolution, a liaison, that the body of Saint Teresa "lived undecayed in tomb"; there is the humanist version, which Yeats praises as Tradition and gives in "Quarrel in Old Age" as "All lives that has lived"; and there is love to match:

"Uplift those eyes and throw
Those glances unafraid:
She would as bravely show
Did all the fabric fade;
No withered crone I saw
Before the world was made."

There is the "stillness" of the lovers in "Chosen," adduced in evidence of total being; as the woman says,

I take
That stillness for a theme
Where his heart my heart did seem
And both adrift on the miraculous stream
Where—wrote a learned astrologer—
The Zodiac is changed into a sphere.

If all else fails, one returns to a plain sense of things, to a vision of life under Blake's auspices and attributed now to Tom the Lunatic:

"Whatever stands in field or flood,
Bird, beast, fish or man,
Mare or stallion, cock or hen,

> *Stands in God's unchanging eye*
> *In all the vigour of its blood;*
> *In that faith I live or die."*

One lives with miracle, if a miracle comes; if not, one still lives. Joy is available if the attributes of Self can swell and overflow, like Blake's fountain, and fill up the hollows left by Soul; or if Soul, in loneliness, "descends" into the mire of humanity. Either way, the values declared in *The Winding Stair,* by a casting vote if not unanimously, are those of time, place, and human limitation. A partial list would include the following: the mounting swan, "so lovely that it sets to right / What knowledge or its lack had set awry"; the holy bird of "Lullaby"; the innocent and the beautiful; "the strength that gives our blood and state magnanimity of its own desire"; Tradition, "Thoughts long knitted into a single thought, / A dance-like glory that those walls begot"; "a woman's powerful character" —Lady Gregory's; "the book of the people"; Anne Gregory's yellow hair; the human liberty Swift served; the shells from Rosses Point, not those "in Newton's metaphor"; the passion of "A Woman Young and Old"; the unchristened heart; the love sung by Mohini Chatterjee; all other loves; beauty, wherever found; mere Life, "I am content to live it all again"; the stir through the countryside in "The Crazed Moon," "What manhood led the dance!"; the high breeding and "style" of Coole Park, Lissadell, and their inhabitants; and the great dance, the dance of the human imagination, "Men dance on deathless feet."

Indeed, the heroes of this book—tragic heroes, most of them—are men and women who with dignity conducted a war between the mind and sky—Stevens's phrase: Blake, silently invoked throughout; Homer; Swift "beating on his breast in sibylline frenzy blind / Because the heart in his blood-sodden breast had dragged him down into mankind"; Goldsmith; God-appointed Berkeley; Burke; Lady Gregory, "an aged woman and her house"; Douglas Hyde; "that meditative man, John Synge"; Shawe-Taylor; Hugh Lane; the anonymous woman young and old; Crazy Jane; Eva Gore-Booth; Con Markiewicz; Kevin O'Higgins; Tom the Lunatic. And the imagination which Yeats praises is not that "loose imagination" of "An Acre of Grass" but something much closer to the "old man's eagle mind" of the same poem:

> *Grant me an old man's frenzy,*
> *Myself must I remake*

Till I am Timon and Lear
Or that William Blake
Who beat upon the wall
Till Truth obeyed his call.

—an exorbitant stanza, indeed. (How many Blakes are there, such that William needs emphasis?) What we hear in *The Winding Stair* is a man beating upon a wall.

III

In the Diary of 1930 Yeats meditates upon these themes, in one or two passages with particular intimacy:

> I am always, in all I do, driven to a moment which is the realisation of myself as unique and free, or to a moment which is the surrender to God of all that I am. . . . could those two impulses, one as much a part of truth as the other, be reconciled, or if one or the other could prevail, all life would cease. . . . Surely if either circuit, that which carries us into man or that which carries us into God, were reality, the generation had long since found its term.

In prose-moments Yeats was prepared to concede, of Self and Soul, that one is as much a part of truth as the other, but in most of the poems he enlisted under one banner and for the time being served it zealously. In *The Winding Stair,* when it came to a choice between the circuit which carried him into man and that which carried him into God, he chose man; but even as he voted he felt the burden of misgiving, loss, sacrifice, waste. The longing expressed in the Diary points directly to "Byzantium" and *The Resurrection.*

It is customary to read "Byzantium" as a parable of the poetic imagination, placing it in the company of similar parables from Coleridge to Stevens; where the blood-begotten spirits are the human experiences, broken and forged by the creative imagination and refined to the "glory of changeless metal." Read in this way, it seems a small poem enough. I should prefer to take it more literally. Indeed, the scenario for the poem is given, a few pages later, in the first stanza of "Vacillation":

> A brand, or flaming breath,
> Comes to destroy
> All those antinomies
> Of day and night.

The landscape of "Byzantium" is very like that of the third section of "Blood and the Moon": the tower, the odour of blood on the ancestral stair, and the unstained shaft of moonlight upon the floor chime with the city, the fury and the mire of human veins, and the disdainful starlit or moonlit dome. Recall, too, in reading "Byzantium," the tone of

> Odour of blood on the ancestral stair!
> And we that have shed none must gather there
> And clamour in drunken frenzy for the moon.

The first stanza is all Soul, and the rhetoric favours Yeats's second "circuit," that which "carries us into God" or, in alternative idiom, into the thirteenth cone. The crime of death and birth is not forgotten, but it trails out from the second circuit and barely survives the second stanza. The image which floats before the poet is identified with the superhuman:

> I hail the superhuman;
> I call it death-in-life and life-in-death.

He does so because Heraclitus, or so Yeats fancied, had already vouched for this relation: "God and man die each other's life, live each other's death," as the Greek student of Heraclitus says in *The Resurrection*. But our emphasis must be upon God, since the speaker—all Soul—has "a mouth that has no moisture and no breath." The third stanza produces a correlative eikon, the golden bird, "more miracle than bird or handiwork" because it issues from the "shade more than man, more image than a shade." The golden bough which sustains the bird is nearer the second circuit than the tree half flame and half foliage of "Vacillation"; so this is a commitment, not a resolution. The changeless metal is not that of Sato's ancient blade; it is assimilated to the metal of the moonlit dome and exhibits a corresponding scorn. But at least the "complexities of mire or blood" are recalled. Recalled, only to be refined and simplified, the antinomies of day and night now destroyed by the brand or flaming breath, flames that no faggot feeds, because this is still the second circuit, the Way of the Soul.

The triumph of the Soul would be complete but for the dolphin, the beast of burden totally committed to the Self, to mere "Life." As the dolphin carries the human soul to Paradise, the reality of the first circuit breaks in; the vatic poet looks back at the waves of this poor reality breaking upon the marbles of the dancing floor:

> *Those images that yet*
> *Fresh images beget*

—as one wave of human reality begets another, answering in their kind the superhuman "flames begotten of flame," and the Way of the Self, the first circuit, "that which carries us into man," carries us into the cycle of nature, honey of generation, mire and blood and time, "that dolphin-torn, that gong-tormented sea."

The antinomies of day and night, Self and Soul must be brought to the most crucial of all tests, the antinomies of God and Man. The aphorism attributed to Heraclitus links "Byzantium" to *The Resurrection* and both to the central preoccupation of *The Winding Stair,* but Yeats did not need Heraclitus for this incitement, it was implicit in the logic of his terms. Given the antinomies already deployed, he could not have avoided bringing them to this definitive test. It is easy enough for Crazy Jane to reflect, in her Sabbath voice, that "Men come, men go" but *"All things remain in God."* Yeats could not answer so readily. For one thing, he had to dramatize the issue before he could face it. So he needed *The Resurrection.*

In the Preface to the play Yeats is concerned with the question of the supernatural. "What if there is always something that lies outside knowledge, outside order? . . . What if the irrational return? What if the circle begin again?" and, a few pages earlier,

> Even though we think temporal existence illusionary it cannot be capricious; it is what Plotinus called the characteristic act of the soul and must reflect the soul's coherence. All our thought seems to lead by antithesis to some new affirmation of the supernatural.

In the play itself the voice of Soul is the Greek, to whom the reality is God-but-no-man; a phantom:

No god has ever been buried; no god has ever suffered. Christ only seemed to be born, only seemed to eat, seemed to sleep, seemed to walk, seemed to die.

Furthermore, the gods

can be discovered by contemplation, in their faces a high keen joy like the cry of a bat, and the man who lives heroically gives them the only earthly body that they covet. He, as it were, copies their gestures and their acts.

The Greek's lesson is exactly the opposite of Ribh's, in the later "Supernatural Songs": things below may indeed be copies, as the Great Smaragdine Tablet said, but Ribh has just declared,

Natural and supernatural with the self-same ring are wed.
As man, as beast, as an ephemeral fly begets, Godhead begets Godhead.

In the play the voice of Self is the Hebrew, to whom the reality is still Man-but-no-god: Christ "was nothing more than a man, the best man who ever lived":

He preached the coming of the Messiah because he thought the Messiah would take it all upon himself. Then some day when he was very tired, after a long journey perhaps, he thought that he himself was the Messiah. He thought it because of all destinies it seemed the most terrible.

What a relief, then, that the second circuit can still be evaded; that the first constitutes whatever reality we are ever likely to bear.

But there is a third voice, the Syrian; the one who believes and thereafter contains within himself the great disorder which, as Stevens says in "Connoisseur of Chaos," is itself an order. This is an approach to "the meaning," the resolution, and the next step is the climax of the play, when the Greek, a doubting Thomas, touches the side of the "phantom" and feels there a heart beating:

O Athens, Alexandria, Rome, something has come to destroy you. The heart of a phantom is beating. Man has begun to die. Your words are clear at last, O Heraclitus. God and man die each other's life, live each other's death.

The song with which the play ends "certifies" Christ's humanity in terms remarkably close to the idiom of Self in *The Winding Stair:*

> *Odour of blood when Christ was slain*
> *Made all Platonic tolerance vain*
> *And vain all Doric discipline.*

The final commitment is to the cycle of nature:

> *Everything that man esteems*
> *Endures a moment or a day.*
> *Love's pleasure drives his love away,*
> *The painter's brush consumes his dreams;*
> *The herald's cry, the soldier's tread*
> *Exhaust his glory and his might:*
> *Whatever flames upon the night*
> *Man's own resinous heart has fed.*

"Byzantium" invoked "flames begotten of flame." In "Coole Park and Ballylee, 1931," Yeats suddenly asks, "What's water but the generated soul?" because the racing waters which dropped into a hole suggested the death of the elements—Heraclitus again—and particularly the death of fire (the soul) in water which is therefore the generated soul. But the song at the end of *The Resurrection* moves from Heraclitus to Swift and Blake and the cry of mutability; with this difference, that the exhaustion now seems purposive, no longer waste but a cycle of exhaustion and regeneration. The regeneration is in the flame and the actions of painter, soldier, herald, lover. T. S. Eliot, writing of these matters in "Little Gidding," says, "Between melting and freezing / The soul's sap quivers"—which is one way of putting it; and the Chorus of the Four Elements in the second part of the poem recites a Heraclitean lesson in apocalyptic terms:

> *Water and fire succeed*
> *The town, the pasture and the weed.*
> *Water and fire deride*
> *The sacrifice that we denied.*

> *Water and fire shall rot*
> *The marred foundations we forgot . . .*

—another version of the moonlit dome disdaining all that man is. So
Eliot directs his ephebe toward the refining pentecostal fire; Yeats sends
him to Swift and Blake.

For several reasons. First, because Yeats himself has been to school at
those masters: Swift, who "served human liberty," the freedom and
uniqueness of the first circuit; Blake, who in *Vala* spoke of divisions and
antinomies:

> *Daughter of Beulah, Sing*
> *His fall into Division & his Resurrection to Unity:*
> *His fall into the Generation of decay & death, & his*
> *Regeneration by the Resurrection from the dead.*

Second, because Blake and Swift will help Yeats—and therefore his
ephebe—to know that man is in love and loves what vanishes and to
know also that "all lives that has lived."

IV

Yeats thought well of *The Winding Stair.* In the Introduction to *A Vision*
he claims that the poetry of *The Tower* and *The Winding Stair* is a gain in
"self-possession and power," and, some pages later, glosses this claim with
another, that of holding in a single thought reality and justice. When we
bring these terms together—power, self-possession, reality, justice—we
see that Yeats's claim amounts to nothing less than this, that in those
books his doctrine of the Mask has been realised, certified. In "Hodos
Chameliontos" he says:

> And as I look backward upon my own writing, I take pleasure alone
> in those verses where it seems to me I have found something hard
> and cold, some articulation of the Image which is the opposite
> of all that I am in my daily life.

In a dozen places he speaks of the assumption of a mask in similar terms; it
is conscious, creative, theatrical. The doctrine itself is merely the applica-

tion of theatrical metaphors to the common idea that the human imagination is "creative"; "every creative act can be seen as fact," as Yeats says in *A Vision.* The only difference between Yeats's doctrine and the general Romantic theory of the creative imagination is that it takes very little stock in the idea of the art-object safe beyond time, the poem as a well-wrought urn. Instead, it aspires to the condition of drama, incorrigibly in time, and it capitalises upon the ambiguities of such terms as role, action, gesture, mask, and play. This is at once the strength and the limitation of the doctrine; when it is utterly dedicated to reality and justice, it is powerful, self-possessed, and humane, always aware of the crime of death and birth. To assume a role and accept the discipline of living it is splendid; but the temptation is merely to flaunt a pose, to strike a gesture, to cut a dash. The great poems in *The Winding Stair* seek reality and justice and let the photogenic figure take care of itself. The weaker poems are hardly concerned with justice at all and treat reality as a mere instrument in the service of a spectacularly cut dash. Sometimes the finest poems are tainted in this way.

I have in mind, as a case in point, "Coole Park and Ballylee, 1931," especially a moment in the second stanza:

> *Upon the border of that lake's a wood*
> *Now all dry sticks under a wintry sun,*
> *And in a copse of beeches there I stood,*
> *For Nature's pulled her tragic buskin on*
> *And all the rant's a mirror of my mood:*

Yeats, not Nature, has pulled the tragic buskin on, and the rant is his own. One has only to recall Coleridge's "Dejection" to see that Yeats's lines are a Romantic commonplace devoid of Coleridge's tact. Yeats is planting himself in front of a suitably grandiose backcloth; he is worried about the decor, not about reality and justice. When he sees the mounting swan he says:

> *Another emblem there! That stormy white*
> *But seems a concentration of the sky;*

—and for the present he is more interested in self-exalting emblems than in swans. As the poem proceeds, blessedly, he returns to the particulars of reality and the images of justice.

But he was always liable to cast himself in "interesting" roles; the randy old man, the Blueshirt singer, the Fascist Celt. In *The Winding Stair* he cast himself, all too often, as Swift. In the Introduction to *The Words upon the Window-Pane* he said, "Swift haunts me; he is always just round the next corner"; when he really meant "in the next poem." Because Swift had a fanatic heart, Yeats had to have one too.

There are two or three texts which bear upon this. When we think of Yeats's reality and justice; how he served them and, in days of weariness, forgot them, turning to his mirror; we recall "The Circus Animals' Desertion," where he speaks of certain masterful images floating before him as compensating dreams for a life gone sour: "and soon enough/This dream itself had all my thought and love." It was the dream itself, he says, enchanted him:

> *Players and painted stage took all my love,*
> *And not those things that they were emblems of.*

The man, the actor, the role, Life as a drama in place and time; Soul and Self; God-made-man; the Greek, the Hebrew, the Syrian; Heraclitus, Blake, Plotinus, Swift: in his later years Yeats was often in a mist, wondering where, in all this, truth and value might reside. And how much truth consisted in a "great performance." (But at least he anticipated, in self-knowledge, everything that might be said against him.)

Another text comes from *A Vision*. In the discussion of Phase 16, with instances drawn from Blake, Rabelais, Aretino, Paracelsus, and "some beautiful women," Yeats says that people of this Phase run between extremes, now full of hate, now liberated by a symbolism that expresses "the overflowing and bursting of the mind." In these people, he says, there is always

> an element of frenzy, and almost a delight in certain glowing or shining images of concentrated force: in the smith's forge; in the heart; in the human form in its most vigorous development; in the solar disk; in some symbolical representation of the sexual organs; for the being must brag of its triumph over its own incoherence.

The last phrase is the one we need. Yeats was never quite sure what form the triumph would take, and the "frenzy" is a problematic force not necessarily to be identified with that for which Yeats prays in "An Acre of

Grass." When reality seemed beyond imaginative redemption, and justice a chimera, he often turned to the mirror and saw that with an hour in the green room he could give another farewell performance. It would have to be a little broader than the last version, its effects puffed out a little, an extra dash of rant; for he must brag of his triumph over his own incoherence.

But at other, stronger times Yeats would hold in a single thought reality and justice. Notably at Algeciras, meditating upon death; when reality was acknowledged by the images, the cattle-birds, the trees, the mingled seas, the tangible shells of Rosses' level shore; and justice by a grace of tone, a propriety of cadence and measure. Or again in "Coole Park, 1929," an example to stand for many in *The Winding Stair.*

"Coole Park, 1929" moralises a landscape—the swallows, a lime tree, a sycamore, the great house itself; then the fine things done and said and thought within its walls, "a dance-like glory that those walls begot." As in "The Municipal Gallery Revisited" and "In Memory of Major Robert Gregory," the "genius of the place" is given through the people who visited or lived there: Douglas Hyde, Yeats himself, Synge, Shawe-Taylor, Hugh Lane, and the great lady:

> *They came like swallows and like swallows went,*
> *And yet a woman's powerful character*
> *Could keep a swallow to its first intent;*
> *And half a dozen in formation there,*
> *That seemed to whirl upon a compass-point,*
> *Found certainty upon the dreaming air,*
> *The intellectual sweetness of those lines*
> *That cut through time or cross it withershins.*

The certainty found upon the dreaming air is the "accomplishment" invoked in "Meditations in Time of Civil War," a splendour flowing through the generations into a house, a person, a deed, a thought. The lines cut through time not to destroy it but to mark its possibilities, like a flare. In a difficult poem called "Stars at Tallapoosa," Wallace Stevens posits lines "straight and swift between the stars" which have nothing to do with the sea-lines or the earth-lines; they are pure intellectual acts, performed by man's imagination for its own pleasure. But the lines which Yeats praises in his poem are continuous with the earth-lines and the sea-lines, they are made articulate in speech, style, grace, accomplishment.

Lest all this be lost through a breach of tact or a defect of memory, as in a broken tradition, he introduces a qualified witness, of a later generation, to remember what should be remembered:

> Here, traveller, scholar, poet, take your stand
> When all those rooms and passages are gone,
> When nettles wave upon a shapeless mound
> And saplings root among the broken stone,
> And dedicate—eyes bent upon the ground,
> Back turned upon the brightness of the sun
> And all the sensuality of the shade—
> A moment's memory to that laurelled head.

The shade is everything included in Hopkins's "dapple," in Whitman's "drift," in Stevens's "Summer," in Yeats's "dark declivities"—it is the felt plenitude of things; and the sensuality is Yeats's "love's play" or Eliot's "brown hair over the mouth blown." Whatever it is, it is in time and place and known upon the body's certitude. In the first stanza Yeats speaks of "Great works constructed there in nature's spite," figuring yet again the strain between perfection of the work and of the life. Even at Coole Park in a landscape which lends itself to parable this strain persists; there is still a dispute of Self and Soul. The dispute is resolved not by recourse to an idea, a Hegelian synthesis, or a categorical imperative stronger than the disputants. It is resolved by appeal to a person great enough to resolve it: Lady Gregory herself, who embodied Self and Soul in her own reality and justice. Santayana performed a similar service for Wallace Stevens. To Stevens he appeared, in those last months, "a citizen of heaven though still of Rome," Self and Soul in poise. The question with which we began—in a world of mutability, where does value reside?—is answered in Yeats's memorial poem: "a woman's powerful character," rooted in place, assenting to time. All lives that has lived.

An Honoured Guest: New Essays on W. B. Yeats, edited by Denis Donoghue and J. R. Mulryne (London: Edward Arnold, 1965).

TWO

Joyce

THE EUROPEAN JOYCE

In the fourth chapter of Joyce's *Portrait of the Artist as a Young Man,* the young man Stephen Dedalus is walking along the wooden bridge down the Bull Wall. "He drew forth," Joyce reports, "a phrase from his treasure and spoke it softly to himself:

—A day of dappled seaborne clouds.
The phrase and the day and the scene harmonised in a chord. Words. Was it their colours? He allowed them to glow and fade, hue after hue: sunrise gold, the russet and green of apple orchards, azure of waves, the grey-fringed fleece of clouds. No, it was not their colours: it was the poise and balance of the period itself. Did he then love the rhythmic rise and fall of words better than their associations of legend and colour? Or was it that, being as weak of sight as he was shy of mind, he drew less pleasure from the reflection of the glowing sensible world through the prism of a language many-coloured and richly storied than from the contemplation of an inner world of individual emotions mirrored perfectly in a lucid supple periodic prose?

The part of his treasure from which Stephen has drawn the phrase—a day of dappled seaborne clouds—is a book by a minor early nineteenth-century American writer, Hugh Miller, called *The Testimony of the Rocks; or, Geology in its Bearings on the Two Theologies, Natural and Revealed;* it was published in 1857. The book is an attempt to reconcile the biblical account of creation with the new arguments from geology. At one point far out in the book, Miller imagines Satan contemplating the divine creation but unable to comprehend it; least of all to comprehend that God has created the universe as a home, Miller says, for "higher and higher forms of existence." How must Satan have felt, he says, "when looking back upon myriads of ages, and when calling up in memory what once had been, the features of the earth seemed scarce more fixed to his view than the features of the sky in a day of dappled, breeze-borne clouds. . . ."

You'll notice that Stephen has not recalled the phrase quite accurately: "breeze-borne" has become "seaborne." But no matter. What is more to the point is that the phrase has floated free from its context and lodged in his mind as an independent particle of language, as if it were a phrase in music, which in a sense it is. Stephen is not averse to satanic contemplation, but it is the phrase as such that has occurred to him, not even the sentence in which it had participated.

When Stephen starts questioning himself about his relation to words, he comes upon several possibilities, but mostly to dispose of them. The colours of words: it was a standard speculation, especially in nineteenth-century French poetry and poetics, that syllables might be related to one another as in the relation of colours, shades, and tones; that the syllables of a word might stir into action the several senses, and not merely the mind intent on replacing the word by its meaning. Stephen puts aside the notion, at least for the moment, and he thinks of his preference for the rhythmic rise and fall of words rather than "their associations of legend and colour." I have always interpreted that phrase as pointing to the early Yeats, and to his cult of what Ezra Pound called "the associations that hang near words." If so, Stephen's preference is an occasion, one of many, on which Joyce distanced himself from a Yeatsian aesthetic which he had to guard himself against, as against an exotic temptation. The poems in *Chamber Music* show how real the temptation was.

The third possibility Stephen considers is the most telling one: that he derives less pleasure from "the glowing sensible world" reflected in language than from "an inner world of individual emotions mirrored perfectly in a lucid supple periodic prose." It is itself a glowing preference, but a curious one. The sensible world glows and is sensible only to a mind interested in seeing it in that character; interested to the point of seeing it "through the prism of a language many-coloured and richly storied." There is no question of merely seeing the world as in itself, severely, it really is. We are free to think that Stephen, short-sighted or not, sees the glow of the world enough to be afraid of seeing it too keenly; as if he were afraid that the "inner world" of his purely individual emotions might have to take a secondary place in his sensibility. So he moves from the colours of language, its glows and associations, to whatever quality is enacted in "a lucid supple periodic prose."

It sounds as if he means a style chiefly characterised by its syntax, and means to praise the flexibility of its performances; which is very odd, since the phrase which started the whole speculation has no syntax at all and is all poetic diction. But I think Stephen is urging himself to move beyond the rich adhering words of a poetic diction, to escape from his lyric prison to a life of decision and action, much as Yeats had to put behind him the entrancing associations that hang near words before he could write the far more resilient poems of his middle books.

How much Stephen has to urge himself to leave the lyric prison is shown on the next page, his mind still occupied by Miller's phrase. "Disheartened, he raised his eyes towards the slow-drifting clouds, dappled and seaborne. They were voyaging across the deserts of the sky, a host of nomads on the march, voyaging high over Ireland, westward bound. The Europe they had come from lay out there beyond the Irish Sea, Europe of strange tongues and valleyed and woodbegirt and citadelled and of entrenched and marshalled races."

That is not a style in which a writer goes forth to do anything. Stephen's diction is drawn from literature, from anthologies of prose style, and diverse translations of Latin, Greek, and German texts. But I would make much of his sense of Europe, which extends, a few pages later, into more particular affiliations: references to the plays of Gerhart Hauptmann, Newman's prose, "the dark humour of Guido Cavalcanti," "the spirit of Ibsen," and a line of poetry recalled from Ben Jonson.

I have gone into the episode in the *Portrait* mainly to emphasise that to Joyce, as to Stephen, language always seems to offer itself as a countertruth to the truth of reality. Of course, among his many senses of language he had a journeyman's sense, too. He was quite willing to treat sentences as useful instruments to disclose a reality not itself linguistic. One of the stories in *Dubliners* begins: "Mrs Mooney was a butcher's daughter. She was a woman who was quite able to keep things to herself:

a determined woman." These sentences are not as straightforward as they sound. They tell us not necessarily the truth about Mrs. Mooney or what God or the world thinks of her, but what she thinks of herself. It is her accent we hear, the precise degree of assertiveness her voice would deliver, if the question of her character were to be raised in her hearing. But the sentences are still predicated on the assumption that there is a world which language merely negotiates: dappled seaborne clouds would persist even if the English language did not.

Granted. But Joyce was deeply susceptible to the opposite notion, too, that words as such far surpass the character by which they usually denote things and help us to administer them. It was Samuel Beckett and not Joyce who wrote: "Words have been my only loves, not many." But Joyce might have written it, for the sentiment that finds words purer and richer than anything they merely denote. Some of his styles acknowledge, like Mrs. Mooney, a world more or less given; its reality can be manipulated but not, in the end, transformed. But he has other styles which testify not to worlds and realities as given but to another world sustained only by the desire of it. In Joyce's early poems and in the *Portrait,* this world that exists only in the desire of it is represented by poetry, or by phrases of it, remembered and fondled. Sometimes the beauty of the phrase depends upon Stephen's removing it from its context, as if from every mere historical condition, as at one point he removes Luigi Galvani's phrase, "the enchantment of the heart," and lets it dominate his sentences: "An enchantment of the heart! The night had been enchanted. In a dream or vision he had known the ecstasy of seraphic life. Was it an instant of enchantment only or long hours and days and years and ages?"

If the world is, according to Wittgenstein, "everything that is the case," then in reading Joyce we have to assume also a second world, everything that is not the case but is so intensely desired that, so far as the imagination of desire is in question, it amounts to its own case. The two worlds are not, indeed, totally separate; they couldn't be. The first world, even in a life like Joyce's of much grief, is likely to give forth a few consolations, appeasing some old wounds. The second world, as it takes a linguistic form, has to admit many echoes from the world it otherwise repudiates. But if there are writers who accept the given world to the extent of annotating it and finding their satisfaction in doing little more, Joyce is not one of them. He is intransigent in desiring a world that never was, or that was only in the poetic fragments that would replace it.

But I have to qualify this report, if only to take account of such a scene as the one in *Ulysses,* the second chapter, where Stephen helps the boy Cyril Sargent with his sums: "Ugly and futile: lean neck and tangled hair and a stain of ink, a snail's bed. Yet someone had loved him, borne him in her arms and in her heart. But for her the race of the world would have trampled him under foot, a squashed boneless snail." Richard Blackmur, I recall, quoted that passage, and distinguished between Stephen Dedalus and Leopold Bloom largely on the strength of it, saying that the passage shows Stephen at his most tender. "He transcends his intransigence, and comes on the conditions of life—which is where Bloom is all the time." There again we have the two worlds, and only a different vocabulary for them. Leopold Bloom accepts the conditions of his life and wants only to succeed in forgetting their most painful embodiments—his father's suicide, his son's death, fears for his daughter, and at four o'clock the certainty that Molly is taking Blazes Boylan to her bed. Still, Bloom remains in his conditions and makes the middling best of them. But Stephen resents every condition, and would accept life only if it were another life, of his own making; except for rare lapses into a more general acknowledgement.

The question is: what form does desire take, in this intransigent sense, when it comes into language and disdains the chore of annotation?

I want to come upon an answer to this a little roundabout. Several years ago the critic Kenneth Burke proposed a certain pattern in the development of a writer. His notion was that most writers start off by writing of themselves and giving every privilege to their own feelings. The ideal form of this phase is the short lyric poem, or the lyrical fiction which is hardly fiction at all. Some writers never escape from this phase, but the major writer escapes at least far enough to acknowledge the existence of other people and to let them live their own lives. Better still if he can imagine other lives, and best of all if these lives are vigorously distinct from his own. If the chronology could be bent a little, we might take Joyce as a case in point. Starting out with early fragile poems, the first version of the *Portrait,* the *Portrait* itself, and the luridly imagined episode that took the form of the play *Exiles.* Then the crucial development in his career would be the diversion of privileged interest from Stephen, the hero of lyrical experience, to Leopold Bloom, who sustains the middling perfection of putting up with things. But *Dubliners* breaks the symmetry of his development, a very early work largely written in 1905 from jottings earlier still. So we have to say that there were at least early stirrings, even in the lyrical or self-expressive phase, of the recognitions that issued fully in *Ulysses.* But the pattern has further to go. It sometimes happens, even in a book which takes communication as its morality, that a writer in the process of imagining lives other than his own will come upon possibilities purely internal to his medium, possibilities which surpass the morality of communication. Some writers may glimpse those possibilities and decide to leave them alone, presumably because they find security in the bond of communication and would not want to be released from it. But there are other writers who, coming upon those possibilities, will insist on exploiting them as if "to the end of the line." To those writers, if something is glimpsed as possible, it becomes an aesthetic necessity; it must be done.

You see already how the pattern might be called upon to explain Joyce's development in his later work. In *Ulysses,* for the most part, he keeps the promise of communication. At least in the first half of the book he rarely affronts his readers, or confounds them. But it is clear that as the book proceeded Joyce indeed came upon purely internal possibilities, which offered themselves as a pun might offer itself to someone in a conversation, and in some of the later chapters of the book, tentatively, he explores those possibilities. Several years later he develops them with full panache in *Finnegans Wake,* where he sees a possibility and never looks back.

In *Ulysses* the two worlds I have referred to—we can now call them the world of conditions and the world of desire—are generously projected. Every reader of the book warms to its presentation of the sights, sounds, and smells of Dublin, the noise of its streets, the lore and gossip, both eloquent to the pitch of exorbitance. If you want an example of reality which gives the impression that it hadn't to be imagined at all but only transcribed, think of Paddy Dignam's funeral, and the man in the macintosh who turns up in Glasnevin. Bloom wonders who he is: "Now who is that lankylooking galoot over there in the macintosh? Now who is he I'd like to know? Now, I'd give a trifle to know who he is. Always someone turns up you never dreamt of." Bloom counts the mourners at the graveside, and makes the man in the macintosh number thirteen. The reporter Hynes is listing the mourners, and after a misunderstanding with Bloom he puts the stranger down as Mr. M'Intosh. And so on. The stranger turns up again, indeed several times, later in the book; or at least he enters into Bloom's meanderings. So he can readily stand for the supreme condition of there being life at all, a life that has to be lived rather than imagined.

Now the world of desire is so pervasive in *Ulysses* that there is no point in giving an example of it; it is incorrigible. It is there in every daydream, every swoon of apprehension, every poetic phrase which surpasses whatever it denotes. It is there whenever an event at large is seen and pondered and fondled in someone's mind to the point at which it is no longer merely an external event but has become an internal event of still richer account in that character. The Marxist critic Fredric Jameson has gone so far as to say that the fundamental device of *Ulysses* is a technique by which events in an alienated world are converted into inwardness, where they are reconciled by the tone in which they are received. Jameson resents the technique, for obvious reasons. As a Marxist, he wants to change the world of conditions. He does not want to further the possibility of leaving the world as it is by having its conditions end up, accepted for the most part, in Bloom's meandering mind. If everything that crosses Bloom's path can be transposed into himself, converted into inwardness, there is no urgent reason to change the world. It is for this reason that a Marxist resents the stratagems of consciousness, the techniques of inwardness by which a reconciling tone displaces every political incitement.

The particular possibility Joyce came upon in writing the later chapters of *Ulysses* was that of dissolving the barrier between one world and another, a procedure which might correspond to dissolving the distinction between the conscious and the unconscious phases of the mind. Language is not responsive to transitions, states of feeling which melt or merge into one another beyond rational discrimination. The reason is that words in conventional forms are separated from one another, and tend to divide states of feeling into particles which do not correspond to the history of the feeling the words are supposed to denote. Music was the most fascinating art to writers in the last years of the nineteenth century because it showed itself then to be extraordinarily good at transitions. Think of the "natural history" of feelings as we hear them in Wagner and Debussy; there are no fractures, no clear demarcations between one feeling and another. The deficiency of words is not the indeterminacy which is said to afflict them but the abrupt demarcation between one word and the next, which corresponds to nothing in anyone's experience.

Suppose you wanted to write a book, a kind of dream-play, in which the conscious and unconscious phases of the mind would be blurred beyond rational redemption; in which the conventional distinctions on which we rely would be dissolved—distinctions between past and present, the dead and the living, one person and another, history and myth, animal and human. When Joyce walked through the British Museum and looked at the Assyrian and Egyptian monuments, he felt, as he told Arthur Power, that "the Assyrians and Egyptians understood better than we do the mystery of animal life, a mystery which Christianity has almost ignored. Since the advent of Christianity," he said, "we seem to have lost our sense of proportion, for too great stress is laid on man." Mark L. Troy has argued that it was the Egyptian *Book of the Dead* which most inspired Joyce to write a book in which such conventionally useful distinctions would be dissolved. Sir E. A. Wallis Budge's *Gods of the Egyptians* and several other similar books gave Joyce the motif of death and resurrection in a tradition far removed from the Christian one, and therefore free of the historical complication in a doctrine too familiar for his purposes.

Finnegans Wake is Joyce's *Book of the Dead.* It is indeed a book in English, of a sort. Or rather, the structure of such divisions as it allows, whether we call them sentences or phrases, is recognisably English. But the words are confounded by taking to themselves diverse linguistic affiliations and echoes from fifty or sixty languages. Some parts of it are more speakable than others, notably the famous section we can still hear in Joyce's recording of it, the scene in which washerwomen gossip as they do their chores on the banks of the Liffey. But by and large, the book remains a private place for scholars.

That situation may change. *Ulysses* was many years in the world before anyone but a professional student thought of reading it; even though it had the glamour of an underground reputation as a questionable book. Now it is widely read, not merely studied. The history of Radio Telefis Eireann will document as a notable exploit the reading of the entire book, an act sure to gain entry to the *Guinness Book of Records* not only for its length but for its bravado. *Finnegans Wake,* too, may have such a future, though many of its sequences seem to defeat the speaking voice. But I doubt if the *Wake* will ever be readable unless we extend our notion of language to accommodate its procedures. Instead of receiving words as tokens of reference and vehicles of a meaning separable from the words, we would have to think of words as what the *Wake* once calls them, "words of silent power," for which the required authority is not the dictionary but the history of magical practise. If we want a motto from the *Wake* itself, there is one on page 570, a reference to Thoth, the God of speech, magic, and writing, secretary to the Gods, and, as Mark Troy has pointed out, responsible for the writing of the *Book of the Dead.* So we read on page 570: "Well but remind to think, you were yestoday Ys Morganas war and that it is always to-morrow in toth's tother's place. Amen."

I have mentioned "words of silent power" for a more available reason. There are some artists who need restlessness as others need peace: as Goldsmith said of someone, "he only frets to keep himself employed." Joyce did not say, as Stephen did, "My soul frets in the shadow of his language," but Joyce, too, cultivated a fretting if not a fretful relation to everything that presented itself as an available condition. In that respect, if not in many more, Joyce and Stephen are close kin. Joyce seems always to have needed conditions which another writer would have regarded as irritations: he needed conditions which could only be met by an exertion of will and other forms of power. In a sense hard to describe, he needed to refuse his "mother-tongue," or to accept it only on his own terms, as Stephen needed to reject his mother's death-bed request.

Joyce's exercise of will and power is clear in several aspects of his career. He wrote in an English which he thought of as something to be mastered. He did not think of his work in that language as collaboration with the great writers in the English tradition, or in any Irish tradition available to him, or with the values those traditions embodied. F. R. Leavis often maintained that William Blake's genius was most fully manifested in his sense of being an English poet, a poet, that is, engaged in "a continuous creative collaboration" with and within the English language. There is nothing of such a sentiment in Joyce's relation to English. Or to any other language. He was engrossed in language as such, but entirely opportunistic in his sense of a particular language.

But he also exercised his power nearer home and homelessness. If he had been willing to subdue his pride, he could have aligned himself with the aims of the Irish Literary Revival, a movement, after all, hospitable to the extremely diverse purposes reflected in George Moore, Yeats, Douglas Hyde, Lady Gregory, and J. M. Synge. But he was never willing to subdue his pride for such a cause. Indeed, while his work is full of Yeatsian echoes and allusions, he took Yeats as his chief antagonist. There is a current theory of literary history, best recommended by the critic Harold Bloom, that a strong writer turns his strength to account by choosing a great precursor—a major writer different in the kind of his genius and incorrigible in its degree—and engaging him in a struggle as if to the death. In that sense, Yeats is Joyce's chosen and fated precursor. Joyce had to swerve from Yeats's way of being a genius, and disown its forms to accomplish his own.

So it was only inevitable that Joyce would choose not any of the Irish ways of being a genius, but the European way. I have never felt inclined to lose much sleep over Joyce's exile, or the conditions which allegedly drove him from Ireland. The truth is that he was not driven, unless we mean that he was driven by a fretting and chafing sense of any conditions offered him. The collusion of chance and choice made Joyce the kind of artist he became: chance, by making him an Irishman and keeping him in that condition; choice, by which I mean his choosing to become an artist of European scope and grandeur, blood-brother to Dante, Shakespeare, Swift, Flaubert, Pater, Wagner, and Ibsen.

A European, in that sense, is something you choose to become. You cannot be born to it. You are not a European merely by being born in France or Germany. Yeats chose Plato and Plotinus for friends, but the choice recognised a temperamental and philosophic affinity, it was not otherwise a matter of principle. Joyce's election of Europe was indeed a matter of principle: or, if you don't want to see it enhanced by that word, call it a matter of ideology. I think he wanted to live in such a spirit as to make home whatever he chose to remember, and thereafter to have a chiefly nomadic relation to life. This suggests that he wanted the unsettled conditions from which the artistic detachment which we associate with Flaubert would emerge. His recourse to Wagner was more than ideological. Opera meant more to him than any other art. His mind was suffused not with ideas and theories but with arias. Verdi, Puccini, and Wagner meant to him everything he didn't need to invent. But I have been persuaded by William Empson to emphasise rather the example of Ibsen. Empson has argued that Joyce's belief "that in Ibsen Europe was going ahead with its own large development was what prevented him from being an Irish Nationalist." There's much to be said for that view, and a good deal of biographical evidence in its favour, starting with Joyce's learning enough Norwegian as a young man to read Ibsen in the original, and publishing a high-flying article in the *Fortnightly Review* in 1900 to praise Ibsen and, I think, to tell the world where his own artistic eyes were turning.

But in any case Joyce gave definitive form, starting with the last pages of the *Portrait,* to the desire which begins in Ireland and defines itself in Europe, seeking not its fortune but its providential form. In his domestic life he spoke more Italian than French, more French than English. *Finnegans Wake* is Irish of necessity, European in its diction,

Egyptian in its major mythology. That should be enough to be going on with, if an art of European or even global scale is in question.

As an Irishman by necessity, Joyce set astir a fiction, as in Flann O'Brien's *At Swim-Two-Birds* and *The Third Policeman,* of comic ingenuity, the words on the page in blatant disproportion to any use they might be turned to. As a European on principle, he set a pattern for the uncommitted occupation of space, its chief exponent Samuel Beckett, a writer as different from Joyce as he could reasonably be, given so many similarities. But as soon as you start naming names to denote such consequences and consanguinities there is no end to it.

Meanwhile we proceed. *Finnegans Wake* is clearly the next item, after forty-four years in which most of us have left it well alone. Is it an example of language secreting itself from resources as promiscuous as Europe itself? Or, beneath every surface, is it a story not much different from any other? The most recent suggestion I have seen is Hugh Kenner's, that the book started out from some sense of Erskine Childers's execution in 1922 and became a story about a family in Chapelizod, ending in the dormant mind of the mother, widowed now, the morning after, "trying not to awaken to awareness that her husband lies beside her no longer." The notion doesn't seem plausible, but that is not a decisive consideration in this peculiar case.

The Genius of Irish Prose, edited by Augustine Martin (Cork: Mercier Press, 1985).

POUND/JOYCE

In December 1913, Ezra Pound and W. B. Yeats were living in Stone Cottage, Coleman's Hatch, Sussex, "by the waste moor / (or whatever)," as Pound recalled that winter in *Canto LXXXIII.* The plan was that Pound would act as Yeats's secretary. In the event, he also gave Yeats instruction in the art of fencing. They read "nearly all Wordsworth" and less than all of Doughty's *The Dawn in Britain.* Yeats bore with Wordsworth for the good of his conscience, but he preferred Joseph Ennemosor's book on magic. Pound was labouring with Fenollosa's notes on the Chinese language, writing some new poems, and preparing *Des Imagistes.* One day he asked Yeats "whether there were any poets in Ireland fit to contribute to an anthology of poetry unlike his own"; that is, any Imagists still free from Celtic twilight. Yeats mentioned a poem beginning, "I hear an army charging upon the land," by a young Irishman called James Joyce. It is clear now that Yeats liked the poem mainly because it resembled his own "I hear the Shadowy Horses."

Pound wrote off to Joyce, who was in Trieste. He had not yet read Joyce's poem, but Yeats's word was good enough. Pound introduced himself as a literary man connected with serious magazines like *Poetry* and *The Smart Set.* Perhaps Joyce might like to send some pieces for publication. "I am *bonae voluntatis,*" Pound assured the young man. A few days later he had read the poem; "we are both much impressed by it." "Despite the old lavender of his *Chamber Music*," Pound recalled many years later, "this poem, because of the definiteness of the visual image it presents, had an affinity with the aims of the then nascent Imagist group." Joyce replied at once, giving Pound permission to use the poem, and sending him a batch of stories from *Dubliners*. Within a few weeks he sent him the first chapter of *A Portrait of the Artist as a Young Man*. Pound was delighted, sent the stories to *The Smart Set*, and the chapter to *The Egoist*.

Between 1913 and 1920 Pound wrote about eighty letters to Joyce. Sixty-two of these have survived and are now the property of Cornell University Library. Joyce wrote about sixty letters to Pound during the same period, but most of these have been lost. Pound also published several essays on Joyce's work; some of these are readily available, but other pieces have not been reprinted. A few items in fugitive magazines are hard to find. *Pound/Joyce* gathers together, as the editor Forrest Read says, "all of Pound's surviving letters to Joyce, most of which are published for the first time, all of his essays and articles on Joyce's work, his radio broadcast, various anecdotes of the time, and a number of miscellaneous pieces and extracts."

It is a great pity that Joyce's part in the correspondence has been lost. Pound's part was always practical, energetic, selfless. He sent Joyce's stuff to the magazines, lobbied influential men for money, encouraged Joyce in his work, put *Ulysses* into the *Little Review*. He was, in short, magnificent. He offered Joyce advice, but was not visibly annoyed when the offer was refused: he gave more. When he read the "Calypso" chapter of *Ulysses*, he thought parts of it excessive. "Leave the stool to Geo. Robey," he advised, "he has been doing 'down where the asparagus grows' for some time." The *Little Review* had just then been suppressed. If Wyndham Lewis's *Cantleman's Spring Mate* could not get through the law, there was no hope for Leopold Bloom at the jakes. Besides, Pound was not convinced of the artistic necessity. "The contrast between Bloom's interior poetry and his outward surroundings is excellent, but it will come up without such detailed treatment of the dropping feces." Lest two inoffensive editresses should go to jail in a doubtful artistic cause, Pound excised about twenty lines from the description of Bloom in the lavatory. Joyce insisted, of course, that they be restored for the book. When the "Sirens" chapter arrived, Pound had the same misgivings about asparagus. Joyce had gone down "as far as the lector most bloody benevolens can be expected to respire." The subject was "good enough to hold attention without being so all-bloodily friccasseed." As a general principle: "One can fahrt with less pomp & circumstance." Finally, Pound expressed a preference for phallic rather than excremental concerns: "purely personal—know mittel europa humour runs to other orifice." Nevertheless, he continues: "I don't arsk you to erase."

It was all quite urbane. Pound never moved far from his sense of Joyce as a prose Imagist, and he lost interest in the man when he found that sense impossible to maintain in the queer light of *Work in Progress.* The great modern artist in prose was the author of *Dubliners,* the *Portrait,* and *Ulysses.* Pound's position was clear. "Mr Joyce writes a clear hard prose," he said in July 1914, giving in one sentence the gist of his entire commitment. He had very little more to say on the subject, but he said the same thing ten times:

> It is a joy then to find in Mr Joyce a hardness and gauntness, like the side of an engine; efficient; clear statement, no shadow of comment, and behind it a sense of beauty that never relapses into ornament.

There was very little English prose worth reading alongside Flaubert: James, Hardy, perhaps Conrad, Joyce, and Ford were the new masters. "Mr Joyce is the best prose writer of my generation in English." By these standards, Shaw was trivial, "the intellectual cheese-mite," Arnold Bennett was cheap, H. G. Wells's style was "greasy in comparison with the metallic cleanness of Joyce's phrasing," D. H. Lawrence was inferior with his "loaded ornate style heavy with sex, fruity with a certain sort of emotion."

The same standards, and many of the same phrases, are enforced in the *Imaginary Letters* which Pound took over from Wyndham Lewis. In prose, Joyce was the civilized master, the cosmopolitan, "the stylist," like Ford in *Mauberley.* Indeed, it was probably Joyce's example which prompted Pound to a theory of prose which he outlined in the Henry James number of the *Little Review;* that "most good prose arises, perhaps, from an instinct of negation; is the detailed, convincing analysis of something detestable: of something which one wants to eliminate." Poetry, on the other hand, "is the assertion of a positive, i.e., of desire, and remains, endures for a longer period." The real function of good prose is to get rid of mush.

Flaubert pointed out that if France had studied his work they might have been saved a good deal in 1870. If more people had read the

Portrait and certain stories in Mr Joyce's *Dubliners* there might have been less recent trouble in Ireland. A clear diagnosis is never without its value.

The date of that: 1917.

So Pound attended to his discovery. In return, Joyce took very little interest in Pound, except as a wonder-working impresario. There is no evidence that he cared, one way or another, for Pound's poetry. He ignored Pound's criticism. It was prudent to keep in with Harriet Weaver, since the patron should be assumed to be in the right unless demonstrably in the wrong, but Pound's assertions could be disregarded:

> I never listened to his objections to *Ulysses* as it was being sent him once I had made up my own mind but dodged them as tactfully as I could. He understood certain aspects of that book very quickly and that was more than enough then. He makes brilliant discoveries and howling blunders.

In any event, Joyce was engrossed in his own case. Pound might be *il miglior fabbro* to Eliot, but he had no such contract with Joyce.

Things began to cool off, as far as the public record shows, in 1926, when Pound received samples of *Work in Progress*:

> I will have another go at it, but up to present I make nothing of it whatever. Nothing so far as I make out, nothing short of divine vision or a new cure for the clapp can possibly be worth all the circumambient peripherization.

Work in Progress was an extreme case of Gongorism. Worse, it looked back, and the true direction was forward. Joyce was Lot's wife. Pound never came to terms with the work, "that diarrhoea of consciousness," and he resented the fact that Joyce had closed his mind to the twentieth century. At a time when imprudent men were quarrelling over politics, Mussolini, Hitler, economics, American presidents, Major Douglas, Russia, and other contemporary matters, Jim the Penman was otherwise engaged. The rebuke was still couched in Imagist terms. "Joyce's mind has been deprived of Joyce's eyesight for too long," Pound wrote in 1934:

He has sat within the grove of his thought, he has mumbled things to himself, he has heard his voice on the phonograph and thought of sound, sound, mumble, murmur.

In effect, it was the same criticism that Yeats made of both Pound and Joyce in his essay on Berkeley: they were enslaved to whatever images happened to enter their minds. Wyndham Lewis made a similar report in *Time and Western Man* and *Men without Art*. Pound thought himself guiltless in the matter, perhaps because of the purity of his intention, his Imagist conviction, and his concern for the new world of politics. But Joyce, he thought, was guilty. Pound turned away toward Lewis, Ford, Eliot, Brancusi, and Cummings. "I prefer *The Apes of God* to anything Mr Joyce has written since Molly finished her Mollylogue." Cummings was good, *Eimi* was a new thing, looking ahead.

But the cooling off had begun long before *Work in Progress*. When Pound and Joyce met for the first time, in Desenzano and Sirmione, June 1920, the occasion went off well. "Joyce—pleasing," Pound reported to John Quinn:

> After the first shell of cantankerous Irishman, I got the impression that the real man is the author of *Chamber Music,* the sensitive. The rest is the genius; the registration of realities on the temperament, the delicate temperament of the early poems.

But the two men were not really kin. When Joyce arrived in Paris in July, he began to move away from his impresario. New adjuncts to the Muse's diadem had little or nothing to do with Pound's interest: Sylvia Beach, Adrienne Monnier, Valery Larbaud, later Eugene Jolas. Pound himself soon tired of Paris, longed for Italy. In 1924 he was in Rapallo. In 1926 he refused to help Joyce in an international protest against Samuel Roth's piracy of *Ulysses*. In 1927 Joyce consulted him on the question of a new collection of poems, the verses he had written since *Chamber Music*. Pound read them, and told Joyce they belonged with the family album and the portraits. No, they were not worth reprinting. Joyce was hurt. But he already felt that he and Pound lived in alien worlds. Writing to Harriet Weaver in 1928, he said:

> The more I hear of the political, philosophical, ethical zeal and labours of the brilliant members of Pound's big brass band

the more I wonder why I was ever let into it "with my magic flute."

The answer is that he was let into the band because his music reminded Pound of certain indispensable sounds once heard in Flaubert and Gautier. The proof is in "James Joyce et Pécuchet," one of Pound's last and ripest acknowledgements, printed appropriately in the *Mercure de France* in June 1922. It was enough for Pound to discover in Joyce the temper of *Chamber Music* and the style of *L'Education sentimentale*. What he could not bear, in the later Joyce, was the egotistical sublime; or the mushy form it took.

He moved away from Joyce, but he never lost his affection for him, or devotion to his genius. *Ulysses* was indelible. The *Portrait* showed how prose should be written. *Dubliners* was the thing itself. Even *Exiles* had its point, though Pound seriously exaggerated its merit when he read it first, thinking that anything by this author must be excellent. Gradually he came to feel that the play was a necessary error, a transition. At the end, he knew it was not much good. Still, it did not matter. The great work was accomplished, and Pound had helped to bring it out. Perhaps he felt that his labour in Joyce's behalf might have been more richly acknowledged. Certainly Joyce's indifference to Pound's own struggles in the *Cantos* was a shabby thing. The only point to be made is that he treated Pound as he treated other writers who befriended him.

It was an interesting relation, up to a point, but beyond that point its shallowness begins to emerge. Pound's relation to Eliot was of an entirely different order, much deeper. It is appropriate to reflect upon Pound's critical role in the making of *The Waste Land;* to think also of Eliot's magnanimity, the grace with which he received that favour. To think of Joyce sending chapters of *Ulysses* to Pound is to realise that he treated Pound as his literary agent, his messenger boy, nothing more. There is a certain splendour in Joyce's arrogance; it inspires awe. But Pound's self-lessness, care, and generosity inspire affection.

But even in the later years the relation was not completely lost. In December 1931, Pound wrote to Joyce from Rapallo, taking care to add the words "Anno X" to the address, the tenth year of the Fascist calendar. He wanted to know something more of Blarney Castle than could be divined from the well-known ballad. Was the custom of kissing the Blarney stone a survival of some fecundity ritual?

I mean when did fat ladies from Schenekdety or Donegal first begin to be held by their tootsies with their hoopskirts falling over their privates to in public osculate . . . Whose stone, in short, was it?

Joyce replied:

Dear Pound: There is nothing phallic about the Blarney Stone, so far as I know. The founder of the castle was cunctator (or perhaps it was the defender of it). He kept on inventing excuses, parlays etc., during its siege, I think in the time of Essex. The stone is flat and so far as I can remember let into the wall a few feet below a window. I never understood why it could not have been kissed from a ladder. I heard there were double bands of elastic to fasten the women's dresses. I did not kiss the stone myself.

That seemed to dispose of the matter. But many years and many sorrows later Pound recalled the little incident. In *Canto LXXIV,* one of the *Pisan Cantos,* he rehearsed old affections:

> Lordly men are to earth o'ergiven
>   these the companions:
> Fordie that wrote of giants
>   and William who dreamed of nobility
> and Jim the comedian singing:
>   "Blarrney castle me darlin'
>   you're nothing now but a StOWne."

So the affection endured, at least on one side. And maybe on both sides.

Times Literary Supplement, 6 March 1969.

On the Text of Ulysses

Joyce's *Ulysses* was published on his 40th birthday, 2 February 1922, in a limited edition of 1,000 numbered copies. The text was full of misprints, as Joyce irritatedly knew. As late as November, he had been tinkering with the last chapters, getting further detail from Dublin—"Is it possible for an ordinary person to climb over the area railings of No 7 Eccles Street, either from the path or the steps, lower himself down from the lowest part of the railings till his feet are within 2 feet or 3 of the ground and drop unhurt?" he wrote to his Aunt Josephine—and the galleys were demanding attention he couldn't give. On 6 November, he complained to Harriet Shaw Weaver that "working as I do amid piles of notes at a table in a hotel I cannot possibly do this mechanical part with my wretched eye and a half." He evidently decided that he couldn't do much about the printer's errors in time for the birthday, but he hoped they would be corrected "in future editions." This particular birthday was more important than textual precision.

Joyce wrote *Ulysses* by hand, and his arrangements for having the manuscripts typed were so loose that errors were inevitable. Some of the typists thought the writing would be improved by more orthodox punctuation. Further errors were made in the printing-press. None of the compositors at Dijon knew English, except the foreman, Maurice

Hirchwald, who knew only enough to decide that he could correct
Joyce's vagaries. Joyce tried to undo some of the damage, but the job was
too much for him. He corrected thousands of misprints on the galleys,
but missed about two thousand.

Later editions of *Ulysses* haven't been much better. Between 1922
and 1933, the book couldn't be published legally in the United States, so
there was no merit in doing heavy work on the text. When Judge John
Woolsey lifted the ban on the book—6 December 1933—Bennett Cerf
set about issuing a new edition. But the text he gave his printers was a
copy of Samuel Roth's facsimile pirated edition, printed in New York; its
errors remained to corrupt Cerf's Random House edition of January
1934.

I needn't recite the history of the publication of *Ulysses* in England.
The gist of the matter is that the editions which most people read, the
Penguin "reprinted with corrections" in 1971 and the Random House
Vintage Books edition, "corrected and reset" in 1961, are about equally
erroneous: seven errors to a page, according to Hans Walter Gabler's
count. Some misprints are common to both editions, but each edition has
its own errors, too.

On 6 December 1966, Jack Dalton gave a lecture at Cornell University on the text of *Ulysses,* quoting several instances of its corruption, and
promising to produce, on contract to Random House, a new and satisfactory edition. In the event, he didn't live to keep his promise, and the work
passed to a team of bibliographers, led by Professor Gabler.

The main problem in devising a reliable text of *Ulysses* is that there is
no complete manuscript. For some chapters there are drafts, jottings,
notebooks, the British Library Notesheets, fair copies—the most important things are in the Rosenbach Manuscript at Philadelphia, and other
collections at Cornell, Buffalo, and other universities. Rosenbach is the
crucial holding, its holograph notation, as Gabler says, "marks a decisive
point of consolidation in the compositional development." But it doesn't
solve every textual problem. For one thing, Rosenbach is "full of erasures
indicating revisions during the fair-copying." For another, Joyce continued to work on chapters even after he had given the manuscript to a
typist: he did not let the typescript go without further ado to the printer.

Gabler's aim in *Ulysses: A Critical and Synoptic Edition* (New York:
Garland, 1984) has been "to uncover and to undo the first edition's
textual corruption." His main principle has been to distinguish "the

documents of composition"—which he regards as authoritative, unless they can be shown to be faulty—from "the documents of transmission"— which he regards as potentially faulty, unless they can be proved to be authoritative. So Joyce's autographs are separated from the typescripts, the serial versions in the *Little Review* and the *Egoist,* the proofs of the first edition, and the first edition itself. But the distinction is hard to maintain, since transmission becomes composition as soon as Joyce tinkers with it. In any case, Gabler has tried to assemble, as his copytext, "a continuous manuscript text for *Ulysses,* extending over a sequence of actual documents." His principle is a narrative one, as if he were reconstructing a story. Or an archaeological one, deducing a complete structure from related fragments. In the new edition, the left-hand pages record the entire history of each word and accidental, so far as it can be established and indicated by a complicated system of notation: the right-hand pages give the clean text of the book without interruption or comment. Textual explanations and justifications are set out at the end.

I'll give a few examples, in a minute, of the differences the new edition makes. But it's worth saying at once that they're not merely a matter of correcting "Steeeeeeeeeehen" to "Steeeeeeeeeeephen" in the "Telemachus" chapter and "Pprrpffrrppffff" to "Pprrpffrrppfffff" in the "Sirens" chapter, as Craig Raine pretended to think a few weeks ago in the *Sunday Times.* If you are totally indifferent to misprints, you won't even consider buying or otherwise consulting the new *Ulysses.* "On the whole," Raine claimed about misprints, "I couldn't give a fupenny tuck." Not even if the botched printing were of his own verses? More to the point: suppose it were discovered that the printing of *Paradise Lost* is botched, with lines and half-lines dropped, wouldn't English poets, critics, and common readers agree that a new edition should be produced, especially if the hard labour involved were to be done, as it probably would be, by German or American scholars?

I'll quote Penguin, and give page references first to Penguin, then to Vintage.

On 181/181 Bloom is helping the blind man to cross Dawson Street, and wondering what it feels like to be blind: "How on earth did he know that van was there? Must have felt it. See things in their foreheads perhaps. Kind of sense of volume. Weight. Would he feel it if something was removed?" The new edition has, instead of "Weight": "Weight or size of it, something blacker than the dark. Wonder would . . . " (I can't summarise

Gabler's reasons for these changes: consult the left-hand page.) Same page, 13 lines down, same Bloomian theme:

> Sense of smell must be stronger too. Smells on all sides bunched together. Each person too.

Insert, between the second and third phrases, this new one; "Each street different smell." The last "too" has its force justified.

On 568/648 Bloom and Stephen are reading the *Evening Telegraph,* Stephen the letter on page two from Mr. Deasy about foot-and-mouth disease, Bloom an account of the third race at Ascot:

> While the other was reading it on page two Boom (to give him for the nonce his new misnomer) whiled away a few odd leisure moments in fits and starts with the account of the third event at Ascot on page three, his sidevalue 1,000 sovs., with 3,000 sovs. in specie added for entire colts and fillies. . . .

"Sidevalue"? No such thing. Delete and replace by "side. Value." Bloom's side of the newspaper, that is. About the misnomer: the *Telegraph's* report of Paddy Dignam's funeral included among those in attendance at Glasnevin one "L. Boom." The misprint comes into its poignant own 126 pages later when Molly thinks of the *Telegraph* report—Blazes Boylan brought the paper when he visited her for love in the afternoon—and recalls the real thing, a military funeral. Gabler's text reads:

> yes they were all in great style at the grand funeral in the paper Boylan brought in if they saw a real officers funeral thatd be something reversed arms muffled drums the poor horse walking behind in black L Boom and Tom Kernan that drunken little barrelly man that bit his tongue off falling down the mens W C . . .

But the point is lost on 694/773, where "Boom" is printed as "Bloom."

In the "Nausicaa" chapter, 368/370, Bloom is watching Gerty McDowell on Sandymount Strand:

> Suppose I spoke to her? What about? Bad plan however if you don't know how to end the conversation. Ask them a question they ask you another. Good idea if you're in a cart.

Replace the relevant bit by: "Good idea if you're stuck. Gain time. But then you're in a cart." Meaning that you're between the shafts of the conversation, and you can't get out.

On 261/262 Lenehan moves into conversation with Simon Dedalus in the bar of the Ormond Hotel: "Mr Dedalus, famous fighter, laid by his dry filled pipe." A libel on the man: what Joyce wrote was "famous father," a reference to Lenehan's salute, six lines back, "Greetings from the famous son of a famous father," to which Dedalus responds: "Who may he be?"

Stephen, 46/41, walking along Sandymount Strand:

> Unwholesome sandflats waited to suck his treading soles, breathing
> upward sewage breath.

Gabler changes the stop to a comma, and adds: "a pocket of seaweed smouldered in sea-fire under a midden of man's ashes."

In the National Library, 196/195, Stephen has been high-talking about Shakespeare and *Pericles,* fathers and mothers and daughters: "Will any man love the daughter if he has not loved the mother?" Two lines later, after an interrupted interruption by Mr. Best, Gabler inserts the following:

> Will he not see reborn in her, with the memory of his own youth
> added, another image?
>   Do you know what you are talking about? Love, yes. Word
> known to all men. *Amor vero aliquid alicui bonum vult unde et ea quae*
> *concupiscimus. . . .*

Scholars have been delighted with this addition, since it solves the conundrum of a passage in the "Circe" chapter, 516/581, where Stephen says: "Tell me the word, mother, if you know now. The word known to all men." Richard Ellmann virtually solved it in *Ulysses on the Liffey* (1972) with his chapter called "The Riddle of Scylla and Charybdis," which argues that "the answer to the sphinx's riddle was man, the answer to Scylla-Charybdis's is the act of love." (The Latin comes from St. Thomas Aquinas, *Summa contra gentiles,* Book I, Chapter 91, as John T. Noonan, Jr., has pointed out. Thomas declares that for the truth of love, it is required that one will the good of someone as his own. He continues, in the passage Joyce has shortened:

> By this, that we understand or rejoice, we must have in some way an
> object. For love wills something for someone. For we are said to love
> that for which we will some good, as said above. Hence, those
> things which we want, we are said, properly and absolutely, to
> desire, but not to love—rather to love ourselves for whom we want
> these things.

Joyce is referring to the contrast between true, selfless love and the
derivative love by which we are really loving ourselves.)

But that addition to 196/195 raises a problem about Gabler's editorial principles. The three lines he adds to the text turned up in an early
fair-copy. The fact that they don't appear in a later typescript is easily
explained, he says, as "a typist's eyeskip in copying from the final working draft, where two phrases ending on ellipses and underlined for italics
followed one another in close succession." The typist's eye dropped from
one set of dots to another. Still, Joyce didn't restore the dropped passage,
though he had plenty of opportunity on typescript and galleys. He may
not have noticed that the passage was gone: or he may have spotted it and
decided it was no great loss. But Gabler's procedure sets aside the editorial
principle that you should print the latest text the author corrected.

He sets it aside in many decisions, two of which I particularly regret.
On 105/104 Bloom at the graveside in Glasnevin is thinking about the
bad air in such places:

> Down in the vaults of saint Werburgh's lovely old organ hundred
> and fifty they have to bore a hole in the coffins sometimes to let out
> the bad gas and burn it. Out it rushes: blue. One whiff of that and
> you're a goner.

All the early versions—Rosenbach, typescripts, early proofs, and even the
serial version in the *Little Review* (Vol. V, No 5, September 1918) have
"doner." The change to "goner" was made on the last set of proofs, which
Joyce corrected. But Gabler has stuck to "doner." It's a good enough word,
as slang goes, but—at least to Dublin ears—far inferior to "goner," which
sounds the true note. Partridge's dictionary gives both, but "goner" has a
much richer currency.

In "Eumaeus," 573/653, Bloom is discoursing to Stephen about the
superiority of sculpture to photography in the representation of the
female nude:

Marble could give the original, shoulders, back, all the symmetry.
All the rest, yes, Puritanism. It does though, St. Joseph's sovereign . . .
whereas no photo could, because it simply wasn't art, in a word.

Puritan suspicion of the body gives St. Joseph his high repute for chastity,
and discourages sculptors from showing a woman's sexual parts. The
Buffalo typescript leaves a big gap after "sovereign," presumably to give
Joyce space to write out the indecipherable words more legibly. In the
event, he didn't. He even eliminated the three dots of the galley and
joined "sovereign" to "whereas." But Gabler has found in Rosenbach an
early, obscure phrase which Joyce didn't choose to add to any later
typescript or galley. The new version reads:

Marble could give the original, shoulders, back, all the symmetry,
all the rest. Yes, puritanisme, it does though Saint Joseph's sovereign
thievery alors (Bandez!) Figne toi trop. Whereas no photo . . .

Gabler doesn't claim to have deciphered this new stuff with any certainty.
"Thievery" is evidently Richard Ellmann's suggestion, and while Ellmann
is the best man in the world for some things, deciphering manuscript isn't
one of them. The vulgar French is Stephen's. Gabler comments:

Bloom's narrated speech, it may be noted, carries directly from
"rest." to "Whereas", so that the problematical sentence appears
intercalated. Its sense is admittedly a trifle obscure . . . Assuming
that, as he listens to Bloom eulogizing on the female form of Grecian
statues as an esthetic experience, Stephen remembers what Mulligan
had suggested about the nature of Bloom's curiosity, he would seem
to be silently satirising Bloom.

(In "Scylla and Charybdis" Mulligan insinuated that Bloom was homo-
erotic: "O, I fear me, he is Greeker than the Greeks.") For these reasons,
Gabler says, the French sentence "which Joyce let stand as a transmissionally
corrupted fragment has been editorially restored to the text." Prematurely,
in my view: there must be a point at which guesswork should confess
itself bewildered and report that the text at that point can't be deciphered.
    There are hundreds of emendations in the new edition. Some of
them are inciting readers to argue about the price of a bar of Fry's Plain
Chocolate in Dublin in 1904—a penny is obviously right, by the way,

and a shilling ridiculous—but the samples I've given are enough to show the kind of thing we're dealing with. I gather that Gabler's text will be issued in a popular edition, two years from now.

Now a word about the new edition of Ellmann's biography of Joyce. The book won all the prizes when it first appeared in 1959. The second material that has become available, but it isn't radically different. Indeed, the revision is pretty light. Ellmann has retained the old structure, and has inserted the new stuff at appropriate points. Stanislaus Joyce's diary has provided some detail about the rewriting of *Stephen Hero,* Gogarty's letters to G. K. A. Bell have confirmed what was already fairly well known about Gogarty's side of a contentious relation with Joyce, Louis Berrone's *James Joyce in Padua* (1977) has eked out the little information on Joyce's time in that city, and C. P. Curran's papers have annotated the Dublin years. More is now known about Lucia Joyce's infatuation with Beckett. There are new letters from Ezra Pound and Adrienne Monnier. But none of these items alters the picture to any great extent.

The oddest aspect of the new edition is that Ellmann hasn't allowed his general sense of Joyce to be modified by Joyce's own letters. There is virtually no comment on the extraordinary constriction of Joyce's daily interests. The obscene letters to Nora are virtually kept out of the picture. I'm not saying that there is any merit in being shocked by those letters, but they are part of the record. I'm surprised that Ellmann hasn't quoted them, or—if he didn't want to do that—allowed them to exert pressure upon our understanding of the man who derived occult gratification from writing them. Reviewing the letters, Lionel Trilling referred to Joyce's "delight in the excrementitiousness of the places of love and joy," and he assumed that the letters which released that delight would "cease to be dismaying or amazing soon after they are brought into the light of common day and permitted to assume their institutional status—one might say their prestige—as biographical data." But Ellmann hasn't allowed them to assume that status. The gist of them is indeed well known to scholars, but not to the common reader for whom Ellmann's biography is intended. The result is that readers, common or not, find themselves offered a far blander image of Joyce than a full report of the evidence would sustain. Much the same applies to the treatment of Joyce's notes for *Exiles.* Looked at closely, they make a horrifying document, but Ellmann doesn't look at them closely, he uses them only for local illustration. In his Inaugural Lecture at Oxford on 4 May 1971, Ellmann remarked that "today we want to see our great men at their worst as well as their best;

we ask of biographers the same candour that our novelists have taught us to accept from them." If we do, we are going to be disappointed in Ellmann's biography: it is not, in that special sense, candid.

The only new material of much interest concerns a woman, Gertrude Kaempffer. Joyce met her in Locarno in 1917, and he tried to start an affair, but she didn't respond. He thought it would stimulate her if he wrote a letter telling her of the sexual excitement he had felt one day as a boy when the family nanny went aside to urinate. The letter was a failure. Ellmann says that the only consequence of Joyce's meeting with Gertrude was that the pallid girl who excites Bloom in the "Nausicaa" chapter of *Ulysses* is named Gerty.

Ellmann's corrections and second thoughts are worth noting. (I call the first edition A, the second B, and give the page references to the relevant passages in both.) It now appears that the lecture Joyce prepared on James Clarence Mangan—in Trieste, early May 1907—wasn't delivered: but why not (A269/B259)? The girl Joyce swooned about in Trieste when he was teaching her English "was Amalia Popper" in A353, but "may well have been Amalia Popper" in B342. What Joyce felt for her in A was "overwhelming desire," in B "erotic commotion." In A356 "the poems which Joyce composed between 1912 and 1916 reflect his relationship with Signorina Popper": in B345 they reflect his relationship "with the real or concocted signorina." In A359 Signorina Popper asked and received permission to translate *Dubliners,* "but in the end she did not do Joyce this favour either": in B348 "this was the only favour she conferred on Joyce." (Did she translate the stories, or was her request to translate them the favour?) A462 describes Joyce's first sight of Marthe Fleischmann: on 9 December 1918 he was going back to his flat at 29 Universitätsstrasse when he saw her ahead of him. Not so, according to B448: he first saw her "early in December 1918" when he looked out of a side window of his flat "and saw a woman in the next building pulling the toilet chain"; and a footnote remarks that Earwicker's crime in the Phoenix Park of *Finnegans Wake* "is often indicated to be that of peeping on micturating girls." In A522 Bernard Shaw, declining to contribute money for the publication of *Ulysses,* told Sylvia Beach: "I take care of the pence because the pounds won't take care of themselves." In B507 he tells her: "I take care of the pence and let the Pounds take care of themselves." A527 has Joyce writing to Alessandro Francini: "I've become a monument of Vespasian eminence," and a footnote says that "vespasian" is French colloquial for "urinal." B513 has him saying: "I've become a monument—

no, a vespasian." The reference in both cases is the same: Joyce's letter of 7 June 1921. (Can Joyce's handwriting be read as variously as that?) A714 reads: "When Beckett presented him with a copy of *Murphy,* Joyce replied only by a bad limerick beginning, 'There was a young man named Murphy.' In B701 the limerick is quoted, beginning more dashingly, "There's a maevusmarked maggot called Murphy."

On the question of accuracy, especially in transcribing letters and other documents: I don't think Ellmann's book is always reliable. On A353foll., he quoted bits from *Giacomo Joyce,* Joyce's account, "in his best calligraphy," of his dealings with Amalia Popper. But when *Giacomo Joyce* was published by Faber in 1968, "with an Introduction and Notes by Richard Ellmann," the official text was found to differ at several points from Ellmann's quotations. The woman's "dropping hat" was found to be "drooping." Her body turned out to be "lithe," not "little." "A sparrow under the wheels of Juggernaut, shaking shakes of the earth" became more plausible when "shakes" became "shaker." "The voice of an unseen reader rises, informing the lesson from Hosea" was now found more decorously "intoning the lesson from Hosea." But in B342foll., while the hat still droops, the quoted passages—when they correspond to those in the first edition—are textually identical with A354foll., as if *Giacomo Joyce* had never been published. The woman's body is little again, and shaker is shakes. The unseen reader's voice goes back to informing Hosea. The facsimile pages reproduced in *Giacomo Joyce* show that all the errors of transcription on A359 are retained on B348. It's very odd.

I still love the book. Even though it stays away from the rough stuff, it's continuously engrossing, attentive to what Ellmann regards as the main issues, and most handsomely written. But I wouldn't trust it all the way for accuracy.

Now that textual and biographical matters have been dealt with, it would be well to go back and read the novel. Several questions about it seem to have been left dangling, despite the attention it has received. I'll mention two. Critics regularly quote the most memorable sentence from Eliot's famous review, where he says that Joyce's method "is simply a way of controlling, or ordering, of giving a shape and a significance to the immense panorama of futility and anarchy which is contemporary history." But they don't quote the next sentence, where Eliot says that "it is a method already adumbrated by Mr Yeats, and of the need for which I believe Mr Yeats to have been the first contemporary to be conscious."

Did he mean Yeats's juxtaposition of ancient and modern motifs, of Helen of Troy and Maud Gonne as in "A Woman Homer Sung" and "No Second Troy"? Or had Eliot something else in mind as marking the relation between Yeats's poems and *Ulysses?*

The second matter arises from William Empson's work on *Ulysses.* I've never seen his interpretation discussed. He takes the book to be a story about a young man, Stephen Dedalus, who was saved from violence, crime or craziness by having a quiet affair with an older woman, Molly Bloom. The affair didn't cause any trouble, because it was arranged by the husband, Leopold Bloom—who liked Stephen anyway—in the hope of getting rid of Molly's current lover, Blazes Boylan, the worst man in Dublin. The Blooms have lost their infant son Rudy, and Leopold can't bring himself to try to beget another one; but he thinks he might clear up the jam in his marriage by putting Stephen to bed with Molly. It would do the three of them good. Leopold might be able to father a son, after all, when the new triangle has established itself. He might even be able to fix Stephen up with his daughter Milly, and get her settled down with a decent young husband. In the event, Stephen can't bring himself to a decision, and for the time being he walks away from the invitation. But he may come back, and the Blooms much hope he will.

According to this interpretation, *Ulysses* is a generous treatment of the Eternal Triangle: not at all like *Exiles,* the disgusting shot Joyce took at the theme before he got his emotions into better order. Empson thought that there was probably a basis in fact for the story: that young Joyce had an affair with an older woman before he met and eloped with Nora Barnacle. There is no known evidence of such an affair, but Empson's interpretation doesn't fall on that account. It might be said that motifs of begetting and the Eternal Triangle were too fixed in Empson's mind to let his judgment thrive; but that, too, doesn't dispose of the question. The difference his interpretation would make is that it would modify the general emphasis on son-in-search-of-father and father-in-search-of-son: a reading which has the effect of leaving Molly (Penelope) as a colourful presence, exotic indeed but marginal to the book. The *Odyssey* complicates that issue, but we are reading Joyce, not Homer. The relation between Bloom and Stephen, too, becomes quite different when each is seen in relation to Molly and therefore in a peculiarly ambiguous relation to the other. I'm not saying that Empson's interpretation should dislodge Ellmann's, Kenner's, or anyone else's, only that I haven't seen it seriously considered.

TWO POSTSCRIPTS

1) I thought the "word known to all men" was agreed. Not so. Bernard Benstock, writing in the *Irish Literary Supplement,* Spring 1985, keeps the question open. In "Circe," THE MOTHER says: "You sang that song to me. *Love's bitter mystery.*" To this, Stephen (eagerly) replies: "Tell me the word, mother, if you know now. The word known to all men." In "Telemachus" Stephen recalls that when his mother was dying, he had sung Yeats's song of Fergus, accompanying himself on the piano:

> Her door was open: she wanted to hear my music. Silent with awe and pity
> I went to her bedside. She was crying in her wretched bed. For those words,
> Stephen: love's bitter mystery.

In "Scylla and Charybdis" Stephen's Periclean speech includes the rhetorical question: "Will any man love the daughter if he has not loved the mother?" and after an intervention by Mr. Best, he asks himself, according to Gabler's edition: "Do you know what you are talking about? Love, yes. Word known to all men. *Amor vero . . .* " Now enters Mr. Benstock:

> The question is brought on by her reference to *"love's bitter mystery,"* as it
> logically should be, since his own restoration of the Yeatsian phrase in
> "Telemachus" (after Mulligan departed, singing the song) was contained in
> the memory of his mother's voice: "For those words, Stephen: love's bitter
> mystery." If Love is definitively the Word Known to All Men by early
> afternoon in the library, why is it now necessary late at night to ask the
> question? In the morning, Love to Stephen, as it was to his mother, is a
> bitter mystery, and despite his temporary satisfaction in the afternoon,
> within the particular context and limited by the self-reflexive nature of
> *Amor* as wishing something good for someone and nonetheless something
> we covet for ourselves, the solution does not survive into the night. What
> cannot be known by anyone still alive can also not be retrieved from a dead
> mother Stephen conjures up out of his own guilty imagination. Whatever
> the word known to all men may actually be, the one word that has now
> been disqualified by its very appearance in "Scylla and Charybdis" is Love.

So we have to read it again. A dying mother cries over the words "love's bitter mystery." Later, her son talks of parental love and recalls the motif. Several hours later, in the brothel of "Circe," Stephen—drunk, hallucinated, and generally demented—has a lurid vision of the same scene, his dying mother. She is now dead, and appears to him as if she were in a Jacobean nightmare. The crucial word in Stephen's eager entreaty is not "word" but "now"; as if he were interrogating Lazarus, who has come back from the grave to tell all. "Tell me the word, mother, if you know now." Benstock is right: it can't be Love, it must be the gist of everything she has learnt by dying and coming back. In the event, her answers to Stephen feature three likely words: prayer, repent, and beware! Stephen receives these by smashing the chandelier and shouting, "Non serviam!"

Which suggests that Kenner may be right, after all, in divining that the "word known to all men" is Death. My own second thought is that the word, which is likely to be the mother's admonition in the end, is "Repent!"

2) To complicate things further: In a recent *Times Literary Supplement,* Jeremy Treglown reported that John Kidd, a research fellow at the University of Virginia, has been arguing that Gabler's edition contains hundreds of errors. Kidd claims, apparently, that Gabler has ignored impressions of *Ulysses* published during Joyce's lifetime and containing variant readings. Many of Gabler's readings, including some substantive ones, are—Kidd alleges—incorrect, or unexplained, or both. There, up to June 16, 1985, the matter uneasily rests.

London Review of Books, 20 September–3 October 1984.

BAKHTIN AND FINNEGANS WAKE

Even now, nobody knows how to read *Finnegans Wake,* as distinct from deciphering bits of it. If it is a story, there is no agreed account of what the story tells. Many readers, in the reasonably clear light of *Ulysses,* think the *Wake* an aberration, a freak of culture. Some regard it as fulfilling certain linguistic possibilities Joyce came upon while writing the later chapters of *Ulysses.* Some think the *Wake* presents an extreme version of a technical procedure Joyce commanded, in the seeming innocence of *Dubliners,* from the start. Any of these attitudes is defensible, but the second and third ones are, I think, particularly interesting. I want to consider here the third one: it would be a telling perception if it turned out that Joyce's procedures are continuous rather than arbitrary, and that only the conditions of their employment changed between 1905 and 1939.

Hugh Kenner, adept of this third attitude, has argued—in *Joyce's Voices* (1978), and recently in "Notes toward an Anatomy of 'Modernism' "[1]— that everything Joyce did, every extravagance of his later manner, is traceable to two early innovations: the first, by which he accommodated carefully adjudged discrepancies between narrative and diction; the second, by which he learned, especially in *A Portrait of the Artist as a Young Man,* how to locate his narrative styles on several levels. Kenner treats these innovations as two, but they could as well be taken as one, since the discrepancy between narrative and diction, as he describes it, is maintained by choosing crucial words from several levels of vocabulary, each implying a different level of social class, decorum, and expectation which the vocabulary includes. Many hours of leafing through Skeat's *Etymological Dictionary* showed Joyce that words bear the marks of the particular social experience they seem merely to denote.

Most of the stories in *Dubliners* proceed, as Kenner remarks, by third-person narrative, "imparting a deceptive look of impersonal truth." The look is deceptive because "the illusion of dispassionate portrayal seems attended by an iridescence difficult to account for until we notice one person's sense of things inconspicuously giving place to another's." Often a sentence begins as if its sole business were to tell a disinterested truth, but within a few phrases it leans so far toward the character being described that it receives and accepts the idioms he would use if he were managing the narrative. In "Grace":

> The transept of the Jesuit Church in Gardiner Street was almost full; and still at every moment gentlemen entered from the side-door and, directed by the lay-brother, walked on tiptoe along the aisles until they found seating accommodation.

From the side-door: to avoid drawing attention to themselves by coming late through the main entrance. On tiptoe: because they have the delicacy of gentlemen, now that they are in a church where delicacy is the sign of virtue. Seating accommodation, rather than mere seats: because, as Kenner observes, "seating accommodation" would be their kind of phrase in this kind of place, at a Jesuit Retreat, the Jesuits catering "for the upper classes"; hence the phrase is "a fumble after polysyllabic elegance."

In the *Portrait:*

> Every morning, therefore, uncle Charles repaired to his outhouse but not before he had creased and brushed scrupulously his back hair and brushed and put on his tall hat.

After five disinterested words, scrupulously indicative, the sentence continues to observe the grammar of third-person narrative but resorts to the diction Uncle Charles would use if he were reporting his activities. "I repaired to the outhouse," he would say.

But Kenner's account of the matter doesn't make it clear, as I think it should, that the discrepancy isn't between narrative and diction but between two or more types of diction. What he calls narrative hasn't sprung spontaneously into the English language and the indicative mood. "Until they found seats" doesn't differ from "until they found seating accommodation" as nature differs from culture but as one social formation differs from another. Neither phrase is translucent.

But we need a much more elaborate theory than Kenner's if we are to go further with the technique of discrepancy he has described and find it still active, extravagantly flourished, in *Finnegans Wake*. Bakhtin's theory seems to me to offer the best hope of this reward. So I will make a wide detour to give the gist of it, and see whether or not it helps us to read the *Wake*.

II

Bakhtin's theory of language and style is predicated upon the privileging of social or communal life. The world of things is already given, and consciousness transforms it into actions and projects. But the criteria for such transformations are provided by sociality. There are obvious difficulties in regarding intersubjectivity as preceding subjectivity, but Bakhtin gets over them by concentrating on language as the already social means by which any act of consciousness is performed. We are social by virtue of being verbal. Bakhtin separates himself from Freud on this consideration. Freud "explains processes that are essentially social from the perspective of a purely individual psychology": he derives "the entire ideological series, from the first to its last component, from the simplest elements of individual psychic life, as if we existed in a social void."[2]

It follows that the normative character of speech is what Bakhtin calls "dialogic." Even in solitary musing, I imagine another self whom my speech invokes: every utterance is part of a dialogue. It would be possible to reconcile Bakhtin's theory of speech with Saussure's, but only if Saussurean *langue* were to be construed as the available expressive resources of a language, and *parole* as each act of a specifically social and dialogical intention. Failing that, a linguistics involving only the relation of a sign to other signs would be inadequate. It would also be possible to think of Bakhtin's dialogism as corresponding to Kristeva's idea of intertextuality, and to use her term as marking the widest considerations of sociality in language: "dialogism" could then be retained for the narrower reference to "the exchange of responses by two people," as Todorov proposes in his study of Bakhtin.[3] This would ease the problem of "monologism": otherwise, the distinction between monologism and dialogism could only be one of degree. Kristeva is obviously troubled by the distinction. In her first essay on Bakhtin she insists that the objectivity of monologue can't withstand a psychoanalytic or semantic analysis. "Dialogism is coextensive with the deep structures of discourse." Hence, in order to describe "the dialogism inherent in the denotative or historical word, we would have to turn to the psychic aspect of writing as trace of a dialogue with oneself (with another), as a writer's distance from himself, as a splitting of the writer into subject of enunciation and subject of utterance."[4] Monological discourse would be possible only by an act of self-censorship, such that the discourse never turns back upon itself or enters into dialogue with itself.

Confusion is probably inevitable among these terms, because not every monologue carries the sinister marks Bakhtin would ascribe to monologism. I'll try to clarify the point in a moment, but it is crucial to begin by emphasising that, to Bakhtin, monologism does not mean the mere recourse to the forms of monologue, but rather the refusal of the acknowledgements implicit in dialogic. A monologue turned toward sociality and the value of dialogic would be entirely free of any sinister imputation. But the point is hard to enforce, if only because Bakhtin thought of poetry as essentially the lyric cry, and of the novel's prose as far readier than poetry to make the acknowledgements guaranteed by dialogism. It is impossible to defend this association of sentiments from such critics as Ransom and Brooks who think of lyrical poetry as "dramatic," spoken as if in the voice of an imagined speaker in an imagined situation. Bakhtin's understanding of poetry was extremely slight; he always regarded it as the lyric voice of monologism.

It should be clear that monologism and dialogism are not neutral or merely descriptive terms; they are terms of, respectively, rebuke and praise. Each denotes an attitude to life which comes into discussion as an attitude to language.

A monologic artistic world is one which is controlled at every point by the artist who has projected it. In such a world, every thought is a function of the artist's consciousness: it either gravitates to him and becomes a sign of his power, or it is admitted only so that it can be degraded and repudiated. Bakhtin associates monologism with philosophical idealism, which transforms the unity of existence into the unity of consciousness, and that, in turn, into the unity of a single consciousness. At that point, as he says in his book on Dostoevsky, idealism recognises only one principle of cognitive individualization: error. Monologism presupposes that consciousness is placed above existence; it takes for granted the self-sufficiency of a single consciousness, the inviolacy of the "point of view." Tokens of freedom which may be assigned to other minds are specious: the verdict has already been decided. Later in the book on Dostoevsky, Bakhtin describes the monologic word as the word that gravitates toward itself and its referential object: it is as if the word lived alone in the world, except for the object to which it refers. "In the presence of the monologic principle, ideology—as a deduction, as a semantic summation of representation—inevitably transforms the represented world into a voiceless object of that deduction."[5]

The dialogic principle is most elaborately described in Bakhtin's account of Dostoevsky. His novels feature "a plurality of independent and unmerged voices and consciousnesses, a genuine polyphony of fully valid voices." What unfolds in Dostoevsky's novels "is not a multitude of characters and fates in a single objective world, illuminated by a single authorial consciousness; rather a plurality of consciousnesses, with equal rights and each with its own world, combine but are not merged in the unity of the event." Dostoevsky projects "a world of autonomous subjects, not objects." Every act a character commits is in the present: there is no recourse to explanations from history or environment. No act is predetermined; it is conceived of and represented by Dostoevsky as free. In a monologic novel, the novelist casts a mantle of objectivity over every point of view he does not share, turning it into a thing, an object to be disposed of; but in a dialogic novel, every contending attitude is extended to its supreme form, and always remains a free subject among free subjects.

Bakhtin sometimes thought of Tolstoy as a master of monologic, comparable to Dostoevsky as a master of dialogic. In Tolstoy's story "Three Deaths" (1858), the three lives and deaths illuminate one another, but only for the author, who is located outside them and takes advantage of his external position to give them a definitive meaning, a final form.

But the names are not important: indeed, Bakhtin changed his mind about Tolstoy. What is important is Bakhtin's distinction between the two attitudes: monologic is godlike in exerting continuous power over its creation; if dialogic is godlike, it is in choosing not to exert its power. But

Bakhtin doesn't claim that Dostoevsky's consciousness is not to be found
in his novels—a claim René Wellek has taken him as making. "The author
of a polyphonic novel," according to Bakhtin, "is not required to renounce
himself or his own consciousness, but he must to an extraordinary extent
broaden, deepen, and rearrange this consciousness in order to accommodate the consciousness of others." Presumably Bakhtin would concede—
though I don't recall the particular concession—that the form of a
Dostoevsky novel embodies the degree of control the novelist wishes to
exert. Limits are imposed by the story, the disposition of the characters,
the fates they meet. In a strict sense, there is a last word, even though it is
a mark of dialogic to proceed as if no word were ever the last one.

  The distinction between monologic and dialogic appears in Bakhtin's
criticism in several forms. Sometimes it is given as the distinction between
centripetal and centrifugal forces; between common, standard, or orthodox speech which tries to exert control over its matter and insists on
coinciding with itself, and "heterological" speech which is far more
concerned to provide a space of freedom and diversity than to enforce the
unity of a normative language.

  In another version, the distinction separates epic from novel. The
epic poem, according to Bakhtin, "has been from the beginning a poem
about the past, and the authorial position immanent in the epic and
constitutive for it—that is, the position of the one who utters the epic
word—is the environment of a man speaking about a past that is to him
inaccessible, the reverent point of view of a descendant." The past is
inaccessible except through tradition: it is tradition which has the responsibility of maintaining the one system of belief on which the epic is
sustained. The source of the epic's creative power is therefore memory,
not knowledge. For that reason, the epic as it has come down to us "is an
absolutely completed and finished generic form." It is a monologic form
because the order it recites is closed upon itself; the hero is merely a
function of his destiny. The novel, on the other hand, is as open as the
knowledge and experience in which it revels. The matter of the novel is
the spontaneity of the inconclusive present, a present that is felt far more
keenly as it reaches toward the future than as it takes up the burdens of
the past. But the novel is dialogic above all because the distance between
itself and its matter is virtually set aside by the proximity of popular
speech and the informalities and familiarities it ensures. "The novelist is
drawn toward everything that is not yet completed," as Bakhtin says in
"Epic and Novel."[6]

At this point one begins to wonder whether Bakhtin's distinction between epic and novel is not merely opportunistic: it seems to have little to do with the experience of reading particular epics and novels. Indeed, Todorov has good reason to suspect it, and to point out that virtually all the characteristics of the novel, in Bakhtin's account, are taken from Goethe, Friedrich Schlegel, and Hegel, "as if a failure to achieve genuine integration of the notion into his own system authorized such a massive and uncritical borrowing."

In yet another version, the distinction between monologic and dialogic separates myth from "heteroglossia." Bakhtin associates myth with "an absolute bonding of ideological meaning to language." Categories of language are congealed, and meaning—in a particular society—is correspondingly enforced. In "Discourse in the Novel," Bakhtin speaks of "the absolute hegemony of myth over language as well as the hegemony of language over the perception and conceptualization of reality." Later in the same essay he refers to "a mythological feeling for the authority of language and a faith in the unmediated transformation into a seamless unity of the entire sense, the entire expressiveness inherent in that authority." Heteroglossia, by which he means the sense of many languages and many diversities of perception, goes some distance to undermine the authority of myth:

> The resistance of a unitary, canonic language, of a national myth bolstered by a yet-unshaken unity, is still too strong for heteroglossia to relativize and decenter literary and language consciousness. This verbal-ideological decentering will occur only when a national culture loses its sealed-off and self-sufficient character, when it becomes conscious of itself as only one among other cultures and languages.[7]

At that point, no one would conceive of his language as being sacrosanct, or as having privileged access to truth as if by natural law or providence.

Finally, the distinction is given historical manifestation. In *Rabelais and His World* and again in the revised version of *Problems of Dostoevsky's Poetics,* Bakhtin distinguishes between official culture and the culture of laughter in medieval and Renaissance society. Medieval man, in a sense, led two lives: an official life, "monolithically serious and somber; beholden to strict hierarchical order; filled with fear, dogmatism, devotion, and piety"; the other, a life of carnival and the public place, "free; full of ambivalent laughter, sacrileges, profanations of all things sacred, disparagement and unseemly behaviour."[8] Medieval laughter "is the social consciousness of all the people." The Renaissance, in this character, is a direct carnivalization of human consciousness, philosophy, and literature. Instead of orthodoxy, there are pageants, comic shows of the market-place, parodies, grotesqueries, and billingsgate. Carnival is street-theatre, a show without footlights in the sense that it doesn't distinguish between actors and spectators. Rabelais is the master of these comic ceremonies, the third Book of *Gargantua and Pantagruel* a riot of popular uncrownings, cuckoldry, thrashing, and mockery.

I am not concerned with the validity of Bakhtin's historical description, or indeed with its originality. Some of his account is familiar from such books as C. L. Barber's *Shakespeare's Festive Comedy* and Enid Welsford's *The Fool.* The chapter on Rabelais in *Mimesis* shows that Auerbach and Bakhtin arrived independently at much the same sense of him. Auerbach, too, refers to Rabelais's promiscuous mixture of styles, his polyphony, his source in Lucian, the multiplicity of viewpoints wantonly juxtaposed, "the creatural concept of the human body," Rabelais's nonchalance among the attitudes he describes, and his "grasp of life which comprehends the spiritual and the sensuous simultaneously." No matter. What Bakhtin emphasises is that high or official culture is, almost by definition, monologic, to the extent to which it insists on maintaining itself as a separate and privileged culture. Carnival is dialogic because it mocks such pretension.

But I should emphasise that Bakhtin is not interested in carnival and grotesquerie as mere themes. I infer from the excellent biography of him by Katerina Clark and Michael Holquist[9] that he is concerned with these explosions of energy only insofar as they are tokens of an available social institution, a second life alongside the first. It is superficial to refer to Bakhtinian carnival on every occasion of local satire and mockery. I have heard David Lodge making such a reference when the event in question was the ITV programme *Spitting Image,* a puppet show which mocks British politicians and the Royal Family. That is not what Bakhtin meant at all. *Spitting Image* and *Monty Python* are satirical shows comfortably accommodated within the institutions they deride: they are not ways of life, or social practises on the margin of the official culture. Indeed, it would be easy enough to regard them as bolstering the culture they apparently attack; by showing that the culture is liberal enough to see itself laughed at. These shows reinforce the law they mock.

Similar considerations would indicate that the reception of Bakhtin's work in the West should direct a little irony upon itself. It is evident that he has been turned into a hero for our time for reasons mostly sentimental. It is indeed impressive that he developed a rhetoric of dialogic, polyphony, and carnival during the years and in the country in which such thoughts were most virulently suppressed. In itself, the theory merely urges that the imagination should exert subversive pressure upon the official myths and ideologies. Kenneth Burke said it briefly in *Counter-Statement:* "When in Rome, do as the Greeks." We should honour Bakhtin for preserving such a stance in Russia during the 1920s and thereafter, surviving the Stalinism his theories must be interpreted as attacking. It is edifying, while reading the Clark and Holquist biography, to think of Bakhtin, ill, exiled, working out a theory of the novel as transgression—or rather, in Kristeva's phrase, a theory of dialogism as "transgression giving itself a law," a law of becoming and not of being, of analogy and not of causation. But it is easy to exaggerate the significance of the theory, as Kristeva did when she wrote of Bakhtin in 1966 and thought his dialogism might well become "the basis of our time's intellectual structure." It won't: indeed, in certain moods I could be persuaded that dialogism is merely a footnote to Nietzsche's Dionysianism. The monologism of the West will hardly be defeated by the one if it has survived the other.

What I value Bakhtin's theory of dialogism for is a more tangible merit. The theory implies an alternative sense of "the meaning of meaning"; not the mind's imposition of order upon sentiments and images that can be forced to allow such attention; but meaning as recognition of all the constituents of the scene, including most particularly those which are in danger of being suppressed. Stated in this form, the theory isn't especially original: it could be deduced, in its essentials, from Blake's attack on Bacon, Locke, and Newton—"Single vision & Newton's sleep." But it is more useful than Blake's in providing a sense of the ways in which Cartesian idealism and Newtonian sleep could be construed as merely one form of the mind's activity among many. More specifically, and in preparation for a return to *Finnegans Wake:* Bakhtin's account of heteroglossia, or of what the essay "From the Prehistory of Novelistic Discourse" calls "polyglossia," suggests the conditions in which the hegemony of a single language may be undermined. In that essay he points out that the Roman literary consciousness was, in effect, trilingual: Roman literature was born "in the interanimation of three languages," Latin, Greek, and Oscan. So it was natural for a Latin writer to see his words in the light of Greek and sometimes of Oscan, too. He would see his words as if out of the corner of his eye. One of the effects of this particular relation to his language was that he would construe it not on the assumption that it was transparent to reality but, on the contrary, that it was one way among several of seeing the world. Bakhtin quotes the passage in which Wilamowitz-Moellendorff, writing of Plato, says that "only knowledge of a language that possesses another mode of conceiving the world can lead to the appropriate knowledge of one's own language." A writer with such knowledge would see his own language not as natural but as already, in part, stylized. "Where languages and cultures interanimated each other"—Bakhtin recurs to that verb as if it contained his whole meaning, which it does—". . . in place of a single, unitary sealed-off Ptolemaic world of language, there appeared the open Galilean world of many languages, mutually animating each other." In a passage quoted by Clark and Holquist, Bakhtin speaks of the corresponding necessity of breaking up old fixations of words and concepts—the argument is akin to Remy de Gourmont's on the dissociation of ideas—"by freeing them temporarily of all semantic links, and freely recreating them."

I should add, what is perhaps clear enough, that heteroglossia and polyglossia name the conditions in which people no longer assume that discourse must be authoritative, and that the supreme token of authority is the recognised voice. The question of voice is always a question of authority. When we refer to a young writer as finding his voice, we mean that he has devised a style such that, his sentences once uttered, we recognise a distinctive voice. There is no reason why his achievement should be celebrated in these terms; their unearned assumption is that we want to hear a distinctive voice so that we can accept its authority.

But the trouble with these sentiments is that they issue, in Bakhtin's phrase, as the attributes of monologic: a clearly recognised voice, an unquestioned sense of self, a firmly enforced point of view, an impression of continuous control of the materials. Insofar as we read in the spirit of these assumptions, we are inevitably bewildered by a book—*Finnegans Wake*—in which Joyce chooses not to exert the authority he exerted in *Ulysses,* disowns the finality of a single voice, dissolves the demarcations between one thing and another, and goes as far as possible to undermine the imperium of the language—English, it is worth saying—in which the book is, however deviantly, written.

III

Here is a passage from the *Wake,* selected not at random:

Where the lisieuse are we and what's the first sing to be sung? Is it rubrics, mandarimus, pasqualines, or verdidads is in it, or the bruise-livid indecores of estreme voyoulence and, for the lover of lithurgy, bekant or besant, where's the fate's to be wished for? Several sindays after whatsintime. I'll sack that sick server the minute I bless him. That's the mokst I can do for his grapce. Economy of movement, axe why said. I've a hopesome's choice if I chouse of all the sinkts in the colander. From the common for ignitious Purpalume to the proper of Francisco Ultramare, last of scorchers, third of snows, in terrorgammons howdydos. Here she's, is a bell, that's wares in heaven, virginwhite, Undetrigesima, vikissy manonna. Doremon's! The same or similar to be kindly observed within the affianced dietcess of Gay O'Toole and Gloamy Gwenn du Lake (Danish spoken!) from Manducare Monday up till farrier's siesta in china dominos. Words taken in triumph, my sweet assistance, from the sufferant pen of our jocosus inkerman militant of the reed behind the ear.[10]

A reader bent on deciphering that passage, with the aid of several annotators including Fritz Senn, Roland McHugh, and Adaline Glasheen, would probably start by taking Joyce's word for it—in a letter of June 27, 1924, to Harriet Shaw Weaver—that it comes from "a long absurd and rather incestuous Lenten lecture" delivered by Shaun to his sister Izzy, otherwise Issy, otherwise Isobel. He would also take note of the fact that Book 3, Chapter 2, has 29 paragraphs, of which this one is the fifth; and he might already have noted that the number 29 refers most particularly to the number of children of St. Bride's School to whom, counting Issy, Shaun delivers his sermon.

If we were content to decipher this passage, we would begin by remarking that it is indeed in English: some of the words are odd, but they are all in the places of standard English. Or rather, of the English spoken by Irish priests, their heads full of the ecclesiastical Latin Litany of the Saints, and the liturgy of Holy Week, with special reference to the

Holy Thursday supper and the washing of feet. Assume, too, that the priest is riffling through his mass-book, trying to find the text, a task his server should have made easier by marking the relevant passages with ribbons of several colours. Formal annotation might proceed roughly as follows:

lisieuse: of Lisieux; St. Teresa of the Child Jesus.

rubrics: directions, printed in red, for the conduct of divine service.

mandarimus: obscure. Mandaremus = we might command.
> Mandatum, Latin name of the ceremony of washing the feet.

pasqualines: paschal, Easter-ceremonies, featuring the paschal candle.

verdidads: obscure to me.

bruiselivid indecores of estreme voyoulence: images of Christ crucified.

bekant: German "famous."

besant: unlikely to refer to Annie Besant, famous Theosophist. Otherwise obscure.

the fate's to be wished for: *Hamlet,* "a consummation devoutly to be wished." Also the feet to be washed.

sindays after whatsintime: Sundays after Whitsuntide.

mokst: most.

his grapce: His Grace.

Economy of movement: in theology, the judicious presentation of doctrine, bearing one's audience in mind.

axe why said: XYZ.

hopesome's choice: Hobson's choice.

sinkts in the colander: saints in the calendar.

common . . . proper: as in the parts of the Mass.

ignitious Purpalume: fiery St. Ignatius Loyola, wounded at Pampeluna; his feast-day July 31, hence last day of a scorching month in a hot summer.

Francisco Ultramare: St. Frances Xavier, Apostle of the far-flung Indies beyond the sea: his feast-day December 3, "third of snows" in a rare winter.

terrorgammons howdydos: Latin *te rogamus, audi nos,* one of the responses in the Litany of the Saints.

is a bell: Isobel.

wares: in an earlier draft Joyce wrote "swears," but settled for bog German.

Undetrigesima: 29th, as in Livy.

vikissy manonna: *vicesima nona;* 29th, also.

Doremon's!: possibly Latin *Adoremus.*

affianced dietcess: diocese, the feminine ending suggesting affianced.

Gay O'Toole: St. Laurence O'Toole, Abbot of Glendalough.

Gloamy Gwenn du Lake: Glendalough. Also Thomas Moore's "By
    That Lake, Whose Gloomy Shore." Possibly faint allusion to
    "In the Gloaming," one of Joyce's favorite songs.

Danish spoken: an indelicacy is available in German, but not in
    Danish. Glendalough a tourist attraction.

Manducare Monday: obscure. *Manducare* means to chew or eat.
    In the Gospel for Monday of Holy Week Martha and Mary
    gave Christ supper.

farrier's siesta: the resting time of one who, in Spain, celebrates
    a Feast.

in china dominos: Latin *in cena domini,* at the Lord's Supper on
    Holy Thursday.

Words taken: the formula used by the priest after his citation of the
    text for sermon.

inkerman militant: Inkerman, a battle mentioned often in *F.W.*
    Militant as in Church Militant.

the reed behind the ear: Shem's pen; also allusion, as in the *Portrait,*
    to Thoth, Egyptian god of writers.

Deciphering the book along these lines, it would be possible to turn it
into a fairly ordinary story, as Danis Rose and John O'Hanlon have
paraphrased it in their *Understanding Finnegans Wake* (1982). The reader
would deduce from the words on the page an orthodox English tale, and
would deal somehow with the evidence that Joyce has parodied, perverted,
or travestied his original straightforward text with the result we inadequately understand.

But it is a puny triumph to read the book in that way. Indeed, Joyce's
reference to Shaun's sermon is misleading, because it encourages the
impression that a character is saying certain things which he draws
toward his consciousness. The passage I've quoted doesn't issue from one
recognisable voice, but from a linguistic procedure which suffuses the
distinction between Shaun's voice and the voice of an anonymous priest
whose phantom-personality is dissolved in his priestly duty. Even to put
the matter in these terms is to go too far toward the conventions of

names, characters, roles, and identities. What we have to retain is discrepancy, not unification.

The discrepancy, for instance, between words written and spoken. In 1924 Joyce told Miss Weaver, unmisleadingly, that "with a half a glance of Irish frisky from under the shag of his parallel brows" are the words the reader "will see but not those he will hear."[11] In the event, the marks visible on page 470 became "with half a glance of Irish frisky (a Juan Jaimesan *hastaluego*) from under the shag of his parallel brows." What the reader hears is a glass of Irish whiskey, a John Jameson to be precise, and brows like parallel bars, the collocation of glance, frisky, shaggy eyebrows, and a Spanish salute being enough to keep drink and sex in extrovert alliance. Indeed, the written form of the words in *Finnegans Wake* often defeats the attempt to utter them: the point of the defeat is that the words as you might decide to speak them are not to be taken as decisive. Other senses or degradations of the words are to be retained as well, even though they can't be reproduced by the human voice, an instrument very fine in its way but too single-minded for Joyce's heteroglossic purpose. The reader who encounters "obscindgemeinded" on page 252 can't make his voice utter simultaneously "obscene-minded," "absent-minded," and the German *gemeinde* for community. No voice can produce, on the instigation of vikissy manonna, a sound which will include *vicesima nona,* kiss, and Issy.

The discrepancy between written and utterable words in the *Wake* is a token of discrepancy at large. When the book was published in 1939, readers saw that something of this kind was going on, but they couldn't agree on the significance of the relation between the root-phrases and the words on the page. John Crowe Ransom, in one of the most interesting approaches to the book, took it as a deliberate reaction to the enforced definition of truth in scientific or positivist terms. Science is concerned only with the effective action and the official truth, but a writer might feel special tenderness for the sentiments, however irresponsible, which don't enter into the effective action. Ransom regretted the aesthetic poverty of whatever a scientific mind counts as experience: it seemed to be a miserable thing by comparison with any really human image a poet might imagine. Indeed, Ransom held a theory of poetry by which a poem is taken to be compounded of a more-or-less rational structure and a more-or-less irrelevant texture: that is, "texture" might include many details irrelevant to the strict argument. Nothing in the argument of Marvell's "To His Coy Mistress" required reference to "the conversion of the Jews," but the poet was delighted to find a rhyme for "refuse" which would let him give an outlandish specification to the woman's lengthy hesitation, which in prosaic terms might be perhaps ten thousand years or thereabouts. Ransom delighted in any detail that a scientific or positivist account of the event would declare irrelevant. He was resolutely opposed to the dogmatism which would declare reality to be such-and-such and not other. He particularly distrusted science for its illiberal dictates in this regard. So he urged poets not to give in to the scientists; poets should not be intimidated by an impoverished account of experience, regardless of its authoritarian insistence. So he welcomed *Finnegans Wake* as "the most comprehensive individual reaction we have yet seen to all that we have accomplished with our perverted ideal of perfect action."

More especially, Ransom noted the rule in *Finnegans Wake* "which punctually alters the terms of discourse as soon as discourse has started, and brings its effectiveness to an end." It is assumed, by this rule, that discourse is in the hands of the scientists, and that the only value sought is effectiveness: so the writer sets out to be subversive, and from a scientific point of view he is bound to appear at best mischievous, at worst sinister. As for Joyce's method, Ransom's description of it is the best I have met:

> In Euclid, or for that matter in non-Euclidean geometry, it is said: Let *a* be this, and let *b* be that; the terms remain fixed in their meanings throughout the problem. But *a* has a homophone somewhere, or at least *b* has, and puns are possible since there are terms of like sound to these terms, and by these tricks Joyce is equal to providing enough distraction to drown the original operation. Joyce exploits at least two prime devices for obfuscating discourse. One is stream of consciousness, which is prepared to excrete irrelevances in any situation. The other is the verbal device of going from the relevant meaning of the word to the irrelevant meaning, or from the word to the like-sounding words, and then to the words like the like-words.[12]

Ransom supposes, then, that there is an enemy. Science has captured discourse, and impoverished our lives by imposing a dreary sense of reality upon us. Joyce is coming to our rescue, opening gates where science has closed them. A reader of Bakhtin would take much the same view as Ransom does, except that he would regard as the enemy any and every form of official culture. Such a reader would then conclude that the root-phrases from which the phrases of *Finnegans Wake* have been developed correspond to the high, official culture which Joyce then degrades. The root-phrases are never allowed to retain their dignity, but only whatever little status they can hold on to, travestied as they are. Most of them began as standard constituents of early-twentieth-century Irish culture—phrases of the day, patriotic tags, operatic arias, sentimental ditties, old songs, proverbs, aphorisms. The technique of travesty determines how they will end up. The book might then be read as a *cena,* a work of blasphemy made by scissors-and-paste degradation of sacred words and phrases now removed from the contexts that made them sacred. The procedure would be an extreme version of the technique of discrepancy between dictions which Kenner's essay illuminates. The only difference would be that in *Dubliners* and the *Portrait* the dictions are kept separate within the sentence, while in *Finnegans Wake* they are brought together as a simultaneous gesture: one word or phrase contains both the root and its travestied development. But the difference is more apparent than real, because the reader has to separate the elements which Joyce has brought together. In reading the phrase, he has to deduce the root—the saints in the calendar from the sinkts in the colander—and then return to the phrase as it stands. The problem with deciphering the phrases is that the reader's mind is concentrated on one direction; that is, on deducing the root from the developed form. The deduction once made, it is not clear what he should do next.

There is no alternative to deciphering; unless a reader is content to read the *Wake* "as music" without bothering with the sense of it. The problem is to decide what, in the reader's activity, corresponds to the simultaneity of the verbal events on Joyce's page. Deducing the root from the developed form is a temporal process: clearly not enough, unless the reader can somehow restore the clash of root and form. Here the Bakhtinian motif of official culture and its carnivalesque travesty may be too rigid for our purposes. Ransom's interpretation, too, may have the same disability, that it concedes too much to the myth of science by giving it more authority than it really has. It may be better to think of Joyce's technique in the *Wake* not as setting the language of travesty in a derisive relation to an official discourse but as relativizing two or more forms of perception by confounding the privilege any of them might be expected to have. The elements jostle one another for the same space on the page. Subordination of one to another is always possible, but it doesn't take place. The result is indeed like the Bakhtinian polyphony, except that the effect is rather one of clashing attitudes within the same space of attention. Joyce's procedure is to force words, phrases, and sentences out of the sign-system which they would inhabit in an orthodox novel; they are then displaced, made to participate in two or more divergent systems. The monologic imperative is set aside. No word in the book finds its destiny in referring to an object. Every word invokes another word or words, the syllables are promiscuously available to every impulse of stylization. Transgression indeed gives itself a law, phonetic rather than semantic. Each occasion is provided, as in stylization generally, by something already said or written by someone outside the book. Hence there are no stable images in *Finnegans Wake:* if we insist on having them, we have to dismantle the book and restore it to what we regard as its elements, a procedure that began with the *Skeleton Key* and continues with *Understanding Finnegans Wake.*

In some respects this is odd. We are accustomed since *The Waste Land* to voices issuing from no visible source and changing into other voices without formal indication; since Pound's *Cantos,* to words which can be looked at but not spoken; and, since Crane's *The Bridge,* to words which don't seem urgently concerned with denoting objects or events. We make allowance for these works, because they are poems: the scandal of *Finnegans Wake* is that it looks, in the hand, like a long novel but doesn't answer the expectations aroused by that appearance. It hasn't any characters. ALP and HCE, Shem and Shaun and Issy aren't characters as Leopold Bloom, Stephen, Molly, and Blazes Boylan are, an assertion sufficiently evidenced by the fact that even those characters in *Ulysses* who enter the phantasmagoria of "Circe" are restored to themselves and are not, in the end, metamorphosed. *Finnegans Wake* registers the matrix of general experience, but with only enough differentiation to distinguish male from female, mountain from river, trees from stones. In this, Joyce and Lawrence are kin: both writers want to come upon life before it has been differentiated into stable egos and personalities insisting on their identity.

Where then do we find "the story of the night"?

Perhaps in the conversation between Joyce and Arthur Power which I have already quoted, where Joyce said that since the advent of Christianity we seem to have lost our sense of proportion, for too great stress is laid on man.[13] Too great stress is also laid on a strictly human paradigm of history according to linear, progressive, and causative desires. To counter such an emphasis, Joyce resorted to Vico's vision, according to which the intellectual history of the race is a cycle of three stages, the hieroglyphic, the poetic, and the abstract, the last turning into the first again in a new cycle. In a Viconian sense of life, a mind would hold itself open to the possibility that something may turn into something else, the generic categories showing themselves as malleable as any other exemplars of metamorphosis. So *Finnegans Wake* imagines not individual lives insisting on their stability but life as such, patient in its transformations. I have been persuaded by Mark L. Troy's *Mummeries of Resurrection* (1976) that the Egyptian *Book of the Dead* provided Joyce with just enough of a story to count as a story of rise and fall and rise again. The story of the night is Joyce's version of the cycle of Osiris: Osiris, his sister-wife Isis, her sister-shadow Nephthys, Osiris's murderous brother Set, the rebirth of Osiris in his son Horus. "Irise, Osirises! Be thy mouth given unto thee!" (*F.W.* 493.28). The cycle is a myth, indeed, but not in Bakhtin's sense. Whatever the provenance of the cycle of Osiris in ancient Egypt, it does not bind Joyce; but it provides him with a story of life, death, murder, and resurrection, quite enough for a book of Ovidian transformations.

In "Notes toward a Supreme Fiction" Wallace Stevens writes that

> *The poem goes from the poet's gibberish to*
> *The gibberish of the vulgate and back again.*

and that the poet tries

> *To compound the imagination's Latin with*
> *The lingua franca et jocundissima.*[14]

R. P. Blackmur took the imagination's Latin to be the "received," objective, and authoritative imagination, whether of philosophy, religion, myth, or dramatic symbol. Presumably it means whatever is proffered or perhaps imposed as doctrine. Latin had this force in the Christian Church for many centuries and in the Catholic Church till recently: in the passage I quoted from *Finnegans Wake,* it is still in force. In Stevens's poem, it is associated with the vulgate, even though the vulgate is printed in lower case. Superior case, the Vulgate means the Latin version of the Bible as St. Jerome translated it in A.D. 406, a translation moving toward commonness and community by comparison with the original Hebrew. So it is not surprising that the lower-case vulgate gradually came to mean the common speech, the ready vernacular on ordinary occasions. But the equivocation of the word allows us to think that, just as there is an esoteric Hebrew behind the Latin of St. Jerome, so there is an adequate speech unheard behind the audible speech attendant upon daily life. To this it is reasonable to add, from Blackmur's second comment, that gibberish is not a frivolous word in this context: "it is a word *manqué* more than a word mocking." One gibbers "before a reality too great, when one is appalled with perception, when words fail though meaning persists. . . . "[15]

A reader of *Finnegans Wake* has to cope somehow not only with the Church's Latin but with the imagination's Latin; with the Vulgate as well as the vulgate; with the poet's gibberish and the other gibberish of the vulgate; and with the transitions and transformations he has to be ready to meet on any page. It may be that recourse to Bakhtin and to Ransom has several merits but this disadvantage, that it makes us too ready to see Joyce's language as debunking the official Latins and doing nothing else. Isn't it possible that Joyce's gibberish is going behind the official Latins and Englishes not to make contact with some linguistic origin preceding history but, hastening the next Viconian phase, to place us in hieroglyphs, free before any law?

THREE

Contexts

ANOTHER COMPLEX FATE

I n the fifth chapter of *A Portrait of the Artist as a Young Man*, Stephen Dedalus, late for his French class at University College, converses with the Dean of Studies, Father Darlington. The topics include the art of lighting a fire, the definition of beauty, Epictetus' lamp, and the currency of the word "tundish" in lower Drumcondra. The Dean seemed to Stephen "a humble follower in the wake of clamorous conversions, a poor Englishman in Ireland." But Stephen felt "with a smart of dejection," Joyce reports, "that the man to whom he was speaking was a countryman of Ben Jonson." A few pages earlier, passing a marinedealer's shop beyond the Liffey, Stephen had repeated Jonson's song, "I was not wearier where I lay." Now he ponders the question of the English language and the Dean who speaks it:

> The language in which we are speaking is his before it is mine. How different are the words *home, Christ, ale, master,* on his lips and on mine! I cannot speak or write these words without unrest of spirit. His language, so familiar and so foreign, will always be for me an acquired speech. I have not made or accepted its words. My voice holds them at bay. My soul frets in the shadow of his language.

The Dean takes up the distinction between the sublime and the beautiful, but Stephen turns away in silence.

I have recalled this episode from the *Portrait* because it marks one of the fundamental circumstances of modern Irish literature: the writer is Irish, but he writes in English, a language at once "so familiar and so foreign." I believe that many Irish writers who write in English have a bad conscience in doing so, even though they have spent their entire lives among English words. It is not enough; or not always enough. "Stephen Dedalus is my name, Ireland is my nation"; but Stephen does not speak Irish, and sad it is. In Ireland, language is a political fact. Those who do not speak Irish speak English with an intonation of misgiving; they cannot be completely at ease with their acquired speech. Something of this restlessness has produced the irritable syntax of Stephen's mind, the torsion of "his" and "mine," England and Ireland. The Irish writer knows that the language remains an old debt, never settled, and he cannot absolve himself of the responsibility. Like Stephen, the Irish writer speaks and writes in English, but with resentment, fretful in its shadow. Joyce, holding English words at bay, preserved his artistic soul by listening to several languages. When he left Dublin, he went to Paris, Trieste, Zurich, but not to London or New York: at least he did not consort with the enemy. He was not to be found, like Yeats, in the writing room of a London club.

But Yeats attended in his own way to the complex fate of being an Irishman. An Irishman was not merely an Englishman with a difference. In "Literature and the Living Voice," Yeats described the general characteristics of Irish culture, and spoke of restoring "a way of life in which the common man has some share in imaginative art." He continued:

> Irish poetry and Irish stories were made to be spoken or sung, while English literature, alone of great literatures, because the newest of them all, has all but completely shaped itself in the printing-press. In Ireland to-day the old world that sang and listened is, it may be for the last time in Europe, face to face with the world that reads and writes, and their antagonism is always present under some name or other in Irish imagination and intellect.

To Yeats, reading or writing a book was a specialised activity, always pursued at some cost. "When a man takes a book into the corner, he surrenders so much life for his knowledge, so much, I mean, of that normal activity that gives him life and strength." Yeats never doubted that the imaginative life of Ireland was oral, dedicated to speech, and that the literature of print was an alien possession. When he spoke of this theme, he made the kind of distinction which Walter Benjamin made, in a classic essay on Nikolai Leskov, between the novel and the story.

The novel is the work of an isolated writer in league with a printing press: it turns toward the middle-class reader and offers him minute psychological analysis. The story comes from oral tradition and returns to that source: it is concerned with experience passed on from voice to voice, and intelligence that comes from afar. The context of story is natural history, its art is memory, its aim is wisdom—which Benjamin calls the epic side of truth—its procedures are formulaic and proverbial.

Taking this theme in Irish terms, one says that the place of Irish fiction is the small community, the nearly deserted village, the storyteller and his audience are peasants, the theme is life in the shadow of death. Irish fiction is a tale of peasants, landlords, and gods. Yeats thought, for a time, that the "old imaginative life" might be stirred to more life, and that this was the work of the Gaelic movement in one way, the Celtic Renaissance writers in another. The Abbey Theatre was founded on speech and story.

The antagonism which Yeats mentioned in "Literature and the Living Voice" is clear in his response to Joyce. He thought Joyce a print man, a city-writer insensitive to rural ways, a novelist rather than a storyteller or chronicler; Dublin's psychologist. In an essay on Berkeley, Yeats associated Joyce with the "new naturalism that leaves man helpless before the contents of his own mind." Ostensibly, it is a philosophical question, a question of aesthetics: but the particular case of Joyce is grounded, I believe, on Yeats's hostility to the urban culture of print and isolation. The hostility touched Joyce in one way, George Moore in another. Moore, "more mob than man," wrote *A Mummer's Wife,* "the first realistic novel in the language," Yeats called it, "the first novel where every incident was there not because the author thought it beautiful, exciting or amusing, but because certain people, who were neither beautiful, exciting, nor amusing must have acted in that way." Imagination, chief of the active faculties, was obviously in suspense.

It is customary to say that there are two traditions in Ireland. I do not repudiate the custom. If we are thinking of the contemporary situation in political terms, it is proper to speak of Nationalists and Unionists. National-ists hope to see Ireland united, the entire island, thirty-two counties, and they differ among themselves only on the crucial question of the means toward the agreed end, and the price they are willing to pay for it. Some Nationalists insist on having the country united immediately, by whatever means: others are willing to wait, such is their concern for peace. Unionists are determined, in one degree or another, that Northern Ireland will remain distinct from the rest of the country, that their loyalty to the British Crown is indelible: if necessary, they will be more British than the English. Not every Catholic is a Nationalist, or every Protestant a Unionist.

In Irish writing, there are two traditions. One is Gaelic, and for the most part it is Catholic. According to this tradition, Joyce may have been a bad Catholic but he was a good Irishman; he held one of the great Irish names, his blood was pure Irish. An Irishman in this definition would speak Irish or at least he would recall the fact that his ancestors spoke Irish. He might be a farmer or, in a small town, a shopkeeper. If he made his way to Ireland's one city, he would be the kind of person studied in Joyce's *Dubliners*. In this literary context, the second tradition is Anglo-Irish, "no petty people," as Yeats described its members in a famous Senate speech in 1925, when he identified himself with his peers:

> We are one of the great stocks of Europe. We are the people of Burke; we are the people of Grattan; we are the people of Swift, the people of Emmet, the people of Parnell. We have created the most of the modern literature of this country. We have created the best of its political intelligence.

It was a strident speech, more embarrassing to his friends than to his opponents, but it was directly in line with Yeats's claim, in 1914, to the possession of "blood that has not passed through any huckster's loin." Members of the Anglo-Irish tradition do not appeal to the British Crown. They are Protestants, but they appeal to the moral and intellectual authority of their own kind, and they declare that kind to be Irish, no matter which side they took at the Battle of the Boyne:

> *A Butler or an Armstrong that withstood*
> *Beside the brackish waters of the Boyne*
> *James and his Irish when the Dutchman crossed.*

At one time Yeats thought it reasonable as well as beautiful to project a liaison of feeling between such men and the peasants who served them. One of his favourite relationships was that of servant and master, and he often claimed that he would have been satisfied to play either of those roles. In his Platonic form of Ireland, peasant and landlord join in pride to crush the puny bourgeoisie, the gombeen-men "fumbling in a greasy till." It has not happened. The Anglo-Irish aristocracy have lost most of their land and all their power. In that condition, they are the objects of nearly universal affection, welcomed as an adornment, a buttonhole in Ireland's lapel. No charitable committee is deemed complete without a lord or two. But peasants have long forgotten how to stand aside, cap in hand, while their masters pass. The peasants, too, are a dying breed, and those that remain have lost their identity. Many of them have learnt the ways of all flesh and the diverse ways by which money is made. The Catholic Church is no longer the greatest power in the land; the priest's word is not law in his parish.

Yeats told his fellow senators in 1925 that Northern Ireland would not give up "any liberty which she already possesses under her constitution":

> If you show that this country, Southern Ireland, is going to be governed by Catholic ideas and by Catholic ideas alone, you will never get the North. You will create an impassable barrier between South and North, and you will pass more and more Catholic laws, while the North will gradually assimilate its divorce and other laws to those of England.

The validity of this argument is now widely acknowledged in the South. Our Taoiseach, Mr. Lynch, has offered to alter any provisions in the Constitution of 1937 which may be considered obstacles to national unity. A revised constitution would recognize the diversity of our traditions; it would be a plural document and indeed a secular document. There are some people in the South who think that such a revision, for such a reason, would be worthless, it would have no influence on Unionist sentiment. I find it hard to believe that a Northern Unionist would forsake Queen and Country if the South undertook to allow him, in return, free access to contraceptives. But a revised constitution, undertaken for whatever reason, would still be significant in marking the secular direction which the South has taken, especially in the past four or five years.

Irish literature is a story of fracture: the death of one language, so far as it is dead or dying or maintained as an antiquity, and the victory of another, both claiming to be Christian; the divergence of one Irishman from another.

It is possible that these fractures are good for literature, if bad for other purposes. Ireland is changing, and the changes make a chapter in the history of the Catholic Church as well as in the history of Ireland. Perhaps it is premature to say much more—except to remark that an Irish writer might find the situation rich in artistic possibilities, even if he found it distressing in other respects. Allen Tate has described, in his essay on Emily Dickinson, a situation shortly before 1850 when the Puritan idea, New England theocracy, had come to an end: "A great idea was breaking up, and society was moving towards external uniformity, which is usually the measure of the spiritual sterility inside." I have read Tate's essay at least five times in as many years, and each time with a terrible feeling that he is writing not of his country in 1850 but of my country now. He has little good to report of the America of 1830–50, except that it offered Emily Dickinson "the perfect literary situation." The poet was born into "the equilibrium of an old and a new order":

> Puritanism could not be to her what it had been to the generation of Cotton Mather—a body of absolute truths; it was an unconscious discipline timed to the pulse of her life.

I do not enforce the translation into Irish terms, but we have in Ireland, I believe, a situation in which the doctrines of the Catholic Church, accepted for centuries as binding truth, must now be taught to a laity often sceptical and recalcitrant. That is not to say that these doctrines are doomed; they may have a new life ahead of them, beloved once again. But they are not accepted merely by being uttered. There is also a question of the values embodied in those doctrines. But even if the Church's mission in Ireland were to fail, the Irish writer would meanwhile call upon Christian belief as a presence in his own work: he would not have to believe in Christianity, it would be enough if he felt its force. His work would be animated by the tension between feeling and form; feeling, the intimate, nervous life, the quick of perception; and form, the higher dream, the symbolic imagination, the Way.

It is sometimes said that Ireland's memory is too long and too ardent, that we should try the experiment of forgetting ourselves. But it is poor advice. For a small country, Ireland has had a lot of experience, many chances if fewer choices. The best writers in Ireland are those who remember most: I do not mean the oldest writers, necessarily. I mean those who feel immediate experience not merely in itself but in relation to a long perspective, mythological and historical, pagan and Christian. I see no reason why Irish literature should fail for lack of enabling matter.

Times Literary Supplement, 17 March 1972.

TOGETHER

Most of the towns and villages in Ireland are as peaceful as Rupert Brooke's Grantchester. Derry is safe at the moment, but it is not its habit to be quiet for long. Belfast is ugly with fear and hatred, though it is still possible to live an unmolested life there, as Oliver Edwards does, pursuing an interest in the relation between Yeats and the German poet Dautendey. There is a small district in South Armagh where the British Queen's writ does not run and a British soldier is everyone's natural enemy. Yesterday (December 5, 1975), the Secretary of State for Northern Ireland announced the end of detention, formally called internment without trial. This morning *The Irish Times* carried a photograph of a young man released from Long Kesh, taking his child by the hand and walking off into freedom: a charming picture if we could be assured that in a few days he will not take up a gun or make a bomb which will kill without prejudice men, women, Catholics, Protestants, or a child of the same age as his own. *The Irish Times* shows a decent interest in the end of detention, but like nearly everybody it has become weary of the theme and turns, with undisguised relief, to the country's economic problems, the high incidence of unemployment, and current legislation designed to prevent the Irish banks from awarding their employees an increase of salary higher than the terms of the National Pay Agreement.

Meanwhile, men and women in Ireland write poems, novels, short stories, paint pictures, sculpt, and compose string quartets. I have done none of these things and therefore speak of them with impunity. It may be said that the "Troubles" in Northern Ireland since 1968 have been bad for life but good for literature: they have gained for young poets an audience which would not normally be available, and they have provided occasions more demandingly intense than those which generally emerge from a comfortable society. A few poets, including Thomas Kinsella and John Montague, have responded to these occasions directly, getting the horror of it hot, but the resultant poems are hysterical rather than impassioned: it is better for a poet to let such occasions wait in silence for a while. Seamus Heaney has been wiser in his economy, approaching violent themes indirectly, as if his poems composed not a politics but an anthropology of feeling, starting well back and deep down. One of these days the poets from the North will have to be read with an interest not chiefly topical. A reading in that spirit is premature, but I hope its day will come, and that Heaney, Mahon, Deane, Montague, and the rest will be read in the critically disinterested spirit we bring to, say, Geoffrey Hill, Roy Fisher, Charles Tomlinson, A. R. Ammons, John Ashbery, Philip Larkin, Ted Hughes.

It is true that Irish writers work under difficulties and that they deserve the advantages of a compellingly ill wind. When Larkin writes the poems in *High Windows,* he knows what he is doing, discovering his language in relation to the general body of the English language as a secure possession, mediated by Hardy, Auden, Betjeman, and other poets. Larkin's general body of reference is contemporary English society, dismal in many respects but well understood in terms of class and the preoccupations of class. As an economist of poetry he knows what he needs, judges precisely the moment at which his art tempts itself to archness or extravagance. Most of what he knows he has been told by his masters. But Irish writers find it peculiarly difficult to know what they are doing: they live upon broken rather than integral traditions; they do not know which voice is to be trusted, and how far. Conor Cruise O'Brien urges us to accept our experience as mixed and plural and to live accordingly in a spirit of tolerance. We are to repudiate the spirit of Republicanism which insists upon defining the essential Irish experience as that of driving out the English and spilling blood in this noble cause. His arguments may be vindicated in the end but meanwhile the spirit of acceptance which he espouses is attractive mainly to people who are disgusted with the Irish question and want to be rid of it; or to people who are weary, indifferent, interested only in getting on in the world. There are men and women who despise the notion of a plural society and who are ready to kill and be killed for the sake of national purity. O'Brien does not understand such people, or the aboriginal loyalties which mean far more to them than a contemptible liberal peace. He answers that his policy will not cause a single death: it is true. But a Republican will assert that there are things more glorious than liberal tolerance—a martyr's death, for instance. So the old rhetorical battle starts up again.

The real trouble is that our natural experience has been too limited to be true. Our categories of feeling have been flagrantly limited; our history has been at once intense and monotonous. We are still an agricultural country: industry, in any sense that applies to Birmingham or Wolverhampton, has been confined to Belfast and the Lagan Valley. So we have had no Industrial Revolution, no Factory Acts germane to our society, a trade union movement of local but not national provenance: hence the frail basis upon which our Labour Party exists, by contrast with the two major parties which can at least define themselves by asserted reference to our Civil War. A limited history, congealed mythologies, a literature of fits and starts: no continuity from one age to the next. Irish novelists feel the anxiety of influence but not the incitement or the challenge of a tradition. The nineteenth-century writers whom Thomas Flanagan studied in *The Irish Novelists* do not amount to a tradition; there are novelists but there is no tradition of the novel, the force of vision, technique, and precedence available to, say, Angus Wilson when he reads George Eliot and writes *Anglo-Saxon Attitudes*. The contemporary Irish novelist looks for a tradition capable of telling him what has been done and how he ought to proceed: instead he finds Joyce, an overbearing presence.

The price we pay for Yeats and Joyce is that each in his way gave Irish experience a memorable but narrow definition; they established it not as the ordinary but as a special case of the ordinary. Synge and the minor writers of the Irish Literary Revival were not strong enough to counter Yeats's incantatory rhetoric: no writer in Ireland has been strong enough to swerve from Joyce's sense of Irish experience in fiction. As a result the writers we particularly revere are those who encountered Yeats and Joyce and contrived to preserve minds and arts of their own: Beckett, and Flann O'Brien, who somehow deflected the blow of Joyce sufficiently to write *At Swim-Two-Birds* and *The Third Policeman,* books which could not have been written without Joyce's example but which could not have taken their definitive form if O'Brien had allowed himself to be intimidated by that example. I think also of Austin Clarke's later poems, the work of a poet who languished in Yeats's shadow until, late and not a moment too soon, he swerved away from it and struck out for himself.

T. S. Eliot has maintained in "What Is a Classic?" that "every supreme poet, classic or not, tends to exhaust the ground he cultivates, so that it must, after yielding a diminishing crop, finally be left in fallow for some generations." I find this an ambiguous idea, but nothing in it is more significant than Eliot's assumption that we have world enough and time. Certainly there are cultures of which we feel that the question of time is not the main problem: it is possible to think of France, England, and Greece as providing a cadence of feeling which allows for historical change and continuity. To think of Shakespeare and Milton exhausting the ground they cultivate is to respond once again to the plenitude of a literary culture in which that ground may be allowed to remain "in fallow for some generations." But it also exacerbates our sense of the vulnerability of those societies which cannot afford fallow years or quiet generations.

Modern Ireland as a State rather than as a province of England is only fifty years old. The separation of North and South is arbitrary, a politician's device. We have had to concentrate in one generation the experience which more fortunate countries have been able to develop in several; and we have largely been prevented from doing so by the exorbitance of rival mythologies. So we have had to live from day to day and hand to mouth. I mention these facts to explain the impression of spasmodic achievement in Irish literature. Our writers are, for the most part, solitary workers: they do not find themselves as participants in a common enterprise. Henry James said of the solitary writer that, "apt to make awkward experiments, he is in the nature of the case more or less of an empiric." I take it that empiricism is work from hand to mouth. It is remarkable, and a joy, that work as fine as Clarke's *Ancient Lights* has been produced in Ireland by such an unconcerted method.

It is probably idle to posit the conditions in which good work is done. Was it necessary for Brian Moore to leave Belfast and go three thousand miles away to write *Catholics?* He would say yes. Would Michael

McLaverty have developed a more complete art by resorting to the same itinerary? It is common to have the experience and miss the meaning. Who knows? Who knows enough? Anyway, it is my impression that Irish writers sense a rift between experience and meaning, but in reverse: the meaning is premature, already inscribed by a mythology they have no choice but to inherit, and then, if they must, to resent.

———————

Sewanee Review, January–March 1976.

DRUMS UNDER THE WINDOW

S ome months ago Conor Cruise O'Brien, Minister for Posts and Tele-
graphs in the Irish Government, addressed the students of University College, Dublin, on a text from Yeats's "September 1913":

> *Romantic Ireland's dead and gone,*
> *It's with O'Leary in the grave.*

The burden of Dr. O'Brien's speech was that Romantic Ireland is not
dead and gone, alas. The ideology of Romantic Ireland is still active: and
life in Ireland cannot be peaceful until that ideology is abandoned.
According to his argument, we have been schooled to revere as heroes
only the men of violence and blood: our saints are martyrs, our demonol-
ogy English, our modern history is supposed to have begun in 1169 when
Dermot MacMurrough called upon Henry II of England to help him
recover the province of Leinster. From that day to this we have had only
one theme, the hated presence of England in Ireland. One theme, and a
corresponding rhetoric: the true story of Ireland is recited as a sequence
of revolutions, glorious in feeling, heroic in failure. Our educational
system, as practised, for instance, by the Irish Christian Brothers, is
obsessed with this vision of Romantic Ireland. Yeats, great poet as he was,

put his genius at the disposal of a cause which has again brought Ireland to the brink of civil war.

Dr. O'Brien's speech embodies the policy of his government, and of many people who do not support the government in any other respect. "They have gone about the world like wind," Yeats wrote of the fame of Ireland's revolutionary heroes, but in Ireland today it is increasingly common to say that this wind brought good to nobody. Or at least it is common among the bourgeoisie and the intellectuals, who now regard the men of Easter Week 1916 as self-deluded fanatics, driven by lust of sacrifice and blood, including—to be fair—their own.

What the plain people of Ireland think, feel, and believe is harder to discover. They did not protest when Reverend Francis Shaw published, in the Jesuit quarterly *Studies,* an essay demonstrating that Padraic Pearse, archetype of Irish revolutionary sentiment, sought his own death in 1916 so that, perfect in his kind, he would transcend that kind and become for every Irishman an immortal symbol, a type, an indestructible ideal. But the plain people of Ireland do not read quarterlies. They are sick of violence, presumably, and vaguely aware of some connection between a bombed hotel in Belfast and an island already in a desperate economic mess. But I see no evidence that they are ready to go to school again to learn a more congenial version of Irish history. They probably feel that the story of Romantic Ireland is essentially true, and that Dr. O'Brien is practicing an "economy of truth" in his scepticism.

In *The Damnable Question,* George Dangerfield refers to "existential Irish history," meaning the recourse to violence, as distinct from the conventional persuasions of diplomacy and parliament. In its contemporary version, the Republican form of violence is embodied in the two versions of the IRA, the Provisionals (Catholics and Right Wing) and the Officials (Marxist). The fact that initiative has passed entirely to the Provisionals is enough to show how thin and rootless a Marxist political force is likely to be in Ireland. In the North the conflicts between the several versions of Unionism are temperamental and strategic rather than ideological.

Dr. O'Brien has been urging us, since violence broke out again eight years ago, to give up the ideology of Romantic Ireland, postpone indefinitely the question of England's departure from the North, and attend to the chore of making daily life more equable, more tolerant. We are to live by bread alone, but to bake better bread and offer a wider choice among the loaves. Instead of poetry good and bad, he urges us to resort to decent prose. Disgusted by the consequences of a myth, he admonishes us to live in a clear air, humanist and secular, without complaint or nostalgia. His rhetoric offers us a life without passion, unless we are ready to develop a passion for mundane experience.

Dr. O'Brien's colleague, Dr. Garret Fitzgerald, has offered Ireland a new, safe symbol in the ostensible unity embodied in the EEC, but without much success: we are in the EEC primarily for the money. Besides, that institution now appears mean rather than radiant, and pretty hopeless as a potentially sacred object, even if we longed for such a thing. We cannot resort to it for a myth more stirring than our own. The trouble is that Dr. O'Brien's demand that we transcend the past makes him sound as if he really wanted us to disown it. He deplores the Easter Rising as willful and unnecessary; but in deploring it he sounds as if he thought an Irishman in, say, 1914 should have been content to find himself represented by the squires of the Irish Nationalist Party. The point is that in 1914 there were not enough possibilities of choice: Britain's broken promises, a dying party, a war elsewhere, and political passion for which no practical embodiment could yet be found.

Mr. Dangerfield's book shows, if the show were still necessary, that in modern politics there have been only two procedures: parliamentary negotiation between a weak Irish Nationalist Party and a British Government incapable of taking Irishmen seriously; or the gun of Republicanism. In theory, there may be a third possibility, but Irish history has not yet disclosed it: unless it is merely to put up with whatever the Lord has given you. If you were a man of peace in 1914, you found your values embodied in the gullible Wicklow squire John Redmond, a decent man fooled by Asquith and turned into a recruiting sergeant for the British army, about to fight in France. On September 20, 1914, Redmond urged the Irish Volunteers to prepare themselves to fight "not only in Ireland itself, but wherever the firing line extends, in defence of right, of freedom, and of religion." After that, it was inevitable that the Volunteers would split into a Redmondite faction, led by John D. Nugent, and a Republican faction, led by Padraic Pearse, who had no intention of shedding his precious blood for any country, large or small, except Ireland.

The point to be emphasised is that in the months after September 1914 the choice between Nugent and Pearse had to be faced along those lines; it was impossible to transcend it or appeal to a higher idiom. During those months, it would have been perfectly reasonable for a nationalist to support Pearse's Irish Volunteers against Nugent's National Volunteers even if he suspected that Pearse's force was already infiltrated by the gun-loving Irish Republican Brotherhood. Dr. O'Brien speaks as if a patriot in 1916 had a wide range of choices, but the fact is that the Irish Nationalist Party was in ruins, and the collapse of the Home Rule negotiations in the summer of 1916 showed that the British Government had no intention of giving Ireland a genuine form of self-government.

This was clear to the Irish people who rejected the Party and turned to Sinn Fein in the election of 1917. Cogent reasons, rather than a self-deluding ideology, caused Irishmen to vote for Count Plunkett, Joseph MacGuinness, Eamon De Valera, and William Cosgrave, men who had distinguished themselves in the Easter Rising and done time in English jails. There is no merit in maintaining that those who ensured De Valera's victory in 1917 were simply the victims of a crazy mythology: the alternative at that time was to trust England to do the decent thing at the behest of a few exhausted Redmondites. In the face of Protestant Unionism in the North and the barely concealed support of Unionism by the English Tories, the nationalist Irishman had no serious choice: it was Sinn Fein Republicanism or nothing.

I deplore the situation in which Irishmen are killing Irishmen and Englishmen, but I do not think anything is gained by arguing that a mythology of Romantic Ireland is a sufficient explanation of our troubles. The roots of violence in Ireland are far deeper than Dr. O'Brien is willing to admit. It is an embarrassment to him that Irish politics cannot even yet be conducted in a language entirely secular and humanist, but he must put up with that situation as best he may.

Material for debate along these lines is provided by *The Damnable Question*, a study of Irish history from the Act of Union (1800) to the Civil War (1922–1923). The crucial event is deemed to be the Easter Rising. Mr. Dangerfield is in such a hurry to reach the General Post Office in Easter Week that he disposes of the years 1800 to 1908 in forty pages. The only story he wants to tell begins for him on a political platform on November 13, 1913, when the Labour leader James Connolly talked open sedition and brought the Irish Citizen Army into being. The story ends with the collapse of Dail Eireann in December 1921.

Mr. Dangerfield is chiefly interested in political and diplomatic narrative; he does not spend many pages on the social history of Ireland, apart from the Famine. Nor does he concern himself much with the religious question or the fact that Ireland is one of the few remaining countries in which it is possible to find avowed Christians killing one another. Dangerfield is most excited to describe those occasions on which the conflict may be explained in terms of character and will. He gives a splendid account of the occasion, March 1914, on which Asquith forced Redmond, John Dillon, and Joseph Devlin to agree to exclude six of the nine counties of Ulster from the application of Home Rule. The idea was rejected, of course, by Sir Edward Carson and the Unionists, but the fact that it was entertained at all disgraced the Irish Party and, far more serious, gave credence to the notion that Partition of some kind was a possible solution. Seven years later, Lloyd George and his secretary Thomas Jones fooled Arthur Griffith, the founder of Sinn Fein, with the same scheme, selling him the idea of setting up a Boundary Commission to determine the size and shape of a Northern Ireland. The principle of Partition was entertained by arguing about its precise form: a betrayal of the Republican cause today as in 1921.

I shall commit an Irish bull by saying that the Partition of Ireland is acceptable to everybody today, apparently, except those who are ready to kill and be killed rather than accept it. In the South, very few people are ardent in their desire to have the Border removed, unless it could be done without cost or consequence. In the North, the ardent are more numerous, but still a small minority. But there is little joy in these facts. Arm a few die-hard Republicans and a few diehard Unionists, and you get today's killings. If the issue were left to the politicians, I have no doubt that Partition would be accepted on a permanent or at least an indefinite basis: compromise would ensure a few improvements in local government in the North; some face-saving pronouncements would make the diplomats happy. But, for the moment, the politicians have been set aside. Dr. O'Brien's government has just now enacted tougher laws in an effort to defeat the violent men, but no one believes that laws will make any difference.

Mr. Dangerfield's narrative ends with the Civil War, but he adds a little reflection upon the desperate situation of the country since 1968. I do not find his argument convincing. He is sympathetic to the ideal of an independent Ireland, united in its thirty-two counties, and he regards as "perfidious" Asquith's determination to proceed with an Amending Bill granting permanent exclusion from Home Rule to the six northern counties. But I think he is naive in believing that if the Tories had accepted Home Rule for Ireland in 1912 "this constitutional path would have led in the long run to independence without Partition."

I doubt it. Or the run would have been too long to satisfy the passions of men like Pearse and Tom Clarke. Home Rule, even in the paltry form contemplated by Asquith, would have driven Carson and the

Northern Unionists to violence; they would never have accepted it any more than their descendants would accept it now. On the negotiations leading to the Treaty in December 1921, Mr. Dangerfield thinks that the Irish delegates should have called Lloyd George's bluff, refused to sign, and gone back to Dublin to a Dail still intact. The British Government should have accepted De Valera's famous Document No. 2—removing the Oath of Allegiance to the King of England—as an alternative to the official Articles of Agreement. The Irish Revolution, "once its political appetites had been appeased, would become moderately respectable and reasonably safe."

As for the Unionist James Craig and his followers: the British Government should have forced them to accept Document No. 2 by withdrawing from the Northern government the means of governing, namely, the money. Mr. Dangerfield thinks that financial pressure, especially in regard to taxation, would have been enough to force the Unionists to accept the situation. "Ulster had not yet hardened into the Ulster of today," he maintains, on no real evidence. "Thus," he says, "the possibility of a privileged, safeguarded Ulster coming in under an All-Ireland parliament, with all the happy consequences which this would have had for Ulster and the Ireland of today, flits for a moment before one's mind." But the happy vision ignores the virulence of Unionist hatred for the very idea of Home Rule, which men like Craig identified with Rome Rule.

Well, it's too late now, anyway. Partition gives every sign of permanence, or of "such permanence as time has." The English will probably withdraw from the North, sooner or later, since they have nothing more to gain and only lives and money to lose by staying there; but I agree with Dr. O'Brien that British withdrawal at this moment would be incalculably dangerous. The presence of British soldiers in Belfast is not bringing peace to hate-ridden streets, but for the moment it is probably preventing a massacre. Even if the British were to withdraw, the Irish would probably continue killing one another without foreign assistance: killing seems to have moved into its self-propelling phase.

Mr. Dangerfield is concerned with these matters, though his story does not officially include them. He is interested in the origin of the conflicts, and especially in the characters who defined them and suffered their exacerbations. An elegant writer, he is particularly gifted in the composition of "brief lives," succinct accounts of Parnell, Lloyd George, Asquith, Carson, Connolly, James Larkin, Pearse, De Valera. The story he tells is indeed well known to readers of F. S. L. Lyons's *Ireland Since the*

Famine and other studies of the period: there have been many books on the subject incited by events since 1968. It is too late to expect that much new material can be produced. So the merit of Mr. Dangerfield's book is mainly in the telling; the story is told with nuances and inflections enough to redeem its familiarity and to raise again certain questions of interpretation.

Few historians would think of describing Redmond as "a man who, though his principles would never be compromised, might come to accept compromise as a principle." That's worth pondering. Of Asquith and the Chief Secretary for Ireland, Augustine Birrell, Dangerfield says that "they took a somewhat dispassionate view of the world, as if they expected the millennium, should it ever arise, to be run by people very much like themselves." Of the conference held in July 1914 to consider the question of the northern counties, Dangerfield remarks that it got bogged down on the nature of County Tyrone: the statesmen "were endeavouring to settle by Act of Parliament what could only have been decided by Act of God, for Tyrone was so liberally pockmarked with Catholic and Protestant communities that nothing short of an earthquake or a general conversion could have drawn a boundary line." The events of Mr. Dangerfield's narrative are dire, but they have not undermined the vitality of his prose.

Despite the impression of continuous slaughter which television programs ascribe to Ireland, nearly every visitor knows that it is possible to go through the country without being inconvenienced by the men of violence. Edna O'Brien seems to have met, on a recent visit to her native soil, nothing more violent than a verbose taxi driver. True, in *Mother Ireland* she does not appear to have gone North, presumably because the North has not played a role in her drama. Mother Ireland lives in the South and West. Ms. O'Brien is from Clare, and the most dramatic road in her early life brought her to Dublin. Go East, she told herself; so Clare, Westmeath, the midlands, and Dublin provide her with musings in *Mother Ireland* as in her novel *A Pagan Place*.

Her themes include religion, death, sex, superstition, urine, childhood, school, De Valera, the neighbors, and marriage, because *Mother Ireland* is a loose, meandering, self-indulgent book of this and that rather than the travel book for which it may be mistaken. Edna O'Brien, a famous and popular novelist, goes back to Ireland for a spell, a touch of nostalgia, a bit of grousing, making a few obvious points about a Romantic Ireland dead and gone to her: the text conveys these sentiments in a prose she presumably thinks good enough for a sloppy occasion. The style is damnable, the language of the Irish Tourist Board in which, to give a few samples from *Mother Ireland,* women are the fair sex, plans come to fruition, people are souls, the yew tree sheds a dim religious light, girls are exultant dusk-haired beauties, cottages nestle, twenty-five is five and twenty, death is demise, dysentery is rife, deaf ears are turned, ways are wended, and drink is imbibed:

> When it rained and the yard was too wet for playtime, we huddled in the porch—forty or fifty girls—like hens except that we were chattering, huddled next to the reek of turf. Turf can get into one's head, making thoughts brown and sodden and flaky as the stuff itself. . . . Our coats would be on hooks, coats slung on top of one another all threatening to fall off, then pixie caps of multifarious orders, scarfs and wool gloves that had been chewed and re-chewed and were anything but pristine.

Such language attracts to itself the story of Ireland in the guise of romantic fiction.

The most interesting passage in *Mother Ireland* tells of schooldays and the world offered to the girls in history class, a world of "arms, crests, spears," with Owen Roe O'Neill recited as "Him they poisoned whom they feared to meet with steel," and Patrick Sarsfield, Shane O'Neill, Robert Emmet:

> All had sacrificed themselves for the Cause, and each had failed— one went into lowly exile, the other had his head on the castle battlement, the third was executed in the Liberties and made a speech from the dock that wrung our hearts.

Ms. O'Brien assimilates these heroic acts to her lamentably hospitable prose. The mild irony which she exerts upon them does not intend to deprive them of their glamour: she, too, has an interest in romance. There is no joy in this for Conor Cruise O'Brien.

Ms. O'Brien's text is glossed by Fergus Bourke's photographs— charming, touching, decent, responsive to their themes, and incomplete only in one respect: not a gun or a bomb in sight.

DE VALERA'S DAY

In April 1933, W. B. Yeats wrote "Parnell's Funeral," a daring, garish poem which interprets the history of Ireland in the twentieth century as a shameless retreat from the lonely, visionary power of Parnell. O'Connell, not Parnell, was Catholic Ireland's hero; the "Great Comedian" offered Ireland a meagre destiny, not tragic splendour. Now we had De Valera:

> Had de Valera eaten Parnell's heart
> No loose-lipped demagogue had won the day,
> No civil rancour torn the land apart.

I have been thinking about Yeats's poem recently, and placing it beside two new studies of modern Irish history, Joseph T. Carroll's *Ireland in the War Years 1939–1945* and Peter Berresford Ellis's *Hell or Connaught: The Cromwellian Colonisation of Ireland 1652–1660*. De Valera emerges as the hero of Mr. Carroll's book, a major statesman and not merely a politician. It was no loose-lipped demagogue but an extraordinarily gifted and courageous man who maintained Ireland's neutrality during the years of the Second World War. The neutrality was benevolent toward Britain and

America, and strictly decorous toward Germany and Japan; in each respect De Valera defined it with remarkable finesse.

Mr. Carroll's narrative begins in 1938 with the restoration of the Atlantic ports to Ireland, an important extension of the Anglo-Irish Treaty of 1921. Thereafter, his chapters discuss the declaration of Ireland's neutrality, the IRA bombing campaign which started early in 1939, the Offences against the State Act, the pressure exerted upon Ireland to join the Allies and give Britain the use of the ports, Britain's essay in economic punishment in 1941 and 1942, the famous American Note of 1944, Churchill's sneering reference to Ireland in his victory-speech of May 13, 1945, and De Valera's reply. Much of the detail arises from the diplomatic encounters between Britain, the U.S.A., Canada, and Ireland on the issue of neutrality: the participants include Chamberlain, Eden, Churchill, Cranborne, and Kearney. Among such players De Valera was a master; the professional diplomats wilt by comparison with him, the big politicians found that he could not be fooled or intimidated. When the British Government held out to De Valera the vision of a United Ireland in return for Ireland's joining the Allies, he knew that the offer was spurious. Britain could never force Craigavon and the Unionists to accept Dublin's embrace.

It is not clear from Carroll's account whether the British Government was naive or cynical on the question of the Six Counties and a United Ireland. When Craigavon told Chamberlain that he was shocked to hear that Britain was negotiating with De Valera behind Northern Ireland's back, Chamberlain appears to have been surprised by the violence of his attitude, but he must have known that Churchill would oppose any attempt to push Loyalists toward Dublin, and that the whole notion was wild. In any case, De Valera was not impressed or charmed, he knew that Partition would have to remain until time healed the wound: "no solution [in Northern Ireland] can come by force; there we must now wait and let the solution come with time and patience," De Valera told Maffey in 1944.

It is vain to speculate on the form Ireland would have taken in the present century if its leaders had held fast to Parnell rather than O'Connell as their chosen archetype. But Yeats was premature in thinking that the man who had torn the land apart and caused a Civil War had no further service to offer his country.

In the same poem, Yeats, thirsting for accusation, writes of the Irish people:

All that was sung,
All that was said in Ireland is a lie
Bred out of the contagion of the throng,
Saving the rhyme rats hear before they die.

In Ireland during the past few years we have been quarrelling about (*inter alia*) our interpretation of history, particularly our own history. Some people maintain that our schools prepare young boys and girls to join the IRA by presenting the true history of Ireland as a narrative of the revolutionary spirit, embodied for each generation in a glorious revolt against British oppression. Teachers are now to be encouraged to concentrate their minds upon social rather than political history, and upon Europe and America rather than merely Britain as sources of historical relations. I have entertained this revisionist version of our history, and do in part believe it. But some facts are recalcitrant. The story recited in Mr. Ellis's book, for instance, demonstrates not that all our old history-books tell lies but that many of them tell truths. His official theme is the political history of Ireland from September 11, 1652, when Charles Fleetwood arrived in Ireland to confiscate the lands and property of those Irishmen who had, since October 1641, taken up arms against England, to the restoration of Charles Stuart on May 14, 1660.

There is no venom in the narrator, only in the events narrated. On June 22, 1653, the Commissioners for the Administration of the Affairs of the Commonwealth of England in Ireland were instructed to take the ten counties, "and to divide all the forfeited lands, meadow, arable and profitable pastures with the woods and bogs and barren mountains thereunto respectively belonging, into two equal moieties," one moiety for the financiers who supplied money in 1642 to put down the O'Neill revolt, the other for the soldiers in lieu of arrears of pay. Those whose land was due for confiscation were to remove themselves west of the Shannon not later than May 1, 1654. It is hard to see how this episode, or indeed the whole sequence of events from 1641 to 1660, would be sweetened by recourse to a wider social context. Ellis tells the story mainly by reference to the activities of the several Commanders, Fleetwood, Henry Cromwell, and the remarkable Edmund Ludlow. The fact that the Cromwellian colonisation was not particularly successful was due not to any ineptitude in these men but to problems of communication and exchange, in the first instance, and thereafter to the resilience of those whose lands were confiscated.

Not that the story is simple. If, like Yeats in this respect, we thirst for accusation, we may find some incitement in Mr. Ellis's book, where he reports a speech made in Parliament on June 10, 1657, by Major Anthony Morgan, member for Wicklow:

> We have three beasts to destroy that lay heavy burdens on us. The first is the wolf, on whom we lay five pounds a head if a dog, and ten pounds if a bitch. The second beast is a priest, on whose head we lay ten pounds—if he be eminent, more. The third beast is a Tory on whose head, if he be a public Tory, we lay twenty pounds, and forty shillings on a private Tory. Your army cannot catch them. The Irish bring them in: brothers and cousins cut one another's throats.

That has the ring of worldly truth. (Tory, by the way, is derived in some fashion from the Irish "toraidhe," meaning in the seventeenth century an outlaw, bog-trotter, rapparee.)

The Spectator, 15 February 1975.

CASTLE CATHOLIC

Patrick Shea's father, like my own, was born "on a small farm on a steep mountainside in County Kerry." At that time, about 1875, a lot of Irish was still spoken in Kerry, but it was not taught in the schools, so Shea grew up, like my father, fluent in Irish and English, but literate only in English. Some members of the family emigrated to America, but Shea stayed in Ireland and, like my father, joined the Royal Irish Constabulary. He served till the RIC was disbanded, following the Anglo-Irish Treaty of 1921. At that point he went to Newry, County Down, and made a new career for himself as Clerk of the Petty Sessions. My father took up the option of joining the new Royal Ulster Constabulary in his RIC rank as sergeant: he served in various towns and spent most of his later life in charge of a small police station in Warrenpoint, County Down. Patrick Shea attended school at the old Abbey, the Christian Brothers School in Newry, my own school twenty years later.

Although the tradition of the Christian Brothers School was Nationalist, and therefore suspicious of the new Stormont Government in Belfast, Shea competed for an appointment to the Northern Ireland Civil Service in 1926, and was successful. He remained a civil servant till he retired on pension in 1973. His career was remarkable in at least one respect: despite the fact that he was a Roman Catholic, he eventually became Permanent Secretary to the Public Building and Works Department. Only one RC predecessor, Bonaparte Wyse, had ever risen to the rank of Permanent Secretary of a department in the Northern Ireland Civil Service. (It was made clear to my father that, being a Roman Catholic, he should not expect to be promoted at any stage of his career: he ended as he began, a sergeant, on retirement in 1946.)

In his autobiography, *Voices and the Sound of Drums,* Mr. Shea does not explain very clearly how he managed to get promotion. Admittedly, it took him nearly fifty years, and he was passed over on several occasions when, had he been a Protestant and a member of the Orange Order, he would have secured preferment. But it is odd that, during those years, he was allowed to go so far. He was clearly a fine civil servant, intelligent and hard-working. An affable fellow, too. He was a Catholic, indeed, but there was no suggestion that he would prove difficult or disloyal. By his own account, the Nationalism of the Christian Brothers boys was alien to him: in Dublin, people would have called him a Castle Catholic, meaning a Catholic who was ready to be invited, as a safe man, to official functions in Dublin Castle. In my own case, the CBS brand of Nationalism in Newry was fairly congenial. The main emphasis in the school was on Irish and football—Gaelic football, of course. I was good at Irish and helpless at football, but my problems were not ideological. It would never have occurred to me to try for a job in the Northern Ireland Civil Service. Living in a police-barracks on money my father earned from Stormont was hard enough to stomach.

There are several obvious explanations for Shea's good fortune. By 1969, he had done his stint, forty-three years in which he had proved himself amenable to his seniors. Captain Terence O'Neill became Prime Minister in 1963, a decent man who felt that the time was appropriate to improve relations between Belfast and Dublin. In 1968 the protest marches began, with angry scenes between the Peoples' Democracy and the Unionists. The Northern Ireland government started putting a few token Papists into high office to suggest to the world that the bad old years of Lord Craigavon and Sir Basil Brooke were over. A Roman Catholic might now become a judge or even a permanent secretary of a department.

Mr. Shea's account of his early years in the Service is extremely interesting. I am ready to believe that his masters were fine fellows: so were they all, all honourable men. It was easy for them to be fine, when every Papist knew his lowly place. Since 1968, fineness has become more difficult. Shea's last chapters are rather perfunctory. His account of "direct rule" and the closure of Stormont in 1972 is so illuminating that I wish there were more of it. In that year Shea wrote, but kept to himself, a document setting out what he regarded as the crucial issues affecting Northern Ireland. He now adds only a postscript:

> One wondered how men for whom one could feel genuine respect could have acquiesced, even participated in, illiberal practises which, in the end, brought discredit on fifty years of government. I believe the answer lies in the relationship between the Orange Order and the Unionist Party; the influence of Orangeism was, I believe, considerable, often malevolent, and always an impediment to good government.

Shea's last pages refer to the Sunningdale Agreement, brought to a rough end by the so-called Ulster Workers' Council strike, when bullies won because the Westminster Government was afraid to govern:

> Merlyn Rees cannot look back on his handling of the UWC strike with any pride. In at least one household in Belfast he got no marks at all for judgment or courage or concern for the fears of law-abiding citizens.

So we come to today:

> My present political views are different from those of my prejudiced youth, but I am totally convinced that whatever may be said about the righting of past wrongs or the maintenance of inherited power and privilege, there has been no moral justification for violence or the threat of violence for political ends in Ireland at any time in the present century.

On that theme, I don't think Shea's judgment, or mine, counts for much. I left Northern Ireland before it became necessary for me to deal with its wretched system, but I saw my father trying to deal with it, and failing. Shea met the system with his intelligence, charm, and affability; besides, he had the luck to survive till the system-keepers realized that the game was up. His autobiography, after all, is justified chiefly as a success-story: how a Catholic won the keys to a Protestant kingdom. It is a good story, vigorously told, but there is nothing in it to interest either Patsy O'Hara or Bobby Sands. Besides, if Shea's judgment had obtained, there would have been no Easter Rising, no Irish Free State, Ireland would have been united, but as a colony, John Bull's other island. My children and I would now live under a government we could not accept as legitimate. When I think of that, as Yeats said, "my tongue's a stone." Violence is an appalling thing, but Mr. Shea's comfortable judgment is merely a function of his success in accommodating himself to a government many Catholics found intolerable and illegitimate.

Times Literary Supplement, 31 July 1981.

T.C.D.

I n 1591 the Corporation of Dublin set aside as the site for a college
the lands and dilapidated buildings of the Augustinian priory of All
Hallows, which had been given to the city at the dissolution of the
monasteries. A year later, on 3 March 1592, Queen Elizabeth issued
a charter incorporating "the College of the Holy and Undivided Trinity
near Dublin" as "the mother of a university" with the aim of providing
"education, training and instruction of youths and students in the arts and
faculties that they may be the better assisted in the study of the liberal arts
and the cultivation of virtue and religion." In *Trinity College Dublin
1592–1952* R. B. McDowell and D. A. Webb have written the history of
that bizarre institution. [In 1952, Provost McConnell took up office and
directed the College toward its present form.] McDowell is a Senior
Fellow of Trinity and a well-known historian. David Webb is a Fellow
Emeritus of the College and Honorary Professor of Systematic Botany.

"Virtue and religion" meant, of course, Anglicanism. The Fellows of
Trinity were required to take an oath and, in most cases, to take Anglican
orders. Undergraduates were obliged to attend chapel regularly; candidates for foundation scholarships had to be willing to receive the sacrament.
At the end of the seventeenth century, Parliament required candidates for
degrees to take not only an oath of allegiance but an oath repudiating the

doctrine of transubstantiation. Practising Catholics were excluded from Trinity, therefore, till 1794, when the oath against transubstantiation was removed. The rules about chapel were maintained, in principle, but quietly allowed to lapse in practise. Religious tests weren't formally abolished till Fawcett's Act of 1873, when a Catholic was elected for the first time to a foundation scholarship. The first Catholic to reach the Board of Trinity as a Senior Fellow achieved that distinction in 1958.

Trinity College and the University of Dublin are for all practical purposes one and the same institution. In theory, other colleges could be added to the University. In 1907, when provision had to be made for the higher education of Irish Catholics, there was talk of simply adding a Catholic College, but the Trinity people wouldn't have it. They set up a Trinity College Defence Committee, collected money for the cause, issued pamphlets, and eventually put a stop to the idea. The Irish Universities Act of 1908 set up the National University of Ireland with three constituent colleges, in Dublin, Cork, and Galway. They are not Catholic colleges. For fifty years the Catholic bishops complained that the new colleges were barely acceptable and fell short of the ideal of Catholic education, but the complaints have long since been dropped. For the past several years there have been plans and counterplans for a merger of Trinity College and University College, but the notion has apparently died—ousted in any case by more urgent political and social problems. University teachers have wasted much time discussing the proposed merger, but their time is not supposed to matter.

Trinity is an odd institution. There it is, smack in the middle of Dublin, its surly front turned upon the Bank of Ireland and the traffic dividing for Dawson Street and Dame Street. Tourists turn up in busloads to see Trinity's great treasure, the Book of Kells. But for most of its history it has been the symbol of Protestant domination and the English presence in Ireland. McDowell and Webb say that Trinity people voted and campaigned against Home Rule because they saw in it "the frustration of their reforms and their hopes." Perhaps: but for a less high-minded reason, too—they feared for their own privilege. At High Table they sang "God Save the King," and drank the King's health: the first of these gestures was called off in 1939, the second in 1945.

I sometimes wonder: what would have happened in Easter Week 1916 if the rebels had seized not the General Post Office but Trinity College? Militarily, it might have been difficult. Trinity had a direct line to the centre of British authority, Dublin Castle: it had an Army School and an Officers Training Corps, who would have defended the College. But the capture of Trinity College would have been a far grander symbolic act than taking the GPO. McDowell and Webb refer to Easter Week, by the way, as "a short-lived and localised but alarming civil war"—which is one version of the event, but not mine. The Rising was not a civil war: it was the revolt of a tiny group of insurgents against the English presence. Our civil war came later, when Irishmen fought against Irishmen. McDowell and Webb say that the general feeling among Trinity students in Easter Week was accurately represented by T. C. Kingsmill Moore's editorial in the magazine *TCD*: "Trinity College, true to her traditions, has played a worthy, if an unacceptable part. To be called upon to defend our University against the attack of Irishmen, to be forced in self-defence to shoot down our countrymen—these are things which even the knowledge of duty well fulfilled cannot render anything but sad and distasteful." They remark, too, that while the attitude of many elders in the College may have been sterner, it was from Archbishop Bernard's Palace and not from the Provost's House that there went out, against the rebels, "the call for swift retributive justice untempered by mercy."

It is hardly surprising that, after the Civil War, when the Free State Government settled down to govern a distressful country, the ministers were in no mood to gratify Trinity College. A request for money got a grudging answer until Trinity threatened to make the correspondence public. The government gave the money and improved their temper. But the Trinity Board knew that it behoved them to keep their collegiate head well down. Trinity was widely disliked: many people coming into their own in the new state saw the College as an alien institution, making much of its Elizabethan charter, its silver plate, and its Protestant tradition. Trinity was then, as it still is in many respects, a remarkably defensive and inward-looking college. Since 1692, every Provost has been a Trinity man: the College has never gone outside to look for a Provost. Indeed, it is well known that, even yet, anyone who has the ambition of becoming Provost of Trinity must take the triple precaution of being born in Ireland, a Protestant, and educated at Trinity. No Papist need apply.

From 1922 to 1946, Trinity spoke in a quiet voice, if at all. Aging Unionists knew that their heyday was over, but that they could still get a fair supply of wine and roses if they ordered them quietly. They had a few anxious months in 1932 when De Valera came to power, but it turned out that he was far more cordial to Trinity than his Free State rivals had been. The Free Staters wanted to let Trinity fend for itself, sell its silver if necessary, rather than reduce by a penny the money to be given to the colleges of the National University. But De Valera was well disposed to Trinity, for reasons not yet clear. True, he knew McConnell well and liked him, but there must have been other reasons. Trinity responded by minding its own business. When De Valera declared Irish neutrality in September 1939, there were some people in Trinity who regretted that Ireland was not joining the Allies in the struggle for freedom, but they kept their sentiments to themselves. There was an incident after the war, when news of the German surrender reached Dublin on 7 May 1945. A few Trinity students hoisted flags, including the Union Jack, on the West Front. There was a scuffle when a number of Republican youths came on the scene, members of Ailtiri na hAiseirighe — according to McDowell and Webb, "one of the nastier of the minute extremist splinter groups which regularly appear on the Irish political scene and equally regularly die after a few years." I don't think the Blimp tone of this description is apt. Ailtiri weren't, in my recollection, any nastier than other people; more naive perhaps. It hardly matters, except as a minor indication of the tone of voice audible throughout this history. McDowell and Webb are nice people, eminently humane and agreeable, but they write on the assumption that Irishmen are mostly daft and that it calls for particular comment if some few of them are nasty. They refer to "the small place that reason tends to play in determining the attitude of Irishmen": a mixed metaphor but an unmixed attitude maintained from start to finish.

Anyway, the flag-burning was ignored or forgotten within a few days. De Valera continued to smile on Trinity, even though by 1952 only 34 per cent of its students came from the South, while 30 per cent came from Britain, 18 per cent from Northern Ireland, and the rest from overseas. Of course, there were reasons. Irish Catholics still disliked Trinity and resented its lofty claims. The Catholic hierarchy forbade its flock to go there. In any case, the quality of the education at Trinity wasn't so wonderful that a Catholic would try very hard to get the Church's permission to enter. Trinity wanted to maintain its connection with the North, since it meant a connection with Britain. And they made a particular virtue out of the circumstance that a fairly large number of foreign students, for whatever reason, came to Dublin. When I taught at University College, Dublin, I felt some resentment toward Trinity, its historical privilege, the complacency of its ethos, its easy and unearned assumption of superiority. It was pointed out that the government grant to Trinity, on a *per capita* basis, exceeded the grant to any of the National University colleges, and that, in effect, the plain people of Ireland were subsidising the education of foreign students at Trinity, which was itself, in another and more acute sense of the word, foreign. More specifically, I resented the policy by which my colleagues and I were required to teach thousands of students, while our opposite numbers in Trinity dispensed sherry to their chosen few. When I protested to the President of U.C.D., he replied that Trinity was an irrelevance to Ireland and its development, it was merely an appendix to the country, the future was in the hands of the thousands of bright young men and women my colleagues and I would train. We would win, without the sherry or the Trinity Ball or the Elizabethan Society.

McDowell and Webb think well of Trinity, and why not? They are so closely identified with the College that to think well of it means to think well of themselves—an understandable pleasure. From time to time they lament the fact that Trinity was "the silent sister" to Oxford and Cambridge, rarely engaging in scholarship. They have to report that many Senior Fellows never published a line, coasted along for sixty well-paid years on the wind of a pamphlet. Half-heartedly, McDowell and Webb offer a few reasons: teaching duties, College administration, outside commitments. But it is a pity, they think, that their elders didn't try a bit harder. Productive themselves, they are rueful about the lazy rascals of earlier times. But they haven't really gone into the question, or considered the full implication of Trinity's character in the country. My own view is that Trinity's vice has always been complacency. For centuries, the Fellows saw themselves as a higher breed, comparable in civility and intellect with their colleagues in Oxford and Cambridge, and surrounded by a populace they despised. Some Trinity Fellows still see themselves in this light, though the delusion is harder to sustain: it needs to be maintained by a great deal of High Table port. But they are great praisers of gone times: nearly every room in the Arts Building is called after some great or ostensibly great man in Trinity's past. To be fair, any university that has lasted nearly four hundred years is likely to have some outstanding people on its list. Trinity has its share, including Berkeley, Swift, Rowan Hamilton, Lecky, Dowden, Bury, Douglas Hyde, J. M. Synge, Samuel Beckett.

Since 1952 and beginning with McConnell, Trinity has gradually acknowledged its responsibility not only to the past but to Irish taxpayers. It has opened its gate to more students. For many years the student population numbered a happy 2,500 or so, but the number has now risen to about 6,000. University College has about 11,000. Trinity has also allowed its campus to be a little cramped: the Arts Building and the New Library are handsome buildings, but already too small for their purposes. Still, many a Senior Fellow must have wept to see his college grounds diminished, the greens reduced, for the sake of demonstrating that Trinity was indeed an Irish university. But it must be acknowledged that Trinity has made these important changes with every show of good will. Indeed, so far as the question of public relations arises, Trinity has now outrun University College. Trinity goes out of its way to be helpful with advice, discussion, clarification. University College is widely regarded as indifferent to the civilities or the amenities of discourse. Trinity is more gracious in its arrangements. If you want to see a fine Henry Moore and a dashing Alexander Calder adorning a campus, see them in Trinity. It begins to appear that University College has adopted Trinity's vice, and has become, for quite different reasons, complacent.

McDowell and Webb have written the history of Trinity as if it were an internal matter. They have told the story as if it were a biography of Provosts. When necessary, they have set internal events against their external contexts, but they seem reluctant to go far beyond the Front Gate. Trinity's happiest years, it appears, were those in which nothing particularly stirring or dangerous was happening outside its walls, and the community within could attend to its genial interests, a decent mixture of College administration, teaching, sport, dining, and—not least—respectable scholarship. When these conditions did not obtain, according to McDowell and Webb, Trinity fell into bewilderment and error. It was ever thus. I assume that 1952 was chosen as the end-date of their history mainly because their account of recent and current events would require an intolerable degree of reticence. It is more comfortable to write about the dead.

Of the Provosts, I find the most interesting not Mahaffy, but George Salmon (1888—1904). McDowell and Webb write splendidly, with great narrative verve and far more wit than I thought their subject would provoke, but they are particularly lively on Salmon and Humphrey Lloyd (1867–1881). There are a few pointless paragraphs. Edward Dowden is absurdly compared with F. R. Leavis because both admired *Middlemarch*. The only error I came across was a reference to Yeats's "no petty people" speech in the Senate in which he declared that the Protestants of Ireland, according to McDowell and Webb, were "the heirs of Swift, Berkeley and Grattan." Not quite: he cited Burke, Grattan, Swift, Robert Emmet, and Parnell, but not Berkeley. On Mahaffy: it may be that McDowell, who joined with W. B. Stanford to write the life of Mahaffy, has tired of the man, but the account of him in the present book makes him appear tawdry and obvious. His views on the Irish University question aren't interesting, his contempt for the Irish language is predictably ignorant, his pretence that he didn't know who Padraic Pearse was is silly. McDowell and Webb, sensing perhaps that Mahaffy comes out as a rather small man, try to enlarge him by Latinising his going. But an epitaph made by Pope John III in the Church of the Holy Apostles in Rome hasn't much bearing upon a man who would have hated to receive it.

The Latin reminds me that there is far too much of it in this book. McDowell and Webb write so well in English that it is supererogatory to resort to Latin for an even grander style. Somebody saw himself as "Hely-Hutchinson *redivivus,*" when a plan didn't work out it was because *dis aliter visum est,* R. M. Gwynn's naivete is glossed with *sancta simplicitas,* the Senior Fellows hoped to find themselves "not so much *in otium* as *in negotium cum dignitate,*" an important topic should not be decided *sede vacante,* McConnell "gave the impression of being the superior of Duncan in *suaviter in modo* and of Parke in *fortiter in re,*" some request or other was "the *sine qua non* of reform," an item in the modern College Calendar "repeated the *ipsissima verba* of 1905." Still, it is a splendid book—even if it doesn't mention the Book of Kells.

London Review of Books, 5–18 August 1982.

AT SWIM

The Crane Bag is a magazine, published twice a year: each issue deals with one theme. In Irish legend, the crane bag contained the alphabet of knowledge. The bag belonged to Manannan, god of the sea: it was made from the skin of his wife Aoife, whom Manannan had transformed into a crane because she tried to steal his secret knowledge and communicate it to the world: it was believed that cranes formed the letters of the alphabet as they flew. The meaning of the letters was available only to the elect. When the first issue of *The Crane Bag* appeared in 1977, its editors brooded upon meanings, metaphors, occult notations, and the like. Only irrefutable evidence of editorial seriousness in the magazine as a whole set aside the question of vanity in its manifesto. *The Crane Bag Book of Irish Studies* reprints the first ten issues: the themes are Art and Politics, a Sense of Nation, Mythology—a double issue, this, as you might expect—Tradition, Anglo-Irish Literature, the Irish Woman, the Northern Issue, Minorities in Ireland, and the Irish Language and Culture. The magazine, after an issue on Joyce and the Arts in Ireland, has now gone international with a Latin American issue and one on Socialism and Culture.

The editors of *Crane Bag* are university teachers, gifted in literature and philosophy, and, it seems, determined to let these commitments take their chances alongside questions inescapably political. They could hardly do otherwise, living in Dublin since 1968. Several of their colleagues are from the North: the poets Seamus Heaney, Seamus Deane, John Montague, Michael Longley. Deane, especially, has been important to them, arguing about Irish literature and the question of tradition, the North, the two languages, the available rhetorics.

I have been reading *The Crane Bag* in association with Hugh Kenner's new book, *A Colder Eye,* a study of the modern Irish writers from Yeats, Joyce, and Synge to Beckett and Flann O'Brien. Kenner encourages his reader, an American apparently, to believe that Ireland is a crazy country from which, believe it or don't, a number of extraordinary writers have emerged. Their emergence testifies to the fact, I gather, that nations sometimes get far more, and far better, than their inhabitants of the day deserve. Yeats tried to coax his countrymen into Unity of Being, but they chose instead the more succulent joys of division, opting for the court-room as the theatre of their pleasure—Irishmen love to sue Irishmen, apparently—the ambush as "the recourse of their plot construction," and "a fine explosion their ecstasy of climax." Joyce wrote of "shattered glass and toppling masonry," but now, Kenner explains, "improved explosives permit local rains of blood and severed limbs." Presumably the argument is that since we don't get enough sex, we have to have our ecstasies outside the bedroom. So that's what we've been up to since 1968, having our orgasms in public.

Leaving that aside—that being a matter on which I don't value Kenner's judgment as much as my own—I have transcribed in my commonplace book the following nine items from *A Colder Eye.*

One: Dubliners do not read the Bible.

Two: in Joyce's day, most Dubliners were Catholic, but that designation "was apt to denote less a state of supernatural conviction than a web of secular allegiances."

Three: one of the differences between Ireland and England is that in Ireland "the conventions of English Romanticism, its blessings in the gentle woods, its brooks that murmur and its winds that cry, were simply implausible." Irish landscape is determined rather by individual acts of will, violent and transient.

Four: "in Ireland nothing moves forward unjeered at."

Five: "the mind of Ireland is held by realities of talk, the most notable reality of which is the presence of others."

Six: the complex role Yeats played included "obligation to some void left by destiny, some body of unimaginable things unsaid." This explains his appropriation of people who did "some not wholly fulfilling thing"—Cuchulain fighting the waves, Robert Gregory taking to the air—their fulfilment to be achieved only when Yeats had emblematised them in strong verse.

Seven: Dublin is a capital city in which "eight decades' experience of the telephone has not yet fostered the habit of returning calls."

Eight: *Finnegans Wake* may have something to do with the execution, on 8 December 1922, of Rory O'Connor, one of the Irregulars.

Nine: "Dublin remains obsessed with the writers it doesn't read."

I have listed these items to indicate that anything you care to say about Ireland is sayable and printable. The more exacting criteria which apply to other nations are voided, evidently, when discourse turns upon Ireland. One of the difficulties such an enterprise as *The Crane Bag* has to face is that there is no reliable context for the matters at hand. In Kenner's book, silliness jostles with exactness of perception, and he has no means of knowing which is which. He can write like Swift or like a shamrock-toting tourist, prevented from knowing the difference by the Babel of discourses which surround the theme rather than by any defect in his extraordinary intelligence. I suppose it says something, though nothing very good, about a country if it attracts, by way of commentary, sense and nonsense which only posterity will discriminate. Meanwhile, *The Crane Bag* has to sound as if the themes it takes up were taken up for the first time. The other times haven't provided either a steady context or a set of criteria.

There is a passage in Yeats's *Memoirs,* though, which suggests that criteria may still be found. Kenner quotes it, but doesn't make enough of it. Yeats is commenting on a dispute he had with Maud Gonne about literature and nationalism. "Practical movements," he says, "are created out of emotions expressed long enough ago to have become general, but literature discovers; it can never repeat. It is an attempt to repeat an emotion because it has been found effective which has made all provincially political literature . . . so superficial." That's worth thinking about. For me, it explains why discussion of Northern Ireland is interminable and frustrating. No one is thinking. Everyone is merely repeating an emotion he has found effective: effective, in the sense of making him and his position familiar. Why does Conor Cruise O'Brien exercise his intelligence when he writes for the *Observer* and several other papers and write far beneath himself when he publishes in *The Irish Times?* Is it merely that he despises the Irish readers who were sufficiently stupid and unworthy as to turn him out of political office? Or that he assumes that what Irish readers want is the repetition of personality, in any familiar form, week by week? Certainly, Irish discourse—not to speak of the action that has arisen from it—has been congealed by the few emotions that have been found effective.

Indeed, it is my impression, now that Yeats has provided the words for it, that *The Crane Bag* is an attempt, on the part of its editors and contributors, not to yield to these few emotions merely because they have been found effective. Which emotions? The emotions that suffuse such words as "history," "myth," "tradition," and "Ireland."

HISTORY: You can go back as far as you like, to Roderick O'Connor, the last High King of Ireland, who in 1175 surrendered to the King of England. Or, if Northern Ireland is locally in question, to the seventeenth-century Plantations of Ulster, the immediate occasion of our divisions. History, Stephen Dedalus instructs Mr. Deasy, "is a nightmare from which I am trying to awake." But a few pages back he made a less famous discovery, that while for his pupils history was a tale like any other too often heard, "their land a pawnshop," nevertheless such facts as the death of Pyrrhus and Caesar's murder "are not to be thought away." Kinsale, the Boyne, and Easter Week are not to be thought away or dispelled by a revisionist pedagogy. What can you do with your history? Put up with it, as with any other ill that flesh is heir to.

MYTH: Kenner was amused to find that at a McDonald's in Dublin a counter-girl wore her name-tag; "Emer-Cuchulain's queen"; from which extraordinary episode arose the admonition that "if you recover an heroic past, then face the fact that you'll have it splattered all around you."

The Crane Bag has much brooding about myth, especially Richard Kearney's essay "Myth and Terror," in which he resorts to Mircea Eliade and Paul Ricoeur to understand and, apparently, to pacify the mythic repetitions—of sacrifice, blood, and apocalypse—he finds in modern Ireland. There is also much meditation on Celtic Mythology, the hero, God and Man, and Yeats's question:

> *When Pearse summoned Cuchulain to his side,*
> *What stalked through the Post Office? What intellect,*
> *What calculation, number, measurement, replied?*

TRADITION: "Discussion of what tradition means," according to Seamus Heaney, "has moved from a sort of linguistic nostalgia, a puerile discourse about assonance, metres, and so on, to a consideration of the politics and anthropology of our condition." Liam de Paor and other writers think of tradition as involving continuities, though not necessarily repetitions. W. J. McCormack writes of tradition as "the guarantee, the demonstration of the real interaction of literature and social life." But there is nothing in *The Crane Bag* quite as telling, on this theme, as the poems collected in *An Duanaire: Poems of the Dispossessed* (Dolmen Press, 1981), gathered by Sean O'Tuama and translated by Thomas Kinsella: there, more clearly than anywhere else, we can see what an Irish tradition means by marking its loss. Seamus Deane comes close to this sense of it when he explains that "the Irish idea of tradition was naturally more inclined toward the notion of continuity betrayed than of continuity retained." He derides, in this essay and elsewhere, the Anglo-Irish filiations— Swift, Berkeley, Burke, and the image of the Big House—which Yeats appropriated with such majesty. For Deane, tradition is "what we have yet to build," not something on which our laurels rest.

IRELAND: What else? *The Crane Bag* has many essays, by Conor Cruise O'Brien, John A. Murphy, and others, on nationalism as a sentiment to be fostered or repressed, and the consequences in each case. But none of the writers has examined the diverse and conflicting relations which Irish people are maintaining with such entities as England, Europe, the EEC—not the same entity as Europe—the Catholic Church, the Protestant churches, the Irish Abroad in America and elsewhere, not to speak of ancient attachments to an Ireland defined only in legend, poetry, and song. The past is another country: yes, but in Ireland it is the same country. It is hard to say what form a coherent life would take: coherent, in the sense of manifesting a decent relation between one's past and present, one's obligations and freedoms. Hard, and in Ireland becoming harder, because most people are finding that their lives are governed by immediacies: unemployment, the cost of daily living (inordinately high), taxation (ditto), the quality of government (abysmal), dependence on the charity of the EEC (shameful), and the wretchedness in the North.

If I am right in supposing that *The Crane Bag* is trying to think of certain issues without repeating the emotions that have suffused them, where is it finding the energy? In books, mainly, despite what Kenner says about the Irish being talkers and not readers or writers. Or rather, in certain books which are invigorating precisely because they have nothing to do with Ireland. Or not directly. The editors have been reading Heidegger, Gadamer, Ricoeur, Chomsky, Marcuse, Vanier, and trying to think of their bearing upon the state of Ireland. Seamus Heaney has been quoting Milosz. The other Seamus has been reading Marxists and neo-Marxists, Lukacs, Benjamin, most of all Adorno. In another essay Deane argues that "the aesthetic heritage with which we still struggle clearly harbours the desire to obliterate or render nugatory the problems of class, economics, bureaucratic systems and the like, concentrating instead upon the essences of self, nationhood, community and Zeitgeist." Now there's something worth arguing about. The short answer is that he's been reading the Frankfurt critics. The longer answer would need a context it is unlikely to get; though *The Crane Bag* is doing more toward that end than anyone, five or six years ago, had cause to expect.

London Review of Books, 21 April–4 May, 1983.

THE LITERATURE OF TROUBLE

I n January 1919 when Yeats was writing "The Second Coming," his mind was recalling a rather dull passage from Shelley's "Prometheus Unbound" and turning it into a series of cultural generalisations:

> *Things fall apart; the centre cannot hold;*
> *Mere anarchy is loosed upon the world,*
> *The blood-dimmed tide is loosed, and everywhere*
> *The ceremony of innocence is drowned;*
> *The best lack all conviction, while the worst*
> *Are full of passionate intensity.*

I shall not refer again to these lines, except to say that they were in Donald Davie's mind when, perhaps in 1952 or 1953, he made a trip to Belfast and wrote a poem called "Belfast on a Sunday Afternoon." It is useful to know that the Orange Order is a fellowship of extreme Unionists or Loyalists in the North of Ireland who celebrate, every year on 12 July, the victory of King William over James at the Boyne. On a summer Sunday afternoon in Belfast, it would be normal to see and hear the Orange bands practising for the great day, marching up and down their famous Shankill Road, or going further afield if they wanted to taunt the Catholics. Here is Davie's poem:

> Visiting Belfast at the end of June,
> We found the Orange Lodge behind a band:
> Sashes and bearskins in the afternoon,
> White cotton gloves upon a crippled hand.
>
> Pastmasters pale, elaborately grim,
> Marched each alone, beneath a bowler hat:
> And, catapulted on a crumpled limb,
> A lame man leapt the tram-lines like a bat.
>
> And first of all we tried to laugh it off,
> Acting bemusement in the grimy sun;
> But stayed to worry where we came to scoff,
> As loud contingents followed, one by one.
>
> Pipe bands, flute bands, brass bands and silver bands,
> Presbyter's pibroch and the deacon's serge,
> Came stamping where the iron Maenad stands,
> Victoria, glum upon a grassy verge.
>
> Some brawny striplings sprawled upon the lawn,
> No man is really crippled by his hates.
> Yet I remembered with a sudden scorn
> Those "passionate intensities" of Yeats.

Davie's scorn is directed against those whose passionate intensities are automatic, unearned, the routine excess of the mob. The poem was published in Davie's little volume *Brides of Reason* (1955). If he were to visit Belfast again now, I don't think he could register an emotion as secure and distanced, as secure in its distance, as scorn. It is twenty years too late for that.

On 17 February 1978, a bomb which exploded in the La Mon Hotel near Comber, County Down, killed twelve people and injured many more. The bomb was placed, it appears, by members of the Provisional Irish Republican Army. There were about 500 people in the hotel at the time, most of them attending the annual dinner of the Northern Ireland Junior Motor Cycle Club; these included several boys who attended to receive their prizes. Other people were in the hotel as members of the Irish Collie Dog Club. A warning was received in the hotel by telephone just as the bomb was about to explode, but too late to do anything about it.

My theme is the literature of such trouble; more especially, the poetry which has been provoked in one way or another by passionate intensities in the North of Ireland since 1968, when violence again became commonplace. But I must begin further back. I shall assume that it is not necessary to say much about the English presence in Ireland for the past seven hundred years, except to remark two facts—that the English and Scots who colonised the country, especially in the first years of the seventeenth century, established themselves most firmly in the north-east; and that the history of Ireland has been taught in Catholic schools as a story of national feeling expressing itself in virtually every generation since the eighteenth century as a revolutionary act to drive the English out of Ireland.

In the past few years, as a reaction to the violence in the North, we have seen a waning of this tradition in many Irish schools. Our children are now told, some for the first time, that Irish history is plural rather than singular, that our country is the result of mixed parentage, that Catholics and Protestants equally share the fate of being Irish. The historical archetype of this sentiment is Wolfe Tone, now regularly quoted in that spirit.

The Easter Rising in 1916 was indeed the culmination of the revolutionary tradition. Like most revolutions, it was the act of a few people who took it upon themselves to represent the essential spirit of Ireland; a gesture to which most Irish people at the time were either indifferent or hostile. The leaders of the Rising knew that in every practical sense it must fail, but they sensed the power of sacrifice, the symbolism of blood yet again shed for Ireland. England executed the leaders, and gave new life to the dead. Many young men and women who were not in the General Post Office in Easter Week felt that the execution of Pearse and his friends defined the destiny of Ireland in revolutionary terms. The ideal of Ireland as "a nation once again" seemed more compelling than ever, and Cathleen Ni Houlihan as beautiful as the dream of her.

It is well known that much of modern Irish literature has been provoked by violence, and that images of war soon acquire a symbolic aura in this country. Our traditions are histrionic and oratorical. The themes of Irish literature are few: if we list childhood, isolation, religion, and politics, we come nearly to the end of them. R. P. Blackmur once argued that "the politics of existing states is always too simple for literature; it is good only to aggravate literature." The institutions of a state, of any state we think of, are never sufficiently complex to animate the difficult purposes of literature. But when he allows that the politics of existing states is good only to aggravate literature, he makes an allowance good enough for Irish writers. It is simple fact that Yeats, O'Casey, and a dozen writers up to Francis Stuart, Brian Friel, Thomas Kinsella, and Seamus Heaney have been aggravated by Irish politics to the point of turning their aggravation into verse and prose.

In August 1915, Yeats told Henry James that he did not feel inclined to write a war poem, even on Edith Wharton's invitation, and he sent James a few verses in that spirit, including the famous disclaimer, "We have no gift to set a statesman right." The plain fact is that Yeats did not feel inclined to put his genius to work in England's cause; but he never thought himself incapable of setting statesmen right if he felt sufficiently exasperated by their follies. A few months later the Easter Rising set his verses astir; he saw no reason to silence himself on that occasion.

Walter Benjamin once wrote that "all efforts to render politics aesthetic culminate in one thing: war." The remark occurs in an essay of 1936 when Benjamin was pondering the Fascist way of organising the proletarian masses without affecting the property structure which the masses, in principle, strive to eliminate. Fascism saw its salvation, according to Benjamin, in giving these masses not their right, but merely a chance to express themselves. Hence the rigmarole of public displays, marches, celebrations, anniversaries, those secular rituals by which thousands of men are given the illusion of living a dramatic life in common.

The introduction of aesthetics into politics is a perennial theme; to consider politics as entertainment, or to ponder the aesthetic aspects of war, blood, and death, is not necessarily self-indulgence, it may be a crucial aspect of modern society. Indeed, modern Irish literature has often been animated by the aesthetic aspect of violence. Padraic Fiacc's recent anthology *The Wearing of the Black* contains many poems, most of them bad in nearly every respect, which testify to the thrill of blood and sacrifice. But it also contains a few poems in which the transfiguring power of violence is recognised, its way of turning boredom into drama; and in one of these poems the poet is tender toward the desire and the need. He virtually withholds his irony from it, while allowing the reader's irony to assert itself. The poet sees how naturally a young man wants to become a dramatic figure in an otherwise wearisome and characterless time. The poem is "Bogside, Derry, 1971":

> Shielded, vague soldiers, visored, crouch alert:
> between tall houses down the blackened street;
> the hurled stones pour, hurt-instinct aims to hurt,
> frustration spurts in flame about their feet.
>
> Lads who at ease had tossed a laughing ball,
> or, ganged in teams, pursued some shouting game,
> beat angry fists against that stubborn wall
> of faceless fears which now at last they name.
>
> Night after night this city yields a stage
> with peak of drama for the pointless day,
> where shadows offer stature, roles to play,
> urging the gestures which might purge in rage
> the slights, the wrongs, the long indignities
> the stubborn core within each heart defies.

It is common for war correspondents to speak of a theatre of war. The aesthetic form most pertinent to war is theatre with its terminology of action, gesture, role-playing. John Hewitt's poem is perceptive in recognising the fact that people can deal with nameless fears only by finding a name for them and objectifying them in a hostile presence; in this case the British Army. He comes close to sentimentalising those stone-throwing youths, I suppose, but he narrowly avoids the temptation. There are many poems which do not scruple to avoid it.

Some poems, like Thomas Kinsella's "Butcher's Dozen," and some plays, like Brian Friel's *The Freedom of the City*, have emerged far too readily from the events that provoked them. It is hard to deny a poet the right to cry and rant and rage when an act strikes him as peculiarly outrageous, as the events of "Bloody Sunday" struck Kinsella and Friel. Yeats spoke of the will trying to do the work of the imagination, and he thought the effort misplaced; but it is hard to be patient.

There is further exorbitance: that of direct, apparently unmediated feeling which has not reached the stage of being either will or imagination; demanding to leap into expression without any mediation. We are told, and we believe, that there is no such thing as unmediated feeling; that the feeling is already inscribed, as if in invisible ink, and that we are never spontaneous. But it is a hard linguistics to act upon. Kinsella's poem and Friel's play come from the primitive demand, the insistence upon unmediated rage. The crudity of these works is not the price these writers willingly pay for the semblance of spontaneity, it is a sign of their rage with everything that stands between them and the feeling of the moment, everything that offers itself as form but could as well offer itself as delay or patience. It is natural for a writer to resent, on such a violent occasion, the admonition that his art is bound to be indirect in its effect and slow to act upon its cause. That poetry makes nothing happen is normally a tolerable fact; but there are occasions on which a poet feels that he must respond to one act with another similar in character and force.

Even in a quieter poet, like Heaney, there are moments of impatience. One of his Northern poems is called "Whatever you say, say nothing," a satirical piece, not one of his better poems but a minor essay in observation. His theme is the Northern habit of keeping one's counsel, saying nothing, intoning the clichés of communication for safety's sake. Heaney recites many of the currencies of such conversation, but at one point he breaks through them into an apparently direct speech of his own:

> *Christ, it's near time that some small leak was sprung*
> *In the great dykes the Dutchman made*
> *To dam the dangerous tide that followed Seamus.*
> *Yet for all this art and sedentary trade*
> *I am incapable.*

"This sedentary trade" is a phrase from Yeats's poem "The Tower," and Heaney's use of it brings him in under Yeats's shadow for the moment, the theme being the poet's general predicament, the gap between writing and action. But the reference to incapacity comes immediately after an outburst of political rhetoric; it's nearly time, Heaney says, the Unionist structures were undermined, and he goes back to the Dutchman William's victory over James at the Boyne in 1690 and the Orange Ascendancy in force in the North since that day. Heaney is more patient than Kinsella and Friel, but there are moments in him, too, when he chafes under the constraints of his trade. Not surprising in an Irish poet. Is it not significant, for instance, that Yeats normally used "violent" as a word of praise, especially when he surrounded it with words of strong heroic cast.

"Some violent bitter man, some powerful man": the power takes the harm out of the violence and the bitterness. "To show how violent great hearts can lose . . ."; greatness and violence are kin. And in "Cuchulain Comforted" there is that line, "Violent and famous, strode among the dead." Indeed, I can recall only one line in Yeats's poems in which violence is repudiated: in "No Second Troy" where Maud Gonne's intentions include teaching "to ignorant men most violent ways," and even in that case it is the ignorance of her pupils that drags the violent ways down to commonplace.

The troubles in the North have been with us now for ten years. Everything that can be said has been said, though much of it has then been forgotten or ignored. So long as the present balance of forces continues, there is no clear reason why the troubles should ever stop. I have long thought that the British Government should make a declaration of intent to withdraw, and ease the transition to the next phase of Irish history. That would mean an end to the British guarantee, regularly given to the Unionists, that the position of Northern Ireland within the United Kingdom will remain intact unless and until a majority of the people in the North want a change. It would also mean either the unification of Ireland or the establishment of an independent Northern Ireland, independent of Britain and of Dublin alike. It is hard to say whether the majority of us in the South genuinely want the country to be united or not; a referendum would return a loud "yes," but in the meantime a common sentiment in the South would say, "Lord, let us be united . . . but not yet."

I have implied that Yeats was not alone in Irish poetry in his ambivalence toward acts of violence. Conflict as such was dear to Yeats because it was the readiest form of his energy: he was more in need of conflict than of the peace that brings it to an end. He feared peace because he feared inertia. I do not mean that he was a propagandist for murder or that he condoned the Civil War; but he was afraid his poetry would stop if conflict stopped within himself; the grappling of opposites kept his art in force. This motive is still active in Irish poetry, but on the whole our poets have been turning their rhymes toward some form of transcendence.

Heaney is the most telling poet in this respect, and the success of *North* makes his case exemplary; it is clear that thousands of readers have found their feelings defined in that volume more than in any other. I shall maintain that Heaney's readers do not see themselves as lords of counter-positions, commanding a perspective in which all forms of conflict are held in poise. Rather, they find release in an area of feeling somehow beneath the field of violence and ideology; or imaginatively prior to such a moment. Heaney's poems in *North* point to such an area. The dominant analogy for his verses is archaeology, not history; his sense of time circumvents the immediacies of historical event by recourse to several different levels of experience, the accretion of cultures. He is, in *North*, a poet "after Foucault," his knowledge archaeological rather than linear or sequential. In the poem "Belderg" he writes of quernstones, millstones discovered in a bog, the hole in the middle of the stone like an eye, a pupil:

> To lift the lid of the peat
> And find this pupil dreaming
> Of neolithic wheat!
> When he stripped off blanket bog
> The soft-piled centuries
>
> Fell open like a glib.

A glib is a thick mass of matted hair, as the *Oxford Dictionary* reports, "formerly worn by the Irish." It is typical of Heaney to represent the experience of the archaeologist as a human discovery arising from a discovery of earth. Archaeology represents for him, paradoxically, the dream of full and immediate presence, time at once historical and perennial, in which the dichotomy between self and other is obliterated. The reconciliation which other poets represent as a vision of landscape is available to Heaney as meaning and value lying under the skin of the earth, waiting to be discovered. Heaney's desire is predicated upon the depth of earth, the levels and sites waiting, like the eye of the quernstone, to be found and seen. And the feeling goes both ways. In "The Digging Skeleton," pictures in medical textbooks are called

> Mysterious candid studies
> Of red slobland around the bones

presumably because the tissue seems alluvial. And generally Heaney's imagination turns toward the bogland which contains and preserves the human past in forms deeper and more secret than history.

The word "bog," Heaney has remarked, is one of the few English borrowings from the Irish language. In Irish, the word means soft and wet, and survives in Hiberno-English in the phrase "a soft day," meaning a wet day, gentle, not cold. He has also reported that in Derry they call a bog a "moss," a word of Norse origin probably carried to the North of Ireland by planters in the early seventeenth century. So he finds in the two words the record of invasion, colonisation, and shift of language in which the Irish word, for once, has held its place. There is a poem, "Kinship," which ponders these affinities. But I think the pondering might go further. It strikes me that bogland, for Heaney, is the meeting-place between mineral and vegetable life, a state of nature which is soft, yielding, maternal, and full of secret lore. He has referred to "images drawn from Anglo-Saxon kennings, Icelandic sagas, Viking excavations, and Danish and Irish bogs." In "Viking Dublin," he says:

> *a worm of thought*
> *I follow into the mud.*

As a motto for the procedures of *North*, the lines would answer very well. Many of the poems in that volume follow those worms of thought into soft bogland. In the poem "Belderg," talking to the archaeologist:

> *So I talked of Mossbawn,*
> *A bogland name. "But moss?"*
> *He crossed my old home's music*
> *With older strains of Norse.*
> *I'd told how its foundation*
>
> *Was mutable as sound*
> *And how I could derive*
> *A forked root from that ground*
> *And make* bawn *an English fort,*
> *A planter's walled-in mound,*
>
> *Or else find sanctuary*
> *And think of it as Irish,*
> *Persistent if outworn.*

Bawn can indeed mean a walled-in fort, if you take its meaning from the English or Scots planter; or it can mean a place for milking cows, if you leave its meaning in Ireland, especially the South. Heaney takes pleasure in these matters, as a poet should.

He also likes to think of his language as issuing from the accretion of centuries. In the poem "Bone Dreams" he writes:

> *I push back*
> *through dictions,*
> *Elizabethan canopies.*
> *Norman devices,*
>
> *the erotic mayflowers*
> *of Provence*
> *and the ivied latins*
> *of churchmen*
>
> *to the scop's*
> *twang, the iron*
> *flash of consonants*
> *cleaving the line.*

"Scop" means a poet, minstrel, or satirist in Old English, so Heaney is invoking the two strongest traditions in the forked tongue of English: the Anglo-Saxon and the Latin. He puts the two dictions side by side in the poem "Kinship":

> *This is the vowel of earth*
> *dreaming its root*
> *in flowers and snow,*
>
> *mutation of weathers*
> *and seasons,*
> *a windfall composing*
> *the floor it rots into.*
>
> *I grew out of all this*
> *like a weeping willow*
> *inclined to*
> *the appetites of gravity.*

It is common to think of vowels as the pleasure principle of language, and of consonants as the reality principle; a thought congenial to Heaney, who writes in the poem "Aisling":

> He courted her
> With a decadent sweet art
> Like the wind's vowel
> Blowing through the hazels.

But Heaney likes to play off vowel against consonant, Latin pleasure against Anglo-Saxon reality, within the grand allowance which is Language itself, a concessive, permeable medium. So the topics or commonplaces on which his language relies are those in which nature and culture meet so harmoniously that we are not aware of a distinction between them.

I think this goes some way to account for the appeal of Heaney's poems. His poetry as a whole gives the reader the satisfaction of believing that nature and culture are not, as he feared, split apart once for all, or that one term has overwhelmed the other. Make a short list of Heaney's themes: salmon-fishing, the blacksmith's craft, the eel's journey, the thatcher's art, threshing corn, pumping water, digging potatoes, water divining. Think of water divining; an ancient skill, beneath or beyond explanation, requiring nothing but a forked stick, two hands, and the gift of divination. As a parable of the still vivid relation between man and nature, it is complete. Writing a poem about it is hardly necessary, since it is already a form of poetry, at once craft and gift. These motifs in Heaney's poetry make a natural symbolism; or rather, testify to the continuing life of such processes. He turns to them as Yeats turned from the reality of civil war to the honey-bees of generation and creative force:

> The bees build in the crevices
> Of loosening masonry, and there
> The mother birds bring grubs and flies.
> My wall is loosening; honey-bees,
> Come build in the empty house of the stare.

The sweetness of the honey-bees represents everything in Yeats's feeling that longs to move beyond the arguments and counter-arguments that make civil wars and keep them brutal. They speak of a natural world prior to history and culture and indifferent to their terrible possibility.

Heaney's version is an appeal to those parts of human life which are still parts of natural life. In the poem "At a Potato Digging," from *Death of a Naturalist,* the gestures of the potato-diggers are assimilated to the seasons:

> *Processional stooping through the turf*
> *Recurs mindlessly as autumn.*

"Mindlessly" is a word of ease and satisfaction in this poem because it points to a custom, a way of work and life, so deeply grained in the lives of farmers that it does not need to be enforced by mind; the "thinking of the body" is enough.

The welcome extended to Heaney's *North* has been remarkably profuse. Part of the explanation is probably the consolation of hearing that there is a deeper, truer life going on beneath the bombings and torture. There are levels of action and responsiveness deeper than those occupied by Protestants and Catholics; there are archaic processes still alive despite times and technologies.

It is a comfort to receive such news, especially in poems such as Heaney's. The outrage of an obscene act such as the bombing of the La Mon Hotel is indeed the denial of humanity which it entails, but it is also its immediacy. What the act gives, without our asking, is immediacy, a quality which we are ready to accept when it comes as an attribute of chance and misfortune but which leaves us baffled when it comes with human motive. This outrage is not diminished by anything we can say of it. Heaney's poems are as helpless in this respect as any editorial after the event in a newspaper or the standard expressions of sympathy from politicians and bishops. But the archives presented as an archaeological site in Heaney's poems offer a perspective of depth upon local and terrible events. Precisely because he does not present history in linear terms, Heaney offers the reader not a teleology implicit in historical interpretation but a present moment still in touch with its depth. The procedure has the effect of releasing the reader—for the moment, God knows, and only for that—from the fatality which otherwise seems inscribed in the spirit of the age. There is little point in fancying ourselves free in space if we are imprisoned in time, but there are signs that poets and readers are turning away from time, having made such a mess of it, and seen such a mess made of it.

The immediate source of Heaney's bog-poems is P. V. Glob's book *The Bog People,* which contains descriptions and photographs of the

Tollund man, who died 2,000 years ago, hanged in Tollund Fen in Denmark; his body was thrown into a bog and it has been preserved to this day by some chemical quality in the bog water. There is little consolation to be found in these facts, but Heaney's poems invoke them, I think, to release the reader's mind from the immediacy of his experience. I find the same motive in many of Donald Davie's poems, and in the poets he especially admires: poets of place and space rather than of time; or poets who find time resumed in space. Davie has argued that modern poets have made a mess of their politics because they have misunderstood their history; history and time have formed an extremely dangerous element which they could not negotiate. Davie has turned from history to geography, to the history that extends from the geographer-historian Herodotus to the geographer-morphologist Carl Sauer and the "archaeologist of morning," Charles Olson, who wrote as the first sentence of his famous meditation on Melville, *Call Me Ishmael,* "I take Space to be the central fact to man born in America from Folsom cave to now."

So what am I saying? Only this: that Heaney is the first of the poets of the North who are turning away from the terminology of time, with its claim to recognise the spirit of the age and to see a divinely inscribed teleology written in what they say is the past. I think I understand the motives at work, and some of their probable consequences. A vision founded on space, depth, archives, levels of soil is likely to emphasise continuity rather than change, and therefore the universality of human life. What his poems mainly give is the sentiment of that universality. But they do not guarantee that we will get our politics right, when it comes to the time in which we have to get them right or wrong. It means that the relationship between history and politics can be disconnected for a while and that this may be a prudent as well as a consoling thing to do. But beyond that, I am not sure. The evidence is not decisive.

A lecture given at Princeton University: abridged version published in *Hibernia,* 11 May 1978.

FOUR

Occasions

AE

On April 17, 1935, a few months before he died, George Russell wrote to his publisher Daniel Macmillan asking him to ensure that the *Collected Poems* would be bound "in dark blue, which is my colour." "This hue," Henry Summerfield reports in the new biography, *The Myriad-Minded Man*, "the colour of the god Mananan whom AE believed to be the Celtic Logos, stands in Theosophy for concentrated abstract thought—thought refined and exalted to the point at which it can apprehend the highest realities: in poetic language this is sometimes represented by a deep blue, star-irradiated sky, a symbol which appears in *The Avatars*." But the god Mananan had not intervened to protect his devotee, AE "the master mystic," from Joyce's mischief in *Ulysses*:

(In the cone of the searchlight behind the coalscuttle, ollave, holyeyed, the bearded figure of Mananaan MacLir broods, chin on knees. He rises slowly. A cold seawind blows from his druid mantle. About his head writhe eels and elvers. He is encrusted with weeds and shells. His right hand holds a bicycle pump. His left hand grasps a huge crayfish by its two talons.)

MANANAAN MACLIR

(With a voice of waves.) Aum! Hek! Wal! Ak! Lub! Mor! Ma! White yoghin of the Gods. Occult pimander of Hermes Trismegistos. *(With a voice of whistling seawind.)* Punarjanam patsypunjaub! I won't have my leg pulled. It has been said by one: beware the left, the cult of Shakti. *(With a cry of stormbirds.)* Shakti, Shiva! Dark hidden Father! *(He smites with his bicycle pump the crayfish in his left hand. On its cooperative dial glow the twelve signs of the zodiac.)*

Presumably a biographer of AE should exhibit an interest in such matters as these: the possible relation between beards, bicycles, and mysticism; reluctance to practise consecutive thought; constant attendance upon the Ever-Living in the hope of receiving messages, however impenetrable, from that source; a disinclination to have one's leg pulled. Mr. Summerfield's interests are not as diverse as they might be, but his book is informative and therefore useful.

George W. Russell was born on April 10, 1867, in Lurgan, where his father worked as a bookkeeper in a linen firm. "I have never been sufficiently grateful to Providence for the mercy shown to me in removing me from Ulster; though I like the people I cannot breathe in the religious and political atmosphere of the North East corner of Ireland," Russell commented. In 1878, his father took a job in an accountant's office in Dublin, and the family moved south. George regularly went back to the North on holiday, and to Donegal to paint, but otherwise he lived and dreamed in Dublin, poet, painter, mystic, editor, a Dublin character if not quite a Dubliner. He worked for several years in Pim's, a large shop, until he joined Horace Plunkett in running the Irish Agricultural Organization Society. In 1905, he became editor of *The Irish Homestead* (Mananan's version: "I am the light of the homestead, I am the dreamery creamery butter"). Later, he edited *The Irish Statesman,* coaxing his friends into print. Meanwhile in a city notable for malice, he was loved.

Russell's position in the history of the Irish Literary Revival is marginal. Mr. Summerfield says that "his greatest accomplishment was the creation of his own character," and it is clear that his published works are inferior to his presence. But character is merely a word for those attributes he always possessed; he never made himself, in Yeats's sense of the word, a personality. Russell's imagination contented itself with the description of virtue; it did not feel impelled to exert itself upon a strictly creative impulse. When he turns up in Yeats's *A Vision,* accompanied by Newman, Luther, Calvin, and George Herbert in Phase 25, his purpose is given as "to limit and bind, to make men better, by making it impossible that they should be otherwise, to so arrange prohibitions and habits that men may be naturally good, as they may be naturally black or white or yellow." His power, Yeats says, "rests in certain simplifying convictions which have grown with his character; he needs intellect for their expression, not for proof, and taken away from these convictions is without emotion and momentum." But Yeats is more severe upon Russell in the *Memoirs.* "He has the religious genius," Yeats remarks, "and it is the essence of that genius that all souls are equal in its eyes: queen or apple-woman, it is all one, seeing that none can be more than an immortal soul; whereas I have been concerned with men's capacities, with all that divides man from man."

Yeats thought Russell a good man but a bad influence. "He has taught many to despise all that does not come out of their own minds and to trust to vision to do the work of intellect; and minds in which there is nothing original turn with arrogance against every talent that does not please them at the first glance." Russell, according to this argument, encouraged his followers in "a luxurious dreaming, a kind of spiritual lubricity," instead of making them use their heads. In *Ulysses,* Bloom sees AE, accompanied by the poet Lizzie Twigg: "His eyes followed the high figure in homespun, beard and bicycle, a listening woman at his side." Holding forth, as Bloom assumes. As for Ms. Twigg: "She's taking it all in. Not saying a word."

Reading AE's poems is like being inside a feather mattress, embarrassed by texture absurdly in excess of structure and ossature: it would be fatal to the experience if the words suddenly decided to go against their character and specify something. Russell's eloquence denotes nothing, and absorbs objects only as stains and oozings. In *Ulysses,* J. J. O'Molloy asks Stephen Dedalus, "What do you think really of that hermetic crowd, the opal hush poets: A.E. the master mystic?" and twenty pages later Bloom thinks it sufficient to say of them that they are vegetarians, "literary etherial people they are all. Dreamy, cloudy, symbolistic." "I wouldn't be surprised," he avers, "if it was that kind of food you see produces the like waves of the brain the poetical." In "A Mountain Wind" the poet is "brother to grass and stones," but the brotherhood does not authenticate the grass and stones by providing a language to denote or discriminate them. Russell's appalling facility makes anything change into anything at the drop of a syllable, according to a poetic procedure once defined, with judicious severity, by Marianne Moore as "the cadence being the sole reason for all that follows":

> *The sombre trees*
> *To cloud change unimaginably; nay;*
> *To fire, to mind.*

Unimaginably: that is, Russell cannot imagine the change, he can only believe in it. In "Transformations," "imagines" becomes "imagineth" to provoke a rhyme:

> *For lips laugh there at beauty the heart imagineth,*
> *And feet dance there at the holy Bridal of Love and Death.*

Reviewing *The Earth Breath* (1897), Yeats said that even when we are in love, AE would have us love the invisible beauty before the visible beauty "and make our love a dream," but he offered the sentence as praise and did not report the fact that AE's poems take for granted an unearned and unquestioned relation between visible and invisible beauty and do nothing to explicate it. Our love becomes a dream because AE's language cannot ascribe to anything its proper density and weight. What he calls transformation is merely the process by which objects and relations lose whatever reality they have had and find themselves dissolved in the aura of Aum and Hek.

The recent exhibition of AE's paintings at the Oriel Gallery, Dublin, provided the agreeable surprise of discovering that they are not as bad as George Moore said they were. "The Donegal dauber" is a formula not entirely adequate to the occasion. AE never acquired a style and found it easier to borrow one from Gustave Moreau: in every other respect he was lazy, careless, the most unBlakean of painters who thought their paintings had something to do with Blake. He told John Quinn:

> What I want to do is to paint landscape as if it had no other existence
> than as an imagination of the Divine Mind, to paint man as if his life

overflowed into that imagination, and to paint the Sidhe as min-
gling with his life; indeed, the unity of God and man and nature in
one single being—an almost impossible idea to convey in paint.

In practise this means that nothing is allowed to assert itself in relation
to anything else: the ostensibly human figures are assimilated to trees, sun-
shine, and leaves, which in turn yield their contours to an atmosphere which
is as much of the Divine Mind as AE's hospitable brush can register. Where
there is nothing but the human face, as in AE's portrait of Iseult Gonne, the
paint retains of her vitality only her patience. The girl's head does not define
itself in relation to space, but waits as if kept alive by the vague possibility of
attending upon a vision. "The supreme question about a work of art," AE
is made to say in *Ulysses,* "is out of how deep a life does it spring": it is not at
all a futile thing to say, especially in the form in which Henry James said it.
But AE's notion of depth, unlike James's, is adequately given in the previous
sentence: "Art has to reveal to us ideas, formless spiritual essences." In painting as in poetry, he thought that to reveal those spiritual essences it was sufficient to show how easily material existences may be dissolved. *Ulysses* again:

> Formless spiritual. Father, Word and Holy Breath. Allfather, the
> heavenly man. Hiesos Kristos, magician of the beautiful, the Logos
> who suffers in us at every moment. This verily is that. I am the fire
> upon the altar. I am the sacrificial butter.

Mr. Summerfield has a good deal to say of AE as theosophist, and of
the influence upon him of Madame Blavatsky, W. Q. Judge, and James
Pryse. "He can do the sidereal alright," Pryse said of AE, displaying the
vulgarity which prompted Yeats to dispose of him in *The Trembling of the
Veil* as "an American hypnotist." Yeats thought AE "the one masterful
influence among young Dublin men and women who love religious
speculation but have no historical faith." It is clear, however, that AE
seemed to Yeats a naif, sacred indeed to all his friends, "as the fool is
sacred in the East," but lazy in the reception of his visions. Yeats wanted
AE to examine and question his visions, and even to write them down as
they occurred, but AE would only interpret them within the self-fulfilling
terms of *The Secret Doctrine.* In *The Avatars* and *The Interpreters* he sets up
an extremely limp dialectic between "the mystic empire" and "the mecha-
nistic maze," but he does not even begin to clarify the nature of vision or

discriminate between one visionary episode and another. His surrogates Paul and Lavelle merely give the standard notion of the imagination a theosophical tone.

In the end, what counts is the practical work: helping people, turning geese into swans, setting up cooperative banks, persuading Irish farmers that, having feet, they should consider standing upon them. *The Irish Homestead* may have presented itself to Joyce's irony as "the pigs' paper," work of a bullockbefriending bard, but it was good work, especially for a man who might otherwise have contented himself with doing the sidereal. AE's journalism, as in his *Imaginations and Reveries* and *The Living Torch* (edited by Monk Gibbon), runs to the high style too often to be convincing, but it includes formidable work, notably the rebuke delivered to Kipling in 1912 on the theme of Ulster. Editorial daring had its limits, of course, especially in the years of *The Irish Statesman*. In 1923, AE asked Yeats for a poem for the magazine, but when the poem turned out to be "Leda and the Swan" he declined the privilege of publishing it on the grounds that his conservative readers would misunderstand it. He favoured good work and encouraged nearly every Irish writer who showed any ability to produce it, but the limits of his taste were denoted by his representing James Stephens, Padraic Colum, and Seumas O'Sullivan as the truly creative forces in modern Irish literature.

Still, the practical work in cooperation and politics brought out the best in AE, and Yeats's explanation is reasonable—that AE's imagination became vivid only in the service of something which he had not created. The language of practical affairs gave him what dialect gave Synge, a value independent of his invention.

Mr. Summerfield's biography is more complete than anything hitherto available, and it is judicious in its sense of AE's worth as an artist: it does not conceal the fact that AE found it possible to be influential without the labour of being great. Writing a book of facts and contexts, Mr. Summerfield cannot avoid the embarrassment of reciting familiar stories. It is dispiriting to tell yet again the historical background in terms of the Dublin lock-out in 1913, Jim Larkin's activities, the First World War, conscription, the Treaty, the civil war, and the years of recuperation. But the real embarrassment is the necessity of presenting a *biographie intérieure* solely on the evidence of visible works and days.

In *Song and its Fountains* AE describes how poems came to him, often from dreams, and he has much to say of psychic experience independent of the bodily senses. In *The Candle of Vision* he testifies to similar events, implying that they are crucial to his development. But these events are so evanescent, their inwardness so much to be taken for granted if taken at all, that they lie far beyond the reach of a biographical method which depends upon public facts, occasions, dates, and places. Mr. Summerfield assumes that there is a relation between outer and inner life, but he cannot claim to explicate it by anything producible. The gap between outer and inner experience remains absolute and we are forced to say of each, this verily is not that. Mr. Summerfield's facts are reliable, and they denote one part of AE's life, but nothing more. So far as the man was a seer, what he saw remains, even after the poems and paintings, a secret.

Times Literary Supplement, 26 March 1976.

JAMES STEPHENS

"Joyce was strangely in love with his own birthday and with mine. He had discovered somehow that he and I were twins, born in the same hour of the same day of the same year in the same city. The bed it seemed was different, and that was the only snag in our relationship." The city was Dublin, the year 1882, the day 2 February, the hour six in the morning, the Joyce James, the speaker James Stephens. The truth of the matter is probably less poetic. In her *James Stephens: His Work and an Account of His Life,* Hilary Pyle tries to show that Stephens was born on February 9, 1880, but I am happy to report that the evidence is inconclusive. In any event, Joyce believed in the poetry; so much so that in 1927 when things were going badly with *Finnegans Wake* he thought of having Stephens finish the work. Stephens's qualifications were indisputable. His name, like Joyce's, was James, he was a poet, a Dubliner, fortunately born, nominally close to the Stephen of *A Portrait of the Artist as a Young Man,* and he had good eyesight. Finally, the lettering on the book would be JJ and S, as Joyce wrote to Harriet Weaver, "the colloquial Irish for John Jameson and Son's Dublin whiskey." The auspices were unimpeachable. Two years later Joyce and Stephens were still discussing the notion. So it petered out.

The first meeting of these Dubliners was a sharp event, if Stephens is to be believed:

> He turned his chin and his specs at me, and away down at me, and confided the secret to me that he had read my two books; that, grammatically, I did not know the difference between a semi-colon and a colon: that my knowledge of Irish life was non-Catholic and, so, non-existent, and that I should give up writing and take to a good job like shoe-shining as a more promising profession.

Thus Stephens in one of the B.B.C. talks with which he filled the vacancy of his last years. In *James, Seumas and Jacques,* Lloyd Frankenberg has gathered these and other memorabilia and they are well worth having. As a critic Stephens was no T. S. Eliot but he was worth listening to while he recalled his friends, notably AE, Yeats, Joyce, Synge, and Stephen MacKenna. The tone of the reminiscences is always genial: Stephens did not traffic in mockery. An occasional slyness keeps the judgment alert. "Still, I'm inclined to believe that Yeats and I were the only poets with good manners that ever lived. When he had finished a poem I always asked him to say it again and when I had finished one he as scrupulously invited me to repeat the last verse." Of Stephens's sing-song method of reading his poems Yeats said: "Stephens has a very original talent, he has discovered Gregorian Chant."

Not that the poems are very good, however you sing them. Stephens wrote a few perfect short pieces, such as "The Goat Paths," "Geoffrey Keating," "Nora Criona," "The Paps of Dana," and "Egan O'Rahilly," but in most of his poems there is less than meets the ear. His most celebrated poems, "The Main Deep" and "The Shell," are sound tracks, too pure to be true. Luckily, there is more to him than the verse.

To begin with, Stephens was a second-rate writer who wrote one first-rate book, *The Crock of Gold* (1912), and showed in *The Charwoman's Daughter* and "There is a Tavern in the Town" that at any moment he might do it again. He never did it again. Instead, he went serious, read books he should have left uncut, and took to big thought on the supposition that it would add cubits to his small stature. He wrote better as a contentedly short man.

To put this in its context. Within ten years or so Irish literature produced Joyce's *Dubliners* and the *Portrait,* Synge's *Playboy of the Western*

World, Yeats's *The Green Helmet,* and Stephens's *Crock of Gold.* None of these is abashed in the presence of the others. Synge and Stephens gave their best in one shot: Joyce and Yeats went on to even greater things. But let that be. *The Crock of Gold* is one of the finest romances in modern literature, a revery sharpened into words for the delight of the thing. Reading it again now I am touched by Stephens's care, his delicacy, his concern to keep life out of harm's way by protecting it with words. Many scenes in the book take the harm out of daily life by bandaging the sore places with words. The relation between the old Philosopher and the Thin Woman, for instance, is as terrible as any human relation could be, if we think of it as a relation beyond the book and postpone the consolation available by needy recourse to the words. Stephens does not dissolve the thing out of existence, but he protects its victims so that the hurt cannot be fatal. The first protection is the genre itself, the second is the full organisation and disposition of the words. At one point the Thin Woman says: "Your stirabout is on the hob . . . You can get it yourself. I would not move the breadth of my nail if you were dying of hunger. I hope there's lumps in it." There are, indeed, lumps in it, because stirabout needs to be stirred. The Thin Woman jumps into bed and tries to give the poor Philosopher rheumatism, toothache, and lockjaw all at once by malignant desire. But Stephens protects him by secreting him in his generic role: if he is a husband, he is nothing but a victim, but he is also and chiefly a philosopher. Hence it comes naturally for him to conclude: "Finality is death. Perfection is finality. Nothing is perfect. There are lumps in it."

This is a blessed recourse in Stephens's writing. He uses words as a nurse uses ointment, to make the patient easier. If marriage is painful, he talks the pain out of it. In "There is a Tavern in the Town" the old gentleman drops a button, picks it up, thinks of his house-keeper, then of the strangeness of housekeeping and matrimony. "Like so many other customs," he says, "marriage is not native to the human race, nor is it altogether peculiar to it. So far as I am aware no person was ever born married, and in extreme youth bachelors and spinsters are so common as to call for no remark." So he proceeds. In Stephens's fiction as long as a man is talking he is doing nothing else; not even suffering. The consolations of speech, like those of breathing and philosophy, are intrinsic, native to the medium. In most writers, language is a beast of burden, content in the knowledge that it is, within its limits, an efficient carrier of sentiments and notions: most of the time it stands and waits. But in

Stephens the language frets if thus restrained: it aspires to the condition of whim. This does not mean that it resents the prosaic attachments, grammar, syntax, and the like. Not at all. In fact, Stephens's language delights in these adornments, now that it has commandeered them for its own purposes. His talkers, like Beckett's, are all grammarians, pedants in strictly linguistic rectitude. Some of them are even aestheticians, despite their amateur status. A few years ago the critic Elizabeth Sewell wrote, in a study of Valéry, that "words are the mind's one defence against possession by thought or dreams; even Jacob kept trying to find out the name of the angel he wrestled with." The sentence was her own and yet I almost think she took it from a story by Stephens: certainly her book *The Field of Nonsense* is the best Introduction to *The Crock of Gold,* though it was not intended for that purpose; with this qualification, that the philosophers in Stephens's romance consider words an entirely adequate defence of the mind against every temptation and hazard. In Stephens's books thought is beaten before it begins, if it dares to live its own life: words, for one thing, have all the elusive advantages of vagary and guile. Thought is a sober citizen, words are libidinous in their conjunctions. So the really destitute people in Stephens's world are the silent ones, like secret drinkers, all thought and not a word. In "A Glass of Beer" the boulevardier sees himself "as a box with nothing inside it": the gods and the devils have abandoned him to his silence.

I have touched on a commonplace, that modern Irish literature is a wordy business. We have had our solid novels, tracts for the times, beasts of burden, but they are not indigenous. The native product tends to be runic, archaic, pedantic, a caprice of words alone. Words alone are certain good, Yeats said in one of his moods, and half believed it. But I have in mind books like *At Swim-Two-Birds,* Eimar O'Duffy's *King Goshawk,* Brinsley MacNamara's *Various Lives of Marcus Igoe,* Austin Clarke's *The Sun Dances at Easter.* Stephens is a crucial figure in this tradition. In such books the motto is: keep talking, and it can't happen. Life is suffered only in the cracks between the words. So in *The Crock of Gold* the sergeant urges Shawn to cut in and keep on talking to prevent the Philosopher from keeping on talking. "Sure, I don't know what to talk about," says Shawn. "I'm sweating this minute trying to please you, so I am. If you'll tell me what to talk about I'll do my endeavors." "You're a fool," says the sergeant: "you'll never make a constable." If Stephens had said that words alone are certain good, he would have meant it, and while reading him we are convinced that it is true. In one of his radio talks he wondered about those people who love music and hate poetry. That this can happen, he said, "flabbers one and ghasts one, than which two nothing worse can happen." Adding, to make it all clear: "To ghast I understand and wince from, but to flabber beats me."

To write the biography of such a man is to fly in the face of nature, because the only significant events in his life were verbal. Hilary Pyle tells us what he did and when, but it is nothing: what he read and with what devotion, but it is little enough. She tells us about the influence of Blake, which I believe was nil. But she never explains what is going on in the only place where anything is going on, in Stephens's pages. As a result, much of her book goes like this:

> Kot and Stephens would also meet at Twinings in Piccadilly. They would go to dinner afterwards in Great Portland Street and end the evening in the Casa Prada, near Warren Street. Another favorite haunt was Ridgeway's, where it soon became a habit to meet on Wednesdays, and a group formed including Ralph Hodgson, Leonard Woolf, J. W. N. Sullivan, Lady Glenavy, sometimes Mark Gertler or W. J. Turner, Lady Ottoline Morrell, Middleton Murry and Lady Huxley. Poetic discussion was lively, and Stephens would often scribble out one of his poems on a piece of paper and give it to Kot, who preserved several among his papers.

(Kot, by the way, is "Koteliansky, the big Russian Jew.")

The ideal reader of Stephens, Miss Sewell excepted, is probably Marianne Moore. Next, the ideal reader of Stephens is anyone who loves to read Miss Moore, and, after that, any reader who is, in Bacon's phrase, a ready man. Even yet, Stephens is the only writer, Miss Moore excepted, who would think of rhyming "tale-spinner" with "Yul Brynner," and he would be the first to congratulate Miss Moore upon the nonchalance of that invention.

He died, of this we are sure, on December 26, 1950.

The New York Review of Books, 26 August 1965.

Synge in His Letters

S ynge's origin was solidly Anglo-Irish, Protestant, upper-middle class: his father a well-got barrister, his mother the daughter of a Protestant parson in Schull, County Cork. Presumably it was a financial blow when his father died, but Synge was too young to feel a difference, and besides there was enough money coming from rented estates in Wicklow. The Synges were landlord-class, with the mentality that went with such privilege. As a young man, John thought himself some kind of radical in a vaguely European sense. In Ireland, he knew that the real issue was the ownership of land. In 1893 he canvassed against Gladstone's second Home Rule Bill on the grounds that it would exacerbate the question of land and intensify strife between landowner and peasant. In Paris he joined Maud Gonne in the Association Irlandaise and stayed in it as long as its talk sounded harmless, but when Maud's journal *L'Irlande Libre* looked as if it would take the *Libre* literally, he resigned from the Association and told her he wouldn't "get mixed up with a revolutionary and semi-military movement." Years later, he accepted an invitation from the *Manchester Guardian* to write twelve articles on the impoverished areas of Galway and Mayo administered by the Congested Districts Board, but the articles, published in June–July 1905, were pretty innocuous. Synge wanted to see local conditions improved, provided the peasants stayed as aesthetically winsome as they were, but he hated the few people who were comfortable enough to have acquired a double chin. Things should change but not yet, O Lord. Synge's political vision, in fact, didn't amount to anything more than Yeats's "dream of the noble and the beggerman." Like Yeats, he hated the small towns and the people who lived in them.

The truth is that Synge was never interested in political issues. As a young man, he much preferred to traipse around Europe, playing the fiddle, enjoying the seasons and the landscapes, learning French, Italian, German, Hebrew, and at Trinity College, Dublin, making a reasonable shot at modern Irish. He had the background of a gentleman and the instincts of an aesthete: spiritualism and theosophy were more in his line than the activities of the Land League. Like Yeats, Lady Gregory, and Douglas Hyde, he brooded over the "spirit of the nation" and thought it would be a fine thing to express it in a theatre, but he didn't want to see it manifested in a rough form. Maud Gonne was too rough. Yeats had to hover about her interests because he was besotted, but Synge had no intention of falling in love with her or letting her bewitch him into dangerous practises.

Besides, he was already in love, supposedly with Cherrie Matheson. His letters to her haven't survived, so we know little or nothing about the relation except that when he proposed to her in June 1896 she turned him down. The letters Ann Saddlemyer has collected give a misleading account of Synge's interests in the years before 1896 when he met Yeats and Maud Gonne. Mostly, such letters as have turned up are carefully composed things in French and German, written to various acquaintances he met on his wanderings. The earliest letter is dated 2 February 1894, and it merely shows that Synge was a young man observing the decencies of discourse. Thank-you notes, a little music, some readings in vaguely Decadent French poetry, and a sense of being abroad made up most of his experience. He was not yet, in any sense that mattered, a writer.

But his constitution was determined to be gloomy. Delicate, morbid, and, after a few years, nearly always ill, he made himself a writer by imagining forms of life as different as possible from his own. No wonder he fascinated Yeats, who took him as the supreme exemplar of the theory he accepted from Wilde, that a writer gains mastery of himself by creating an anti-self or mask and striking through it. Fulfilling the doctrine of the mask, Synge won a place for himself as one of the two representatives of Phase 23 in *A Vision*—the other was Rembrandt. "In

Synge's early unpublished work, written before he found the dialects of Aran and of Wicklow," Yeats wrote, "there is brooding melancholy and morbid self-pity. He had to undergo an aesthetic transformation, analogous to religious conversion, before he became the audacious, joyous, ironical man we know."

Taciturn and dispirited in daily life, Synge filled his plays with gallant lads, tricksters, daring fellows with a gift of the gab. At a time when Dublin audiences were content to see "Mde Rejane in Ibsen, Mrs P. Campbell in Sudermann, Olga Netherstole in Sappho, etc.," as he told Stephen MacKenna, Synge wanted to interest them in unsqueamish plays of rural life, visions of the Aran Islands, the sexual loneliness, the provenance of fear and joylessness and desire. Standard English wasn't gloomy enough to express his gloom, so he invented a style called Synge-song if you don't like it and poetry if you do: a dialect compounded of Irish-English, rural formulae, and—as Declan Kiberd has shown—the Irish of Inishmaan in literal translation. He learned a good deal from Douglas Hyde's *Casadh an t-Sugain* and even more from Lady Gregory's little peasant-plays. But he was interested in these writers only pragmatically and so long as he found them useful: otherwise, he was indifferent.

Yeats was bewildered by Synge till he saw how fully he exemplified his favourite doctrine. In "The Death of Synge" he said that "he had that egotism of the man of genius which Nietzsche compares to the egotism of a woman with child." For a time, Yeats couldn't understand why Synge never complimented him on a poem or a play; why he never said one word of praise to Lady Gregory. He had, Yeats said, "under charming and modest manners, in almost all things of life, a complete absorption in his own dream." He was "that rare, that distinguished, that most noble thing, which of all things still of the world is nearest to being sufficient to itself, the pure artist." He had "no life outside his imagination, little interest in anything that was not its chosen subject." In Paris, Synge and Joyce are supposed to have had lively arguments about literature, drama, language, and such things: or so Stanislaus Joyce reported in *My Brother's Keeper.* But Synge wasn't much interested in Joyce as a writer. In a letter of 26 March 1903, he told Lady Gregory: "I cannot think that he will ever be a poet of importance, but his intellect is extraordinarily keen and if he keeps fairly sane he ought to do excellent essay-writing."

It is a mercy that Synge's plays imagine a life as different as possible from his own, because his own was cripplingly tedious. The natural man in him was a wearisome, fretful, petulant bore. Cherrie Matheson was well rid of his attentions. Early in 1906 he allowed himself to be smitten by Molly Allgood, a light-headed, flirtatious girl who started out as a middling actress and became a good one. Whatever form the relation took, it started in the spring of 1906 and gathered something like momentum in the summer when the Abbey toured Scotland and the North of England. Synge's carrying-on with Molly caused eyebrows to lift and tongues to wag. The management didn't like it. Annie Horniman thought his behaviour scandalous, Lady Gregory thought it at best a nuisance. But the love-birds quarrelled often and loudly enough to take some of the harm out of the situation. As a couple, they were mismatched. Molly was pretty enough to make a good time seem the natural thing. Synge was always jealous. He nearly had a seizure when she went off to a party — I assume the crime was no worse — with some medical students. He hated her to talk to any man. One of the actors, he insisted, had flagrant designs on her. She was silly, childish, she had no taste, she didn't read books; so he lent her *Ivanhoe,* took her to task when he disapproved of her hat, berated her when a day passed and she didn't write him a loving letter. When he got ill, he fretted through every letter, complaining of her carelessness, her thoughtlessness, assuring her that "you need never doubt me, my little heart, if you treat me well." Baby-talk became his norm.

Molly kept his letters, but she didn't warm to their whining rhetoric. On one she scribbled "appalling," on another "frivolous," on a third "presume," whatever she meant by that. When the correspondence began, Synge and Molly were reasonably healthy, but soon he started getting ill. His illness wasn't properly diagnosed: there was talk of asthma and influenza but it turned out to be Hodgkin's disease. After a while, and as if all this talk of illness were catching, Molly, too, started getting ill: she had a lot of trouble with her eyes. When it was clear that he was indeed in bad health, she devoted herself to him, they planned to marry, she visited him with the assiduousness he demanded. He was too sick to be jealous and sick enough to be miserable.

Most of the letters are to Molly, and tedious they are. It is a relief to come to letters in which Synge minds his professional business: when he writes to Frank Fay at the Abbey to find out whether the company is favouring Yeats or Lady Gregory and suppressing *The Playboy of the Western World* and *Riders to the Sea.* Stephen MacKenna brought out the best in Synge. MacKenna was a spirited, malicious character, quite what Synge needed to stir him into life. To MacKenna he entrusted his opinion that one of George Moore's essays was "a misbegotten abortion," and that

John Eglinton was "a fearful instance of pedantic degeneration." Synge was also roused to act with spirit when it looked as if Miss Horniman would coax Yeats into a cosmopolitan rather than an Irish form of theatre. Synge took Lady Gregory's side and preserved Yeats for righteousness. His letters on these occasions are far sturdier than any he wrote from his more intimate life.

Most of the letters in the first volume have been published in other forms. Professor Saddlemyer published in *Letters to Molly* (Harvard, 1971) the correspondence between the lovers in the last three years of Synge's life. In the meantime she has found, by my count, four new letters, and has changed her mind about the dates of a few. But the main difference in the new volume is that she has left the letters in their original form. Synge, like Yeats, couldn't spell, had only the merest notion of punctuation, and let his letters go out in a mess. In *Letters to Molly,* Ann Saddlemyer corrected the errors and made Synge appear more controlled and orthodox than he was. Sometimes the messy letters are hard to read: it takes guesswork to decide that "squal" is supposed to be "squeal." But it's better, on the whole, to see the letters in their native squalor. A few typos are editorial: "coeil" should be "ceoil," "cliat" should be "cliath," "fór" has to be "fós," in one place Shawn is mistaken for Patrick, in another "Eniskerry" should be "Enniskerry." The letters to MacKenna have also appeared in Professor Saddlemyer's contribution to *Irish Renaissance,* edited by Robin Skelton and David Clark (Dolmen Press, 1965), but I suppose that volume is long out of print. So it is good to have all this material brought together, splendidly elucidated by Professor Saddlemyer's notes. The volume also incorporates the relevant matter from Professor Saddlemyer's *Some Letters of John Synge to Lady Gregory and W. B. Yeats* (Cuala Press, 1971), a handsome book treasured by book-lovers but hardly available to the common reader.

The London Review of Books, 1 December 1983.

GEORGE MOORE

In 1901, George Moore decided to conceive a passion for the redemption of Ireland. To form a liaison with the Gaelic League and the Irish National Theatre he left London and settled in Dublin, choosing to reside in a Georgian house in Upper Ely Place a few yards from St. Stephen's Green and the Shelbourne Hotel. Ten years later he cleared out of Dublin and brought his conversations to Ebury Street, London, where he would be free to write *Hail and Farewell*. "A work of liberation I divined it to be," he claimed, "liberation from ritual and priests, a book of precept and example, a turning-point in Ireland's destiny." *Ave* was published in 1911, *Salve* in 1912, and *Vale* in 1914. Moore revised the work for the second edition (1925). So there are no textual problems, the texts are identical in the editions of 1925, 1933 (Uniform), 1937 (Ebury), and the present edition, which justifies itself by virtue of Richard Cave's useful annotations. The book has not changed, but its new readers are deemed to know nothing, apparently, about French Impressionism, Anglo-Irish lore, or a saint named John of the Cross. Mr. Cave's edition is handsome, expensive, informative, and inadequately proof-read. The notes are generally excellent, but I don't see why Mr. Cave is coy about naming Yeats's "Diana Vernon" as Olivia Shakespear, since the name has already appeared in print several times.

Incidentally, Mr. Cave thinks that the Rhymers' Club began in 1891. When I edited Yeats's *Memoirs* I gave the same date, but Karl Beckson has assembled documentary evidence to prove that the right date is 1890.

Moore ascribed to nature the authorship of *Hail and Farewell,* at least in the sense of providing every episode and every character. His own contribution was limited to "what my eye has seen, and my heart has felt," a formula which does not specifically exclude the activity of malice. In the January–February 1914 number of the *English Review* Moore wrote an insolent account of Yeats, Lady Gregory, and Synge. Yeats immediately wrote two "poems of hatred," and included one of them, "Notoriety," as the closing rhyme of his *Responsibilities:*

> *till all my priceless things*
> *Are but a post the passing dogs defile.*

Yeats's father, John Butler Yeats, told him that Moore "was not worth powder and shot," but the poet had powder and shot to spare, and he kept it in good condition for a formal assault on Moore's reputation, holding fire till he was safely dead, in *Dramatis Personae* (1935). It is clear that Yeats was especially stung by the pages in *Salve* in which Moore laughed at his pretensions to high ancestry, all that Ormonde blood: it is easily the funniest part of *Hail and Farewell* in its account of the fur-coated Yeats attacking bourgeois Dublin for philistinism. Yeats's revenge was sweetest, I think, in that section of *Dramatis Personae* in which he told of Moore dining with Edward Martyn in an excellent London restaurant and abusing the waiter for the quality of the soup: by Martyn's standards, not a whit inferior to Moore's, the soup was remarkably fine. In short, Moore was a barbarian, a moral gangster, he had manner but no manners. Nature, according to Yeats who claimed to know such things, "had denied to him the final touch: he had a coarse palate." Witness the soup. No wonder Moore wrote a long preface to one of his books to prove that he had a mistress in Mayfair.

Clean, wholesome fun, at this stage. The tedious parts of *Hail and Farewell* are the routine attacks on Catholicism, Irish priests, the Mass, and so forth. Surely this carefully nurtured contempt did not form the celebrated conversations at Ely Place, where Moore is deemed to have scintillated with AE, Gogarty, and the other dear shadows. Gossip, yes, malice, calumny, detraction, libels, the mocking of absent friends, but I can't believe that Moore's proffered entertainment consisted in reiterated assertions that there had not been a good Catholic book since the Reformation. Yeats called Moore "more mob than man," and certainly Moore had the sensibility of a steamroller, especially when he thought it behoved him to exhibit tenderness. His irony is enjoyable only when it is directed against people whose achievement has rendered them immune to it: so we enjoy the mockery of Newman's style in *Ave,* and of Hardy's in *Conversations in Ebury Street,* and Moore's teasing account of Yeats seeing or failing to see certain wild swans at Coole. With smaller people than these masters, Moore's jibing is wearisome. The anecdotes of Martyn are not very funny—Martyn was too simple to be worth goading. Douglas Hyde gets a severe press from Moore, partly for daring to speak Irish, a language Moore did not trouble to learn but which he recognised when he heard the noise of porter issuing from Hyde's moustache. You had only to listen to Hyde's English to understand why he wanted to revive Irish; but it was not Moore's intention to be fair to a decent man.

Ave ends with Moore's dismissal of England, *Salve* with the announcement of his conversion to Protestantism, *Vale* with his dismissal of Ireland. The entire book is a gesture of riddance. Moore got his keenest pleasure not, apparently, from his attention to women or their attention to him but from the act of disengaging himself from gone enthusiasms. His feelings were not various or deep, and he most enjoyed the pleasure of disowning them. Yeats seizes upon this quality, in the *Memoirs,* where he says that Moore gave himself up to every new impression and quarrelled with everyone who did not share his exaltation, but he could not bear to retain his old impressions or respect their age. "As a woman will speak evil of the lover who has left her," Yeats wrote, "Moore would scorn all other impressions, those of his past life as energetically as the rest." I think he craved the emotion of sublimity and insisted upon finding it wherever he chose to turn. Inevitably, he was disappointed: sublimity did not respond to the likes of Moore. Disappointed, he thought to make his rage sublime in the form of irony and malice. The result is that when he writes of these things they issue as fads: masterpieces assume an air of corruption, their majesty compromised, tainted by Moore's experience of them. When he writes about a painting, we end up thinking it a fraud. Moore preferred the portrait of Rembrandt's wife to the *Mona Lisa:* if any other critic stated the preference it would be worth pondering, consulting its reasons. Since the taste is Moore's, we set it aside, thinking of a palate incapable of distinguishing between a perfect soup and a bowl of dishwater. When we read that he intended writing a book about Ireland called *Ruin and Weed,* "ruined castles in a weedy country," we take malicious pleasure in recalling that Moore's estate in Mayo, 12,371 acres, has passed into more deserving hands. Malice is contagious.

In 1914, stung by Moore's insolence, Yeats started to write his own autobiography, beginning at the safe distance of childhood and youth but moving steadily toward the tendentious years of politics, religion, theatre. It is instructive to compare the two autobiographers. Moore remembers most keenly whatever it is he has decided to repudiate: he recalls people (Russell always excepted: that, at least, is a grace that almost saves Moore) so that he can make their dismissal complete. Yeats remembers people so that he may retain them, and as if he feared that they might otherwise leave him. If an old score must be settled, as in Moore's case, Yeats settles it with the precise qualities which nature denied to his enemy: charm, grandeur, style.

(Yet, the same intolerable man wrote *The Lake, Esther Waters, A Drama in Muslin,* and—as if for Joyce's sake—*The Untilled Field.*)

The Spectator, 1 January 1977.

MAUD GONNE

In 1932, Lawrence Campbell completed a plaster bust of Maud Gonne MacBride and painted it bronze: it was shown at the Municipal Gallery in Dublin, where Yeats saw it. Maud Gonne was then sixty-six years old, and in that phase of her beauty which prompted people to think of her as the most distinguished ruin in Ireland. In the poem "A Bronze Head," Yeats lets his mind play upon several images, without settling for any one of them as definitive. Campbell's sculpture gives Maud almost unnatural finality, but in Yeats's poem she is transformed into his sense of her. It is not necessary for him to distinguish between one moment and another in his relation to her; the moments establish themselves in his mind with as much diversity as the images they have provoked. Even when he wonders "Which of her forms has shown her substance right," he does not pester himself for an answer. It is enough that Maud is a presence, and present in a multitude of forms. Among the forms, Yeats had his favourites; he liked to associate her beauty with apple blossoms and to see her within the frame of a picture, herself picturesque. He writes in his *Autobiography:*

All is but faint to me beside a moment when she passed before a window, dressed in white, and rearranged a spray of flowers in a vase. Twelve years afterwards I put that impression into verse:

> *Blossom pale, she pulled down the pale blossom*
> *At the moth hour and hid it in her bosom.*

When he invoked her among certain "beautiful lofty things," he made another image, equally picturesque:

> *Maud Gonne at Howth station waiting a train,*
> *Pallas Athena in that straight back and arrogant head.*

"Arrogant" was a term of praise, when Yeats was in that mood: it consorted with the noble kind of pride, self-possession, grandeur.

Maud Gonne was born on 21 December 1866, near Aldershot, where her father, Captain Thomas Gonne, was stationed with the Seventeenth Lancers. A few weeks later, he was transferred to Ireland, and the family was soon living in Dublin. Maud's sister Kathleen was born in 1868. In 1871, when Maud was five, her mother died. The girls were reared by their father and various relatives to whom they were entrusted when he was transferred to Vienna and other places as British military attaché. When Maud was twenty, her father died. He left her financially comfortable enough to live where she pleased, travel, order her clothes in Paris, and do things with style.

One of the forms in which Maud's substance was shown, if not shown right, was that of "the colonel's daughter"; an uncharitable phrase from a passage in Sean O'Casey's *Inishfallen Fare Thee Well*. O'Casey didn't like her, I think he resented her social cut and dash. In 1926, he entered into dispute with Maud's friend Hannah Sheehy-Skeffington, who was outraged by the mockery of the 1916 Rising which she felt in *The Plough and the Stars*. O'Casey punished Maud for her friendship by describing that occasion:

> There she sits stonily silent, once a sibyl of patriotism from whom no oracle ever came; now silent and aged; her deep-set eyes now sad, agleam with disappointment; never quite at ease with the crowd, whose cheers she loved; the colonel's daughter still.

She remained the colonel's daughter, in the sense that she knew her place and deemed it high, she took possession of the grand emotions and correspondingly large gestures. While she loved "the people," her love was of the kind that implies superiority to its object. Maud made a point of saying how much she loved the common people, how excited she felt among crowds, and she insisted that this was one of the differences between herself and Yeats. She thought it was good for him to be with people, even in committees and gatherings, but she knew he didn't take naturally to those scenes.

Yeats first met Maud Gonne, if his account of the event is accurate, on 30 January 1889. Maud always maintained that they had already met at John O'Leary's house in Dublin. Neither of them can be praised for historical accuracy. Here is part of Yeats's version:

> I was twenty-three years old when the troubling of my life began. I had heard from time to time in letters from Miss O'Leary, John O'Leary's sister, of a beautiful girl who had left the society of the Viceregal Court for Dublin nationalism. In after years I persuaded myself that I felt premonitory excitement at the first reading of her name. Presently she drove up to our house in Bedford Park with an introduction from John O'Leary to my father. I had never thought to see in a living woman so great beauty. It belonged to famous pictures, to poetry, to some legendary past. A complexion like the blossom of apples, and yet face and body had the beauty of lineaments which Blake calls the highest beauty because it changes least from youth to age, and a stature so great that she seemed of a divine race.

Yeats didn't know that Maud chose to live in Paris because she had contracted a liaison with a French political journalist named Lucien Millevoye. After the defeat of France in 1870, many Frenchmen of Royalist and Bonapartist persuasion gathered under the leadership of General Boulanger. Millevoye campaigned for Boulanger's National Party, and drew Maud Gonne into the cause by comparing Germany's treatment of France with England's treatment of Ireland. Maud joined him in making speeches, writing editorials, and causing as much stir as possible. Her style of oratory ran to somewhat loose comparisons between Irish peasants evicted from their homes and the people of Alsace and Lorraine, seized by Germany as the spoils of an unjust war. She always maintained that it was the eviction of Irish peasants that transformed her from an English colonel's daughter into an Irish rebel; and her most opulent flights of rhetoric were inspired by the vision of Ireland in famine.

Maud stayed with Millevoye for several years: they had a child, a boy, who died of meningitis, and in 1898 a girl, Iseult, who survived. The break with Millevoye came when he urged Maud to exert political influence by distributing her sexual favours. Meanwhile Yeats was in love with her, hopelessly: "my devotion," he said, "might as well have been offered to an image in a milliner's window, or to a statue in a museum." He wrote poem after poem, languishing, full of desire. Maud felt that in some spiritual sense she and Yeats were indeed married, but she declined every proposal of marriage:

> All I want of you is not to build up an imaginary wall of duty or effort between you and life—for the rest, the gods will arrange, for you are one of those they have chosen to do their work.

In fact, she never took Yeats's proposals seriously. Richard Ellmann has reported that there is documentary evidence that Maud and Yeats descended to the fleshly form of union briefly and after several years, but nothing has been published which would count as evidence. Meanwhile they shared visions, dreams, ideals, made occult experiments, read hermetic lore, and found reincarnation credible.

At the start, Yeats was deeply impressed by the image of this beautiful woman making high speeches in France and Ireland. She was immensely gifted in practical matters; she could influence or embarrass a politician, force concessions, press governments into acts of charity, make powerful people feel ashamed of themselves. But Yeats's admiration was reluctant. He didn't like to see women engaged in politics. He didn't like to hear them insisting upon their opinions. Beautiful women should be seen and not heard; and seen, ideally, as the constituents of a noble picture. Their significance should be indistinguishable from their beauty and charm. It was entirely proper for Lady Gregory to help in the creation of an Irish theatre: she was a talented lady, a great personality, but not beautiful; she could reasonably take part in a world managed by men. But Yeats always felt that such beautiful women as Maud Gonne and the Countess Markiewicz paid an exorbitant price for their fame, and destroyed themselves by fanaticism and rancour. When men fought for a cause, they kept some part of themselves intact. But when women fought, they turned their cause into an abstraction and their opponents into monsters. In "The Circus Animals' Desertion" Yeats says of Maud:

I thought my dear must her own soul destroy
So did fanaticism and hate enslave it.

It is hard to know whether Yeats arrived at this interpretation of Maud's career independently, or out of resentment: he was appalled when she married John MacBride, a man of no distinction in Yeats's eyes even though he had come back a hero from the Boer War. (Only when he was executed as one of the Easter Week leaders did Yeats see him transformed.) Maud listened to MacBride's exploits as eagerly as Desdemona to Othello's. He spoke of his fight against England and how the tactics of guerrilla war might be used some day in Ireland against the same enemy. Maud and Arthur Griffith urged MacBride to go on a lecture tour in America to raise money for the Irish cause in general and for Griffith's paper *The United Irishman* in particular. He undertook the tour, and Maud joined him there. Shortly after she came back to Paris, she became a Catholic, and a week later, on 21 February 1903, married MacBride. The marriage was a disaster—there was talk later of MacBride's violence and drunkenness—the only happy result of the union was the birth of a son, Sean, the pride of Maud's later years. The marriage ended in 1905, but legal process in France is a slow business, and Maud had to wait several years for a complete separation which gave her custody of her son.

On 21 January 1909, Yeats wrote in his journal:

We are divided by her religious ideas, a Catholicism which has grown on her—she will not divorce her husband and marry because of her church. Since she said this, she has not been further from me but is always very near. She too seems to love more than of old. In addition to this the old dread of physical love has awakened in her. This dread has probably spoiled all her life, checking natural and instinctive selection, and leaving fantastic duties free to take its place. I was never more deeply in love, but my desires must go elsewhere if I would escape their poison. I am in continual terror of some entanglement parting us, and all the while I know that she made me and I her. She is my innocence and I her wisdom.

Maud Gonne's duties were not all fantastic, though she had a flair for turning them into outlandish symbols. Everything she chose to do was a practical thing, like visiting political prisoners in Portland Jail, but she had a way of turning whatever she did into symbol and gesture, so that it nearly ceased to be finite: she cast a halo about her activities, and those who disliked her or envied her had an excuse for saying that she did everything for the sake of the halo. It was not true; her feeling was genuine, her charity, as Yeats said, was deeper than her hatred. It was simply that she made everything glamorous by attending to it. Some people asserted that she turned up at public occasions to show off her new bonnet. Yeats rejected this judgment, but he thought many of her activities compromised by an impure desire for power, pursuit "of mere effectiveness, or the mere winning of this or that election."

Yeats conceded that Maud's face showed little thought, but it made no difference, because her whole body seemed "a master-work of long labouring thought." He had a theory that beautiful women hate their beauty, not only because it demands constant service but because it calls for "the denial or the dissolution of the self." Presumably he meant that Maud used her beauty for its effect upon the people she confronted, but that she resented it because it imposed upon her a self different from the form of her desire. Yeats wanted such women to take their beauty as a sufficient cause, and to serve it as men serve the cause of freedom or justice or truth. He wanted them not to be beautiful as if by nature but to achieve beauty as if by the discipline of art. It was good for them to become actresses, because that meant devoting themselves to a laborious art, but it was not good for them to be orators and campaigners, because the procedures of public rhetoric were crude, and the crudest often the most successful. The criteria of art were fulfilled, for Yeats, when Maud played the Old Woman in *Cathleen Ni Houlihan* in April 1902. The play is set in Killala in the year of the French, 1798, and the Old Woman is Ireland. It is, as Yeats said, "the perpetual struggle of the cause of Ireland and every other ideal cause against private hopes and dreams, against all that we mean when we say the world." Yeats thought Maud acted the part magnificently and his opinion was widely shared; though it was also said that she acted magnificently because she played herself. Nearly forty years later, when she wrote her partial autobiography *A Servant of the Queen,* she recalled a vision she had experienced on her way home from a famine relief mission to Mayo:

> Tired but glowing I looked out of the window of the train at the
> dark bog land where now only the tiny lakes gleamed in the fading
> light. Then I saw a tall, beautiful woman with dark hair blown on
> the wind and I knew it was Cathleen Ni Houlihan. She was crossing
> the bog towards the hills, springing from stone to stone over the
> treacherous surface, and the little white stones shone, marking a
> path behind her, then faded into the darkness. I heard a voice say
> "You are one of the little stones on which the feet of the Queen have
> rested on her way to Freedom!"

She was always susceptible to metaphor and vision, and uncritical in their
reception. Her patriotism was genuine, but it had no place for critical
discrimination. She showed this limitation when she walked out of the
Molesworth Hall in Dublin during a performance of Synge's *The Shadow
of the Glen,* thinking the play an insult to the women of Ireland. She
disliked Joyce's *Portrait of the Artist as a Young Man* because its characters
were "nonentities." She shared the nationalist resentment against *The
Plough and the Stars* as a libel upon the men and women of 1916. These
limitations in her sensibility arose, I think, from the abstracting tendency
which Yeats saw in her hatred of England: her love of Ireland was so pure
that it could not accommodate anything that she construed as impurity,
any irony or satire directed upon Cathleen Ni Houlihan. The episodes in
her life which characterised her were simple in themselves and notable
only for their intensity: the most typical was the moment in 1918 when
she was arrested on suspicion of having a part in a "German Plot." There
was no such plot, but Lord French was ready to see one even where it did
not exist. Maud, the Countess Markiewicz, and Tom Clarke's widow
Kathleen, were arrested and imprisoned in Holloway. Maud was released
after six months because her health had deteriorated to the point at which
the authorities were afraid she would die. After a few months in London,
she slipped across to Dublin, illegally because she was forbidden to go
back to Ireland. She turned up at 73 St. Stephen's Green, her own house
but at that time rented to Yeats and his wife. Mrs. Yeats was ill, and Yeats,
terrified that the police would hear that Maud was in Dublin, refused to
let her in. It was an appalling episode between them: Yeats convinced
himself that Maud had "a pure and disinterested love of mischief," and
that she flouted the law for no other reason. Maud thought him a
coward. It took several years for the wounds to heal, if they ever healed.
Maud's later life was a disappointment to her, even though it included

the years in which Sean emerged as a formidable politician in the republican tradition. On the question of the Treaty, she believed that Lloyd George's terms betrayed everything that she and her nationalist friends had worked for, but she knew that rejection would lead to civil war. So she remained as close to neutrality as her temper allowed. But in practise she was a Republican like her son: when Cosgrave's government arrested republican Irishmen, she organised committees to look after their wives and children. She never forgave Yeats for accepting from Cosgrave's hands a seat in the Senate. When he won the Nobel Prize, she did not congratulate him. In January 1923 she was arrested and imprisoned in Kilmainham: she went on hunger-strike, and was released after twenty days. She went back to her work for the Women's Prisoners Defence League, and to the street-politics she loved. When De Valera came to power, Maud hoped for better things, but he disappointed her; he didn't tackle the question of Partition, and he outlawed the IRA. In 1936, Maud ran for election to the Dail, and got a miserable vote. In 1938, she published *A Servant of the Queen* and made at least technical peace with Yeats. He died on 28 January 1939. Maud was then seventy-two. She was still ready to speak out, usually in defence of republican prisoners. When Sean McCaughey went on hunger-strike in April 1946, she wrote to *The Irish Times* demanding his release and the release of his colleagues in Portlaoise. In 1948, De Valera lost the election, and the first Coalition Government—an improbable conjunction of men, it must be said—was formed, with Sean MacBride as Minister of External Affairs. Maud continued to do what she could. She recorded three talks for Radio Éireann with the uplifting titles "Innisfail the Isle of Destiny," "Innisfail and Her Golden Age," and "Innisfail and the Figure 3." The point of that last talk was Maud's notion that Ireland was about to produce a third Golden Age, associated with the ideal of Peace. That was in 1951. She died on 27 April 1953.

O'Casey in His Letters

"And oh! dear Sean, don't be too belligerent!" Mrs. Bernard Shaw advised Sean O'Casey in a letter of 27 August 1931. O'Casey refused to accept the advice:

> God be my judge that I hate fighting. If I be damned for anything, I shall be damned for keeping the two-edged sword of thought tight in its scabbard when it should be searching the bowels of knaves and fools. I assure you, I shrink from battle, and never advance into a fight unless I am driven into it.

But he told more of the truth to Harold Macmillan a few years later when he sent him the typescript of *The Flying Wasp*:

> Everything I have written, up to the present, has been "combative," and the sword I have swung so long is now stuck to my hand, and I can't let go.

The letters show that the sword spent very little time in its scabbard. O'Casey was the most quarrelsome writer in Ireland, a notoriously quarrelsome country. Joyce, Yeats, Synge, Lady Gregory are paragons of patience in the comparison, and Shaw a model of forbearance. George Moore is the likeliest contender, but second best after all.

"Though a quarrel in the streets is a thing to be hated," Keats said, "the energies displayed in it are fine; the commonest man shows a grace in his quarrel." I see what he means, though I am not convinced, unless we are determined to distinguish somehow between the energies displayed and the brawling lout who displays them. Reading O'Casey's letters and rehearsing their quarrels, we have to hold simultaneously in our minds the sense in which his energy is fine and the sense in which its occasions are pathetic. It is appalling to see him denouncing anonymous reviewers, correcting errors in the *Sheffield Independent,* setting the record straight in some wretched school magazine. Many of his letters to newspapers were not published, not because they were dangerous but because they were tedious, merely essays in spleen. He could not bear the popularity of his contemporaries: Charles Morgan one day, Noel Coward the next. He was disgusted by the success of *Love on the Dole.* Though an avowed proletarian, he cultivated the bourgeois vice, envy.

Of course the world annoyed him. His later plays were not welcomed, he was never paid enough, he was insulted in Dublin, Limerick, Boston. But his real troubles came from within. He lived to the brittle old age of eighty-four, but his career as an important dramatist came and went within five years. A man who writes *The Shadow of a Gunman* in 1923, *Juno and the Paycock* in 1924, *The Plough and the Stars* in 1926, and *The Silver Tassie* in 1928 should have the luck to continue writing good plays or the prudence to withdraw into dignity and silence while the going is so good. But O'Casey lapsed into wretched plays—think of *The Drums of Father Ned* as one of many—hysterical essays, purpled reminiscences, blasts against the world, benedictions lavished upon communism, atheism, Welsh nationalism.

The letters enact the quarrels in dismaying detail, beginning with O'Casey's first drawn blood in 1912 when, sacked from his job in the Dublin station of the Great Northern Railway, he replied by publishing six denunciations in *The Irish Worker.* The Dublin tram strike in August 1913 gave him not only an opportunity but a vocation. Thereafter he quarrelled with everyone: with Countess Markiewicz for her membership of the Citizen Army, Fergus O'Connor for rejecting his verses, Liam O'Rinn for wrong-headed notions on the compulsory teaching of Irish, Oliver Gogarty for a review of *I Knock at the Door,* Malcolm Muggeridge about the Moscow treason trials in 1938, M. J. Dolan for his production of *Man and Superman,* Mrs. Sheehy-Skeffington who attacked *The Plough and the Stars,* Walter Starkie for his part in rejecting *The Silver Tassie,* George Russell for his views on art, Kingsley Martin for refusing to publish a letter in *The New Statesman,* Yeats for failing to appreciate the *Tassie.* Some of these were good causes, only a coward would have kept silent, but on many occasions silence would have been the right answer. What was the point of trading insults with James Agate, especially if you were likely to be defeated by that master of the genre? ("I am too busy to start a row with Mr. O'Casey, I therefore merely refer him to certain laws governing this question of generosity in criticism laid down by Sainte-Beuve; Mr. O'Casey's secretary will doubtless know the passage.") Or the point of attacking unimportant people, like poor Canon Sheppard whom O'Casey pursued beyond the grave? "The commonest man shows a grace in his quarrel." Not necessarily: O'Casey mainly showed a determination to keep himself exacerbated, outraged, violated.

Still, the letters make a moving spectacle. The waste of spirit and feeling is terrible, but it is impossible to remain unmoved in the presence of such a victim. It matters little that O'Casey brought much of his suffering upon himself or that he insisted on adding his own contribution to the misery God gave him: bad health, useless eyes, no education, no money, no patience. The sole consolation he retained was eloquence. It was never eloquence of the highest quality. Even in the three major plays there are shoddy moments in which the eloquence betrays itself as the form of energy that never knows when to stop. O'Casey's vice of style was the "nimiety, or too-much-ness" that Coleridge ascribed to German philosophers and nearly everybody ascribes to Irish literature. Too much, too loud: O'Casey played all his tunes *fortissimo.* Shaw was right about his style. In 1919, O'Casey sent him the manuscript of a little book, *Three Shouts on a Hill,* composed of three essays on Irish labour, nationalism, and the Irish language. He asked Shaw to write a preface, but Shaw declined: "I like the forward and the afterword much better than the shouts, which are prodigiously overwritten." O'Casey accepted the refusal, but he did not take to heart the comment on his style. In an otherwise colourless life he needed the colour of his prose, the only Mardi Gras he ever enjoyed. He turned the malice of circumstance into a rhetoric of success, vicariously killing his enemies and promoting his friends. Language was a more accommodating home than anything available in Dublin, London, or Devon: in that home he was sole master.

David Krause has done a good editing job on the letters, presenting them with as much elucidation as any reader is likely to need, but I wish he were more judicious in commenting on O'Casey's quarrels. He is always on O'Casey's side, he sees no evil or folly in his hero; everybody is out of step but our Sean. He says that Yeats "disgraced himself and his theatre" by rejecting *The Silver Tassie*. This is an ancient charge, and it is still nonsense. Yeats made a critical error in rejecting the play, but the published correspondence shows that he was scrupulously honest in reaching his decision. It was absurd of O'Casey to say that Yeats and Lennox Robinson had decided to reject the play before they had even received it. It was ludicrous to think that the situation was properly met by mailing insults to Yeats: "You seem, Mr. Yeats, to be getting beautifully worse, you astonish me more and more, there seem to be shallows in you of which no one ever dreamed." The strongest argument against Yeats and his colleagues in the Abbey is that *The Silver Tassie*, whatever its faults, was demonstrably superior to many of the plays the Abbey had already accepted. But Yeats's judgment of the play is formidable, and not at all foolish or shallow. Robinson and Lady Gregory agreed with him, but O'Casey reserved most of his rage for Yeats. For several years he could not hear Yeats's name or advert to his poetry without rushing to display the old scar. When Yeats published *The Tower* in 1928, O'Casey read it as a labour of hate, and sent a grotesque account of it to Gogarty. Eventually he forgave Yeats, but he never forgot an injury.

The first volume of the letters brings a painful but touching story to 1941, the second to 1952, the third to the end, O'Casey's death in 1964. I find myself recalling Yeats's lines from "Remorse for Intemperate Speech":

> *Out of Ireland have we come.*
> *Great hatred, little room,*
> *Maimed us at the start.*
> *I carry from my mother's womb*
> *A fanatic heart.*

O'Casey brought his Ireland with him, and held on to its rancour wherever he happened to be: London, Devon, New York. He was always the man who was sacked from his first job.

The New Republic, 26 April 1975.

FRANK O'CONNOR

I knew some of Frank O'Connor's stories long before I read them. We were living in Warrenpoint, and my father bought a radio—a wireless, as it was then called—so that he could keep up with the news of the War. I couldn't wait to have the wireless delivered, so I pushed a tea trolley across the town and collected the most impressive piece of furniture we were ever to own. We installed the machine and transformed our lives. News of the War was not as memorable as "The Long Road to Ummera," a dramatized version of O'Connor's story, which I heard on Radio Éireann. Sometimes a story was read without change, sometimes it was turned into a little play. I can't remember now in what form the wireless gave me O'Connor's "In the Train."

To hear O'Connor's words without seeing them is an appropriate experience. On the page, they are meant for the ear. O'Connor was always a storyteller. Any of his stories might begin, as one of them, "The Late Henry Conran," does: " 'I've another little story for you,' said the old man." O'Connor never pretended that words came directly from the voice that spoke them, or that they didn't pass through the speaker's mind and the language available to him before coming into their own state, but he wrote his stories, changed them, gave them a different emphasis, a different phrasing, mainly to enhance the reader's sense of listening to a storyteller's voice. In O'Connor's stories the truth of a character is in the telling, the voice, the rhythm.

Frank O'Connor's given name was Michael O'Donovan, son of Michael and Minnie O'Donovan of Cork, where he was born in 1903. A mother's boy, he was estranged from his hard-drinking father, and many years passed before he persuaded himself to make peace with the old man to the extent of calling the second volume of his autobiography *My Father's Son*. Cork was important to "Michael Frank," as Mrs. Yeats liked to call him, but Sligo, where he worked as a librarian for a few years, gave him an even more complete experience of Irish provincial life. In his study of the novel, *The Mirror in the Roadway* (1956), he said that "to have grown up in an Irish provincial town in the first quarter of the twentieth century was to have known the nineteenth-century novel as a contemporary art form." He went on: "The suburban road where we took our walks was the Nevsky Prospekt; Madame Bovary lived across the way." Sligo, even more than Cork, showed him what a small town in Ireland is like, letting him see and hear its conventions of manner, affection, resentment, pride, and vanity.

As a librarian, O'Connor read the books he handled: poems, to sharpen his native sense of language, the relation between speech and silence; but mostly novels and stories, especially the fiction of the nineteenth century: Jane Austen, Stendhal, Dickens, Balzac, Gogol, Thackeray, Turgenev, Flaubert, Tolstoy, Dostoevsky, James, Hardy, Chekhov. One of his stories is called "A Story by Maupassant," because he construed the incident from which it arose in terms he learned by finding them in Maupassant. As for the twentieth century: O'Connor was never at home in it. He read Proust, Lawrence, and Joyce, but with the admiration that is consistent with suspicion and a determination to go a different way. Modernism interested him as something to keep well away from. He distrusted every technique except the ones he inherited from the nineteenth-century masters and, according to his own light, practised. He never doubted that reality was what his eyes and ears told him it was. He did not think that memory and imagination were one and the same, but he had little time for any form of imagination that could not be verified by paying attention to what people did and said.

O'Connor tried his hand at nearly every literary form, but he is most accurately known as a short-story writer. William Carlos Williams used to say that every writer has his own way of breathing: some take long breaths and plan for scale, others short breaths and write to a different rhythm. O'Connor regarded the difference between the novel and the short story as only incidentally a matter of length, scale, and capacity: the real difference, he thought, was in implication, and the rhythm of implication. The novel refers to a world in which it is possible, however difficult, to live: it implies continuity, latitude of possibility, space to breathe. The short story may offer the same implication, but it rarely does: in common practise, it presents life mainly in the form of constraint and through the feelings of tramps, widows, spoiled priests, monks, and only children. O'Connor's affection for the short story speaks of his affection for marginal people, men withering, caught in the duress of circumstance and passion.

But he made distinctions only when he needed them, he was not an assiduous theorist of the art he practised. It was enough for his purposes to think that a short story was the sort of thing you could imagine someone telling you: an anecdote, a reminiscence, told with enough verve to do it justice and enough care to maintain the decencies in its favour. The stories O'Connor liked satisfied these obligations: Joyce's "Ivy Day in the Committee Room," Katherine Mansfield's "Prelude," Lawrence's "Tickets Please," Babel's "The End of the Old Folks' Home," Kipling's "The Gardener," Liam O'Flaherty's "Fairy Goose," Mary Lavin's "Frail Vessel," Salinger's "For Esmé—with Love and Squalor."

Of the several constituents of a short story, O'Connor was most tender toward characterisation. Never indifferent to plots and actions, he was more impelled by a twist of character than by a turn of events. His stories are always implicit in the characters to whom they happen. Circumstance may be fate, but only if fate is indistinguishable from character: chances and coincidences are allowed to bring out only what is already in the character; otherwise the story is rigged. The narrator produces the story, discloses the truth a character could not disclose himself. The character performs his truth, short of knowing it. Often the narrator is in the centre of the story, or close enough to the centre to see the value of what happens there. He is not required to be gifted beyond the talent of seeing the relation between a character and what he does or suffers. That is enough. O'Connor never fusses with omniscient narrators. Enough is better than too much.

The Collected Stories brings together sixty-seven stories, a collection so choice that it would be nice to know who made it. No editor is named. Richard Ellmann's Introduction is charming and informative, but it does not indicate whose good taste has been at work in choosing the stories from many more that could have been picked. Since O'Connor died in 1966, his widow, Harriet, has been tending his work, choosing, for instance, the largely unknown stories recently published as *The Cornet Player Who Betrayed Ireland.* The present collection, the best of a lifetime's work, is presumably her choice. If so, it is carrying modesty too far to withhold her name.

O'Connor's strength, in the best of these stories, is his generosity. Knowing what duress means, and the penury of experience available to most people, he has always wanted to do his best for them, to show the quirky doggedness practised by people who live on the margin. He was not a satirist. Among his contemporaries in Irish fiction, Sean O'Faolain and Liam O'Flaherty are far harder than O'Connor in their accounts of modern Ireland. Among his juniors, Mervyn Wall and James Plunkett have a sense of Ireland far more astringent than O'Connor's. A genial man, O'Connor set his geniality aside only under extreme provocation, and he longed to return to his native mood. He was hard only on people who were soft on themselves.

If he has a weakness, it is a tendency to mistake whimsicality for charm. Like Synge and other writers, O'Connor wrote an English that remembered the Irish it displaced. Many of his phrases are translated from Irish into an English which they render more exotic than their occasion can well sustain. In the weaker stories, like "Song Without Words," what corresponds to the exotic dialect is a whimsical relation to the characters and events. Reading "Song Without Words," I find it hard to avoid thinking of O'Connor's Brother Arnold and Brother Michael as leading eventually to Bing Crosby and Barry Fitzgerald in *Going My Way,* and to their cloying charm.

But it is a minor blemish, all told. At his best, there is no one like O'Connor; at his best, as in "The Bridal Night," "The Long Road to Ummera," "Peasants," "The Majesty of the Law," and another dozen stories just as good as these. I have particular affection for "The Long Road to Ummera" but I suppose Warrenpoint and the wireless have given it even brighter radiance than it deserves. In sober moods I enjoy "The Majesty of the Law" more than any other story of O'Connor's, not only for its humour but, more than that, for its delicacy and tact. When the policeman leaves Dan Bride's house, the long conversation over, and then comes back as if he had forgotten to mention a minor matter hardly worth mentioning (to serve a warrant), I can hardly distinguish between his tact and O'Connor's.

Walter Benjamin says in his essay on Leskov that people think of a storyteller as someone who has come from afar. O'Connor's best stories put the same thought into our heads; how far, in some imaginative sense, he has had to travel to achieve such a sense of life and to accomplish it with such flair.

———————————

The New York Times Book Review, 20 September 1981.

SEAN O'FAOLAIN

The first volume of Sean O'Faolain's short stories brought together seven from *Midsummer Night Madness* (1932), fourteen from *A Purse of Coppers* (1937), and thirteen from *Teresa and Other Stories* (1947). The second has ten stories from *The Stories of Sean O'Faolain* (1958), eleven from *I Remember! I Remember!* (1961), and ten from *The Heat of the Sun* (1966). In the Preface to the Penguin *Stories of Sean O'Faolain* (1970), he said that thirty stories were all he had to show, or all he was content to show, for more than thirty years of story-writing. One thinks, he said, of George Sand turning out volume after volume while never once neglecting a love affair, never missing one puff of her hookah. Well, no matter, O'Faolain has done many other things and written many other books besides his collection of stories. He has been, he is still, a man of letters, a novelist, biographer, autobiographer, historian, critic. But his short stories have a special place in the affections of those who care for good writing.

I should declare an interest, or a prejudice. I much prefer his later stories to his earlier ones. Many of the earlier stories sound as if they were written not only to charm the birds out of the trees but to show that Sean O'Faolain could charm them out of the trees. The reader is forced to believe that life in Ireland was simpler, more beautiful, nobler then than now, that the people were a nest of simple folk, richly expressive, articulate, eloquent, that the grass was greener, the rain softer, the mackerel-crowded seas more mackerel-crowded than any seas a man of my age can describe. It may be true. You're born in Cork in 1900, you grow up with the new century and with a sense of an equally new Ireland. In the dawn of Easter Week some youngsters, including O'Faolain, probably felt it was bliss to be alive, even though Eoin MacNeill was countermanding Pearse's orders and a revolution was dwindling into a revolt. Still, when Republicans were roaming through Cork and Tipperary shooting at the Black and Tans, it was possible to feel heroic. But it must have been hard to feel heroic in the Civil War and the years that followed. Yet O'Faolain's early stories want you to feel that life in Ireland was always a romance and sometimes an epic. I have never been convinced. I'm an agnostic in these sentiments. I don't believe that O'Faolain's early luscious style represents his effort to be equal to the rich occasions he describes. I believe, rather, that the style came first, and demanded incidents, landscapes, and sentiments fit for the style to live in and to adorn.

O'Faolain may agree. In the Preface to the Penguin book, he says that as a young man he was very romantic, that his style took pleasure in such words as "dawn," "dew," "onwards," "youth," "world," "adamant," and "dusk." I could extend the list, but it is already long enough to make the point that his early stories never say "colour" if they can say "hue." He started writing seriously in 1927, several years after "Prufrock" and *The Waste Land* and *Ulysses,* but his taste was still that of Palgrave's *Golden Treasury.* University College, Cork, Daniel Corkery's place, was slow to receive the good news from Eliot, Pound, Mann, Kafka, Valéry, and Joyce. Yeats was inescapable, but there was nothing in Yeats to discourage a young writer from preferring "hue" to "colour." O'Faolain, living among words, chose for company the words he thought were already poetry. Looking back in 1970, he thought the most romantic of all his words were the "and" and "but" which he used "to carry on and expand the effect after the sense has been given." The writer who luxuriates, he says, "goes on with the echoes of his first image or idea." His emotions and his thought "dilate, the style dilates with them, and in the end he is trying to write a kind of verbal music to convey feelings that the mere sense of the words cannot give."

Take, for instance, "Fugue," which O'Faolain wrote in 1927: he thinks it his first successful story—in fact, "a very lovely story." And it is. "I wish I felt like that now," he said in 1970. Which I take to mean: I wish

I were young again, with feelings that chimed with my free-floating style. "Fugue" is about two young men on the run from the Black and Tans: one of them is killed, the other survives to tell the tale and turn it into lyric poetry. The story includes a lonely house, a woman, fear of dying, and landscape strikingly receptive to the hero's desire. It stays in the mind as a very lovely story, and so long as I'm not forced to believe it, I am content. But I don't believe it:

> At last I came upon a lonely ruin upon the mountain, three walls, and I lay on the lee side of it while the rain dripped on me from the remnants of its eaves. When I awoke a dim radiance lit the falling haze, but whether it was the dawn or the sinking moon or any hour past three or before three I could not say. No sound was to be heard: no living thing moved: no bird stirred the wet air: the falling haze made no sound. I rose chattering and trembling, and my feet splashed through the wet earth and the drowned grass, and when I halted there was quiet. I crossed a little stone wall and one of the stones fell with a mighty sound. I might have been the last human creature to crawl to the last summit of the world waiting until the Deluge and the fortieth night of rain would strain him upwards on his toes while the water licked his stretched neck.

I started losing faith with "No sound was to be heard...," its four carefully separated "no's" lovely enough to be loved but not to be believed. Losing faith, I started distancing myself from the rhetoric, and finding the story not in Inchigeela but in Literature. The encounter with the dark woman seemed to come straight from Synge's *The Shadow of the Glen,* the loneliness, the desire, and I was not surprised to find the story ending with a poem in eight lyric stanzas and a word from Yeats: "The dawn moved along the rim of the mountains and as I went down the hill felt the new day come up around me and felt life begin once more its ancient, ceaseless gyre."

The trouble is that O'Faolain, on his hero's behalf, is trying to make me feel more, and more tenderly, than anything the story compels me to feel. He is eking out the story, dilating it as with "and" and "but," in the desperate hope of leaping the gap between the lyrical reach of his style and any merely finite effect the story can have. The style is in excess of any event or sentiment he can remember or imagine for it. It remains a lovely story because we feel in it the void between the hero's feelings and anything the world might offer him to appease them. My trouble with the story is that I believe the endlessness of O'Faolain's desire, because it corresponds to the strain of his style, but I don't believe in his hero as anything but a function of the author. He is not, as we used to say, a real character.

The problem is not merely O'Faolain's: it arises in writers of far larger capacity and greater genius than his. In Conrad, as a special but not unique case: F. R. Leavis has argued in *The Great Tradition* that often in Conrad's fiction, and not merely in *Heart of Darkness,* he tries "to impose on his readers and on himself, for thrilled response, a 'significance' that is merely an emotional insistence on the presence of what he can't produce."

O'Faolain's early stories have two problems, which often merge. There is the large, general problem of Romantic Ireland. In the first years of the twentieth century it was impossible for a young writer to see Ireland "as in itself it really was": he saw it only through a veil of associations, ancient pieties, sagas not entirely forgotten. Corkery's "hidden Ireland" had to be recalled, disclosed. Romantic Ireland called for heroic emotions or, in defeat, elegiac emotions: either way, styles extraordinarily high and grand. The particular version of this general problem, for O'Faolain as a short-story writer, was to imagine characters and situations large enough to contain not only the "object" but the halo, the aura, that already surrounded it, the words that were already poetry, if only bad poetry. His early stories rarely succeed in finding such characters, such situations. So the narrative style has to force the characters to feel more than they could really feel, consistent with the probability the stories claim. The result is that there is always a remainder of sentiment which has to be added, as if between the words, to satisfy the demands of a rhetoric greedy as if by nature. O'Faolain's patriots, young warriors, priests, all those mothers, all their sons, are well enough, but not quite good enough for the rhetorical work they are forced to do.

These problems may explain why so many of O'Faolain's stories show their characters caught in the coils of memory. The past is another country, and memory gives not only free access to it but a further transforming power endlessly ready upon need and desire. It follows, in O'Faolain's early stories, that most of his characters live on their memories while they die otherwise. *I Remember! I Remember!* is the best of his titles, though not the best of his books, and it is all the better, all the richer, when you remember, even vaguely, how the poem goes: "I remember, I remember / The house where I was born, / The little window where the sun / Came peeping in at morn." Morn, yes. Indeed, O'Faolain's flair for memory, and the flare of his memories, were so vivid that he must often have been tempted to proust his way through the Ireland of his childhood and let his art live on that pleasure. But he hasn't yielded, as some of his colleagues yielded. There is a sense in which Frank O'Connor stayed, imaginatively, in the towns of his boyhood, and let the new Ireland mind its own grubby business. Liam O'Flaherty, too, wrote as if his first experiences were definitive and could only be lost if pestered by later matters. Michael MacLaverty, a gifted and largely forgotten writer, nearly broke my heart with a beautiful book, *Lost Fields,* one of the first books I recall caring for. But again he stayed where he started: perhaps the experience of childhood and boyhood was too cherished to admit a rival or the fear of a lapse.

In these respects, O'Faolain has been strong where his colleagues have been timid. He has written well of the mandatory themes, childhood, mothers, first confessions, priests, monks, young girls, but he has forced his art to pay attention to an Ireland which has often disappointed him as a citizen. The stories he has written since 1945 have cast an ironic but not a cold eye upon Dublin, its upper-middle-class life, its lawyers and doctors, the remnants of Ascendancy Ireland, their marriages, their mistresses. This is a Dublin that found its symbol not in a desperate revolt proclaimed from the General Post Office but in a referendum that decided, by a huge majority, that Ireland would indeed join the EEC and grow fat on German money. It has not worked out quite as intended, but for several years the farmers lived high on grants from Brussels, and laundered money kept upper-middle-class life, in Dublin and the smaller towns, as luscious as the wildest dreams of a bourgeois time.

O'Faolain's imagination has kept up with the European Ireland: he has been writing of diplomats and their foreign affairs, of lawyers and their tiresome girlfriends, of Catholics good but mostly bad, of priests and bishops wise in a world they have not made and can't control, of emotions provoked by foreign cities (Turin, called Torino) and dragged back, excess baggage, to Dublin. There is a daring story called "No Country for Old Men" about two cronies, pals from the old IRA days, who make the crazy gesture of taking up Republican arms again and going North. The story doesn't quite convince, mainly because there is a rift—the old problem—between the action and the sentiment. As they try to escape South, the two pals talk of nearly everything under the sun, including the discrepancies between the *Faust* of Goethe and of Gounod. I wish I could believe in such conversations, and feel their latitude, but I can't. "In the Bosom of the Country" is far more convincing in its rambling narrative of sex and religion: as in most of these later stories, the affair has nothing of Grand Opera in it, but an uncertain charm and, inevitably, an undramatic end.

The end of the affair is O'Faolain's later theme, as his earlier one was the conflict between duty and feeling, heroic zeal and the vagary of desire. "I Remember! I Remember!" is a risky story, and I can't quite believe that O'Faolain's Mary Carton would have read Stendhal's diaries and remembered an entry about true feelings leaving no memory. O'Faolain, yes, Mary Carton, no. In the most recent stories, O'Faolain has got over such difficulties by ascribing the stories to a highly qualified narrator, a Jamesian man of the world who has seen, among many things, Bronzino's portrait of Lodovico Capponi in the Frick. The story in which this experience is invoked is "Charlie's Greek," a wonderful story, one of O'Faolain's finest achievements. Imagine a man, a charming rascal, who accounts for the end of an affair by tracing a graceful circle with his hand and saying "we had completed the medallion of our love." It is entirely convincing. I believe in Charlie and feel that I have known him for twenty years, every evasive gesture is persuasive. When he gives the girl what purports to be his telephone number, he chooses one in high standing, taken from a popular book called *I Did Penal Servitude,* by "707070." It is a very lovely story in its way, and very funny, the comedy of Byronism exactly caught and held.

The most famous story in the second volume is "Lovers of the Lake," about two lovers, one of whom, the woman, suddenly decides to do the pilgrimage of fasting and discomfort at Lough Derg. The pilgrimage, which might have been ignored or set aside as a whim, an eccentricity, comes between them, and the affair is wrecked. It is an odd story, dangerously garrulous on occasion, but I have long admired the art of it. O'Faolain's lovers are either too young or too old, they never fully coincide with themselves or their time. They are always decent people, and the feelings they express and act upon are genuine, but they are never exactly the feelings they need at the time. At another time, or in another country, the same feelings would answer beautifully, but in these stories there is a fated disjunction between the feelings and what their tenants need. They need different feelings—poorer or richer, it would not matter.

O'Faolain's attitude to his lovers is tender, rueful, sharp at times but only when an even more extreme sharpness would be fair. His heart is kind, but not soft: no fool where emotions are in question, he is never taken in by the charm he allows his lovers to express. There are no really evil, wicked people in his stories: some are vain, pretentious, silly, but O'Faolain doesn't find satisfaction in observing malice. So, while he is often ironic toward his characters, and agile in detecting their follies, evil is not his theme. He is not a satirist. "I still have much too soft a corner for the old land," he confessed in the Penguin Preface. It is true. In the years after the War, he was much occupied with public issues, the question of censorship, for an irritating instance, and he showed that he could write wounding prose when his ire was up. But that was in polemical vein. In his fiction, he is always ready to see the other side of the situation, and to feel the hidden motives. I mention, as if evidence were necessary, such stories as "A Meeting," "The Confessional," "Unholy Living and Half Dying," "Shades of the Prison House," "The End of a Good Man," "Passion," "Childybawn," "Lovers of the Lake," and "Charlie's Greek."

Thirty? Yes, I could name them, or as many, though they might not tally at every point with O'Faolain's choice. The differences would be slight. To write thirty successful stories, in an extremely competitive art (look at V. S. Pritchett's recent *Oxford Book of Short Stories,* and think of all the stories he had to leave out), is a rare and exhilarating achievement. I salute a master.

The London Review of Books, 4–17 February 1982.

AUSTIN CLARKE

ustin Clarke's repute was a local affair until the publication of his *Ancient Lights* in 1955. Till then, he was regarded as a mildly interesting poet who had not survived the fact that Yeats thought little of him and preferred F. R. Higgins and several other poets. News of *Ancient Lights* was carried beyond the Irish Sea in time for the reception of *Later Poems* in 1961. It is widely agreed that the early poems are worth reading only to see from what improbable source the later poems emerged; or to see how a poet may be submerged by a context unworthy of him. It is also agreed that Clarke moved into his stride only when anger made him a satirist. This was my own impression, too, until I went through the poems again on the occasion of the *Collected Poems,* but I am now convinced that the paradigm is inaccurate. Many of the early poems are indeed tedious. I cannot imagine myself ever again reading *The Fires of Baal* (1921). Only a remarkable sense of duty would send me back to *The Vengeance of Fionn* (1917) and *The Cattledrive in Connaught* (1925). But there are a few good poems in *Pilgrimage* (1929) and the first, premature *Collected Poems* (1936). The first major achievement is not *Ancient Lights* but *Night and Morning* (1938). In fact Clarke's true work is *Night and Morning, Ancient Lights, Too Great a Vine* (1957),

Flight to Africa (1963), *Mnemosyne Lay in Dust* (1966), and a few good poems in an otherwise not very good book, *The Echo at Coole* (1968). The first really memorable poem in the big book is "Celibacy," from the 1929 volume, and with the "Six Sentences" from the first *Collected Poems* Clarke found his voice. He showed himself quite capable of losing it again; there are dozens of later poems both false and *falsetto,* but "Celibacy" and the "Sentences" stand in the *Collected Poems* of Clarke pretty much as "Adam's Curse" stands in the complete Yeats, the place where the reader hears a genuine poetry as distinct from verse merely going through its motions.

A few facts, to begin with. Clarke was born in Dublin on May 9, 1896, and he died there on March 19, 1974; his body was cremated in Belfast, because Dublin lacked a crematorium. A child born at 83 Manor Street is a Dubliner whether he likes it or not. Clarke liked it enough to scatter Dublin street-names throughout his poems, and he always cared enough for the city to be enraged by its folly. His satires are the work of a city poet: his invocations of rural landscape are regularly praised, though not by me. In his apprentice years Clarke went Yeats's way, writing long poems, reciting "the thousand tales of Ireland," and generally proceeding on the assumption that the best way to become a poet was by writing like a Yeatsian poet, at great length. Major influences on Clarke included Herbert Trench for his *Deirdre Wed,* George Sigerson for his recourse to Irish sagas, Thomas MacDonagh for his interest in Irish metres and their relation to a recognisably Irish mode of feeling. Clarke's sense of these matters was far more precise than Yeats's, and I surmise that he committed his talent to these enterprises in the desperate hope of evading Yeats's melody. An Irish poet who published his first long poem in 1917 would have to sell his soul to Yeats or take care to keep out of his way. Clarke's care took him to the Gaelic metres, a safe place because Yeats had no ear for them.

No Yeats, then, if Clarke could help it; but he couldn't help it enough. It is harder to understand why Clarke ran away from Eliot, Pound, the Imagists, the modern French poets, and nearly everything of any force in the new poetry. "Too often I poo-poohed his poems," Clarke wrote of Pound in a late poem, but he never bothered with the "gawky stranger from Idaho" until America charged him with treason. As for Eliot, Clarke's poems show no sign of having attended to *Prufrock and Other Observations* or *The Waste Land.* No Hardy, either. Hopkins, yes, there is evidence of "The Wreck of the Deutschland" in Clarke's ear. But there is no evidence of a sustained relation between Clarke's mind and modern poetry in any of the forms in which it has continued to be audible. He was interested in poems other than his own if they offered him solutions to metrical problems, but normally he taught himself to write by working through the Gaelic poems. He made progress in the art by making mistakes and then correcting them. It took him a long time to discover that he was not created to be an epic poet. Belatedly, he divined that God was trying to tell him something, and then he found that he had something to tell God, namely that he no longer believed in Him, and now resented the expense of spirit in having believed. *Night and Morning* is the magnificent result of those communications, a poetry of faith and fractures, resentments, misgivings, strivings:

> *Knuckle and knee are all we know*
> *When the mind is half despairing.*

In "The Straying Student," Clarke writes of the fleshly siren who drove him from his prayers:

> *They say I was sent back from Salamanca*
> *And failed in logic, but I wrote her praise*
> *Nine times upon a college wall in France.*
> *She laid her hand at darkfall on my page*
> *That I might read the heavens in a glance*
> *And I knew every star the Moors have named.*

That is Clarke at his best. But in 1938 he turned aside from that better self and went into the theatre, under the delusion that he was a playwright: he spent the next fifteen years working with the Dublin Verse Speaking Society and writing verse plays for the Lyric Theatre Company. It was a waste of time and spirit. Clarke was not a playwright. He may have fancied himself Yeats's rival in the theatre, but Yeats survived the feebleness of his early plays to write the *Plays for Dancers* and *Purgatory*, achievements far beyond any of Clarke's. Clarke thought for a time that radio was the coming thing, and that audiences would then be pleased to hear grand syllables recited in the theatre. So the real achievement of *Night and Morning* stayed in abeyance until 1955 and *Ancient Lights*. An appalling suspension of talent; like the chores Clarke had to take on to make a living, reviewing books for *The Irish Times,* producing a weekly poetry programme for Radio Éireann. He did these things very badly because he couldn't bring himself to put even half his mind to them. The reviews were disgracefully slack, a few rambling paragraphs; the radio programmes were tolerated because very few people listened to them and the Irish Government did not then give poets Civil List Pensions. Still, these activities are bad marks in Clarke's copybook, he could have done them well rather than badly: well done, they would have been an inspiration to youngsters in Ireland, not a disgrace. Clarke's sepulchral manner was tedious, and it gave people the impression that poetry, high-mindedness, and low spirits were somehow connected by nature. In the event, he discovered his true power only when he gave himself to bitterness, resentment, and carefully remembered wrongs. In life as in his poetry, there was an enormous gap between the best and the worst of him. As a "local complainer" he was tireless and therefore tiresome. Thank God he was a poet, too.

As a poet, Clarke was fascinated by possibility: it was enough for him that a linguistic act was possible, he did not ask that in addition it be necessary. His mind was full of homonyms, puns, *rime riche,* assonance. He loved making verbs from adjectives: "fierced," "futured," a car "wealthied by," in *Mnemosyne Lay in Dust* (1966) Maurice "feebled against his holders." He loved to make verbs from nouns: stags antler the wind, New York dollars the sky, the sky-blaze noons at Padua. Puns: if it's a liar, it must be a lyre too. *Rime riche:* "sapphired" sparks off "staff fired," "Voltaire" brings the possibility of "volt tear," lightning tearing silence. A question put to a French prostitute, *"Combien?"* is answered not only by *"vingt francs"* but by Maurice wondering "would her comb be an / Ivory one"; "bamboozled" is led by the nose to "bamboo-celled." No marks for the next one: "What woman would rue so / Dearly the pen of Rousseau." And try this for Saigon:

> He heard,
> Far off, phantoms
> Of Buddhist monks,
> Still burning, sigh: "Gone!"
> As he left Saigon.

"Vilified" is nearly always "villafied," especially when Clarke is sneering at Dublin's suburban pretensions, but also in "A Centenary Tribute" when he writes of revisiting Yeats's house at Riverdale:

All had been changed: the stone steps, railings hauled
Away: new side-porch to that Victorian
House: memory of the past evicted.
Contemporary fashion was villafied
Inside.

Sometimes the obsession pays off. A few years ago a cathedral was built in Galway, at enormous expense. If you let your tongue play with "Galway" and then with "gall" you might, with luck and Clarke's talent, come up with this:

Here is the very spirit
Of hard-drinking, sea-mouldering Galway:
A building ugly as sin
To prove the Boys sincere
And still a decent crowd:
Another thorn for the Crown
Of Thorns, a large gall
In the Sponge on Spear.

We judge these procedures by their results, the cackling does not matter if it signals the arrival of an egg. Clarke was not given to ambiguity, certainly he did not seek impressions of indefinitely wide reverberation. He liked his words to have several distinct meanings running happily together but he wanted each meaning to know its own mind and not to confuse itself with its neighbour. He liked to juggle and to keep the meanings simultaneously aloft. His style was not agglutinative, he kept the lines clean, each pointed toward its destination: if a word served two masters, well and good, but Clarke wanted to know each master's name, keeping the record straight. Homonyms pleased him because their meanings went about their business, they did not confound each other, but he took their existence as a good omen and inferred from their proliferation that a poet could still live free:

For something has happened to this eye,
Since it discovered homonyms.
All things shine now, all have nimbus,
Nature displays nimiety;
Though dampness lodge the grain,

> *Vague shadows move around in greyness,*
> *A cloudy lid hide Ireland's Eye.*

Lid: both a man's eyelid and a lid of cloud closing upon Ireland's Eye, a rocky island out from Howth. But each meaning goes its own way, the eyelid turns back to the first line while the other lid settles upon the rock: two meanings for the price of one, nothing is gained by crushing them together. The same goes for homonyms.

But there is more to Clarke's homonyms than that. There is plenty of evidence for associating them with nimiety, natural excess, freedom, but they are more powerfully associated in Clarke's poetry with the freedom of sexual fantasy. Clarke is an erotic poet, and I would be ready to argue that his high jinks in language are related to standard speech as freedom to constraint: sexual freedom, mostly. Homonyms give their speaker a double life, not one life amplified but two separate lives, prosaic and poetic, conventional and exotic, the daily life and the life of fantasy. I call in evidence this passage from "More Extracts from a Diary of Dreams":

> *Why should the aged be unhappy,*
> *Mope in the dark, when the unhappenable*
> *Is theirs and they can glide between the shades*
> *Of meaning in a dream, talk to the shades,*
> *Unchaperoned, watch every jog of nature*
> *That proves the midnight merriment innate—*
> *Fire in the great vein—and when desire has chased*
> *After high boot and bulging stays, be chaste?*

Between the shades: I thought he was going to say "between the sheets." Irish readers find a pun in "the midnight merriment," a reference to Brian Merriman's lusty poem *The Midnight Court*. But consider "chased" and "chaste," riot followed by continence as in the old Morality plays: here the double life. In the poem "Impotence" the word "verb," word for action, means (in its second life) the act of sex:

> *Now that I am almost impotent,*
> *Thought faltering four times out of ten,*
> *And only patience can be tender,*
> *Regular verb is in the past tense.*

Homonyms, when verbs, are both regular and irregular. A few lines later we read how "sinew was tense," and then as the sexual activity gets going the word "fast" becomes a homonym meaning the quickened love-act and the penitential fasting:

> *each second fast*
> *And faster still, we broke our fast*
> *Then sank into a sudden pit,*
> *Knowing that love is but a pittance.*

In some poems an entire line may become a homonym, regular and irregular, the one a constraint, the other a release; as in the last line of "Penal Law":

> *Burn Ovid with the rest. Lovers will find*
> *A hedge-school for themselves and learn by heart*
> *All that the clergy banish from the mind,*
> *When hands are joined and head bows in the dark.*

Homonyms are crucial in Clarke's poetry because he loves to find one sound releasing two words; all the better if one of the words stays at home and obeys the rules while the other one runs wild and makes love upon whim and desire. This points to the dominant motif in Clarke's work, the life of freedom and impulse set against the law of institutions. Since Clarke was an Irish poet, the hated institutions were the Church and State: or rather, the New Church and the New State. His morality is represented by the epic grandeur of the old Irish sagas, "the Irish Gods, who were coarse and mirthful," the stories of Fionn, Diarmuid, and Grainne: later, by the gaiety and freedom Clarke undertook to find in the Irish Church before the Council of Trent. In *The Vengeance of Fionn*:

> *Friend, friend, a song of laughter and of tears,*
> *Of the glad sunlight and the glittering spears*
> *Of springtime rain, my fights and wanderings*
> *Conquest and love and sleep.*

In "The House in the West" the women are pleased by the "laughter, the music and chess-playing." In "Over Wales" Clarke from an aeroplane looks down upon the country, thinking "how Pyll or Gereint had pursued / Big game through forests with pike and gauntlet." Instead of tridentine discipline, an old mythology: Clarke is constantly setting modern Ireland against sweet ceremonies he ascribes to our forefathers. "Eire, clamant with piety" is shamed in the eyes of our epic heroes: we have sold our souls to Brussels, the EEC, America, the Church, the State. England need not have bothered imposing an Act of Union, we have enslaved ourselves:

> *Freedom*
> *Waits, feeble, dumb, for*
> *The gallows rope,*
> *When we are europed*
> *From nape to toe-nail,*
> *Scheduled, natoed.*

The rhetoric is clear enough. In politics we have gone for the mess of pottage. In love we have allowed the Church to pervert us with prohibitions. In poetry we have lost the homonymic freedom of language.

This is only to say what most of the later poems are about. The themes are limited, God knows. I have never known a poet to get more mileage than Clarke has got from the vagaries of the Catholic Church in Ireland, or the vagaries (no less) of our political masters. He is not, indeed, a disinterested witness. His reaction against his early years, his Christian Brothers education and the priests at Belvedere College, was sufficiently violent by itself: it was intensified by the fact that his mother, giving him a house to live in, willed it to the priests after his death:

> *This house cannot be handed down,*
> *Before the scriven ink is brown,*
> *Clergy will sell the lease of it.*
> *I live here, thinking, ready to flit*
> *From Templeogue, but not at ease.*

But Clarke has made the priests pay for it, in poems of extreme nastiness. In "Living on Sin" he maintains that money paid by the state for the rearing of illegitimate children "gives many a nun her tidy bed, / Full board and launderette." In several poems he sneers at religious belief, Lourdes, miracles. In "Right of Way," a particularly ludicrous example, he blames the priests for the suburban sprawl of Rathfarnham:

> *Outlawed by greed, I look down from the Bridge,*
> *Remembering our covetous religion.*

As for our politicians, Clarke thinks they have done nothing but tear down old mansions and crawl into the EEC. His political sense allows him to report upon a brief trip to Yugoslavia:

> *Here no slums,*
> *No beggars, unemployed or wretched poor,*
> *A happy land.*

This was at last, he declares of Yugoslavia, "the happy land / Which Blake and William Morris saw in visions."

Clarke could be just as silly as anyone else, then, when he mouthed things he knew nothing about or took the easy way of hatred: "Hatred's, that well known Irish firm of Contractors." He was evasive and insecure in thought. Nothing in life was allowed to change for the better. If Irish education was nothing but tears and strife in 1903, it must stay that way for Clarke in 1955 so that he can present the priests as obsessed with corporal punishment, "sins against purity," the letter of the Law. Clarke likes to have his ducks sitting, his targets stationary. He is not good with the idiom of process and change. A born satirist, though he was slow to construe his nature, he needs as the objects of his attack things that will stay impaled till he comes to them; or at least he must deal with them as if they were in that condition. Priests must remain "the punishers in black robes." In "The Flock of Dawn" Clarke writes:

> *Satire owns to pride*
> *And poetry is what we dare express*
> *When its neglect has been personified.*

Personified, exactly. Everyone who irritated Clarke was treated as the personification of some horrible Law or Principle. If he stumbled, it meant that he was pushed, probably by the Clergy. He could never distinguish between contingency and law, causalities and symptoms. Reading Clarke, I am reminded of something Richard Blackmur said of William Carlos Williams, that it never occurred to him that reality is other than immediately contingent and equal to the actuality: "sometimes by grace of insight, it is equal; more often, by the fouler accident of mere observation, it is not." Clarke went in for these foul accidents, so he often gives the impression of sitting in Templeogue, a fractious journalist, writing acrid "Letters from Dublin" to some minor newspaper. Poetry is not, after all, synonymous with a sluggish liver.

I am making a fuss about Clarke's dyspepsia to account for the fact that his true work amounts to quite a small list of poems and that he wrote too many poor poems for his reputation's good. The superb poems include these: "Celibacy," "Six Sentences," "Night and Morning," "Mortal Pride," "Tenebrae," "Martha Blake," "Repentance," "The Lucky Coin," "The Straying Student," "Penal Law," "Her Voice Could Not Be Softer," "Summer Lightning," "The Jewels," "Marriage," "Ancient Lights," "The Loss of Strength," "St. Christopher," "Martha Blake at Fifty-One," "Japanese Print," "New Liberty Hall," "The New Cathedral in Galway," and "In Kildare Street." Maybe it was good luck that brought Clarke on these occasions themes so compelling that he was forced to suspend his tricksiness and attend to them. Here are a few lines from "Martha Blake at Fifty-One":

> Waiting for daily Communion, bowed head
> At rail, she hears a murmur.
> Latin is near. In a sweet cloud
> That cherub'd, all occurred.
> The voice went by. To her pure thought,
> Body was a distress
> And soul, a sigh. Behind her denture,
> Love lay, a helplessness.

These are what Blackmur called—missing them from Robert Lowell's poems—loving metres. The elaborate links of internal rhyme and assonance are not made for tricks but for an unrighteous propriety of cadence; the feeling moves into the words and is cared for there. Clarke loved assonance because it "takes the clapper from the bell of rhyme," and he delighted in cross-rhymes and vowel-rhyming, separately, one or more of the syllables of longer words, on or off accent, so that "lovely and neglected words are advanced to the tonic place and divide their echoes." In the lines I've quoted, the internal rhyme links the priest's Latin as it goes by at the Communion rails with Martha's soul, disembodied, a sigh. The cadence is so fully in possession of the feeling that it can accommodate, without the least touch of condescension, Martha's denture as well as the Communion wafer.

If I had to choose one of Clarke's poems, it would be "Martha Blake."

A few mechanical details about the *Collected Poems*. Liam Miller has brought together all of Clarke's verse-books, including the notes which Clarke added when the references were too local to be generally understood. In fact the notes are not as numerous as they should be. Readers outside Ireland are not likely to make much of these lines in "Over Wales"—

> *Passengers read the news:*
> *Singer, the Common Market—turn the pages—*
> *Hire purchase. Shipping. Ford strike for better wages.*

—unless they know that Paul Singer was a famous con-man who pulled off a swindle on the sale of stamps. It doesn't make much difference, but it makes some. The poem "Drumcondra" won't mean anything to a reader who doesn't know that the former Catholic Archbishop of Dublin, Dr. J. C. McQuaid, had his palace in Drumcondra and is reflected upon in the poem as "old Dracunculus." In "At the Dail" the last lines—

> *Above, a tattered Union Jack*
> *Proclaims the haughty rule of Jack-boot*

—make better sense (if no better charity) for a reader who knows that the Jack is Jack Lynch, then our Taoiseach. Clarke's later satires are full of such references, some of them explained, some not.

The New Review, August 1974.

BAIR'S BECKETT

I f you were to read Samuel Beckett's books in the spirit in which they are apparently written, you would not necessarily shoot yourself: if the author has not resorted to the gun, the reader is under no obligation to exceed him in logic or virtue. But you would imagine not only the possibility of your suicide but, more prudently, a change of values by which your normal sense of life would be reversed.

Most of us regard life as, on the whole and with whatever degree of qualification, a good thing rather than a bad thing. We also think of value as plenitude of experience, diversity, a certain liveliness of circumstance. But suppose you were to regard life as chiefly an unchosen evil, a long disease, a boring farce: it would follow that the less you had, the more tolerable your situation. Plenitude would be replaced by penury of experience, attenuation of fellowship, the reduction of daily life to those constituents which a recluse would find congenial: enough food to keep body and soul together, peace, silence, shelter, isolation. Instead of trying to have life more abundantly, you would insist upon having it barely, and on your own choice terms. You would conduct your life by the strategy of negation and good riddance. If something offered itself to your interest, you would exorcise it; like Beckett's Watt, who got into the habit of evolving, "from the meticulous phantoms that beset him, a hypothesis proper to disperse them, as often as this might be found necessary." In *The Unnamable* the compulsive voice banishes all the Murphys, Molloys, and Malones who impeded the only act worth performing—the reduction of expression to its smallest possible form as a preparation for the boon of silence.

The philosophical tradition in which this attitude is praised is not popular, but it is respectable: its motto is that "never to have been born is best." To be cast out of the womb is a disaster. Deirdre Bair reports, in her biography of Beckett, that he once attended a lecture in which Jung said, of a little girl who was brought to him for treatment, that "she had never been born entirely."

Beckett regarded his own birth not only as a disaster in principle but as an incomplete or bungled affair in fact, a mess consistent with the universal mess of human life. Bair has much to say of Beckett's mother-fixation, and I find it persuasive. Clearly, the relation between Beckett and his mother was dreadful, and while she was obviously a tedious, whining woman, she hardly deserved the resentment visited upon her by her son. Beckett's relation to his father was amiable enough and some-times even cordial: he reserved for his mother the venom and then the guilt a more judicious man would direct against life itself. But a mother is only an immediate provocation, the true cause of Beckett's sense of life was his feeling that mind and body were mutually alien.

Suppose this metaphysical notion were taken seriously: suppose you really felt that your mind and your body were separate and hostile forces. Then suppose you identified your true self with your mind, and thought your body a jailor. Such a structure of feelings would certainly result in a general passivity, suppression of the will, the negation of action in favour of indolence, immobility, Oblomov's way. You would reduce life to its basic gestures; doing nothing, waiting, passing the time, letting one damn thing happen after another.

Beckett found philosophic justification for this attitude partly in Descartes, then in Descartes's disciple, Arnold Geulincx, who maintained that since a man can only control his mind he should not waste any time or energy trying to control the external world, which includes his body. Action is transferred to the mind: the logical attitude to everything else is passivity, indifference. But Beckett did not need a philosopher to tell him how to live; his own knowledge, such as it was, was native to him, an aboriginal temper.

Deirdre Bair's account of Beckett's childhood and adolescence is not an essay in psychiatric explanation. She is decorous in such matters. A reader is free to take or leave the mother-fixation and to decide that Beckett's indolence and drunkenness amounted to nothing more than an artist's reaction against a stuffy, bourgeois home in upper-class Foxrock. All the ingredients are available: Foxrock, afternoon tea on the lawn, respectability on every side, Portora, Trinity College, the decencies of Anglo-Irish Protestantism.

Bair provides most of the facts, and leaves the reader to assemble them according to his favourite principle. The precise relation between life and work is left open. Certainly there is a strong autobiographical element in Beckett's writings from *More Pricks than Kicks* (1934) to *Play* (1964). The scene in *How It Is* (1964) where a mother teaches her child to pray is clearly drawn from Foxrock. *Endgame* is, among other things, an "abstract expressionist" version of Beckett's marriage. "I say it as I hear it": this phrase, a constant motif in *How It Is,* does not mean that Beckett takes dictation from life, contingency, or even from the Furies. But it is true to his creative spirit, which never disengages itself completely from childhood and the pain of growing up. In *Endgame* when Clov says, "Do you believe in the life to come?" Hamm answers, "Mine was always that." So was Beckett's, as Bair relates; he was always waiting, in distinguished silence and hauteur, for someone to notice him and publish his books. Meanwhile his life was fertile in vicissitudes.

Reasonably, Bair's biography is mainly concerned with Beckett's life: she is not a literary critic, her account of his art is rudimentary. She spends most of her pages reciting external events, chances, misfortunes, arrivals and departures. Beckett's friendships are duly narrated; mostly with Joyce, Thomas McGreevy, Nancy Cunard, Richard Aldington, Alfred Peron, Jack B. Yeats, Peggy Guggenheim, and Jack MacGowran. When discretion is required, Bair is discreet: an occasional lover is allowed to remain anonymous. Beckett's wife seems to have taken no part in the biography and remains in the shadows: when she is mentioned, the tone of the narrative becomes severe. Time will be more informative than Bair on these and a few other matters.

But on one matter, Bair's narrative is as copious as any reader could wish it to be. I was vaguely aware that Beckett's life has been plagued with illness, but I had no idea what a wretched plague it has been: compounded of boils, cysts, constipation, insomnia, and latterly glaucoma in both eyes. No wonder Beckett often associated himself with Samuel Johnson and tried to write a play about him.

Bair narrates the long disease of Beckett's life, but she does not discuss the bearing of illness upon the question of body and mind. Illness makes it impossible for the sick person to detach his mind from his body. Pain deals hard with such a conceit. But if you were of Beckett's party in the general question of body and mind, you would reject the body more violently than ever, if you suffered from his ailments and survived them. I am guessing now; but if you think of body as ignominiously sick and wretched, and surround it with the general mess and malice of life, you find it easier to understand a man who withdraws as much as possible into his mind and fills it not with things but with the sounds of things, echoes, reverberations, tones, and silence. A mind thus beleaguered would find relief only in Language—as his body would find it in drink. "Words have been my only loves, not many." Many enough, indeed. Reading Bair's biography, I am more convinced than ever that the only thing Beckett really loves in life is Language. "It's here words have their utility the mud is mute"; and on the next page of *How It Is,* "a word from me and I am again I strain with open mouth so as not to lose a second a fart fraught with meaning issuing through the mouth no sound in the mud." The only tolerable part of the bad job of life is Language; the rest is need— body, drink, sex, sleep, things taking their course. No sound in the mud.

Samuel Barclay Beckett was born on Good Friday, April 13, 1906, if we take his word for it. Bair thinks the true date is May 13, and she is severe with his pretension in claiming to have been thrown into the pit of life on Good Friday. The evidence is inconclusive. Beckett's early life was, like Foxrock, extremely dull; Boswell could not make such years interesting. Beckett made what he could of his late adolescence in *More Pricks than Kicks,* but it is not much. Indeed, his life did not transcend the limitations of suburban debauchery until he committed himself to Paris in 1937 and determined to make himself a writer. Bair's account of the Parisian years is extremely interesting, and she is even more rewarding on the war-years which Beckett and his consort Suzanne Deschevaux-Dumesnil spent mainly in Roussillon. After the War, when they went back to Paris, Beckett took up the dreary struggle to write and the even drearier struggle to be published.

Bair's detail on these matters is relentless, and properly so: after reading these chapters we renew our sense of what "waiting" meant for Beckett. Hugh Kenner has suggested that *Waiting for Godot* had its origin in occupied France when the *maquis* would have to send clandestine messages which might or might not be delivered: if not today, tomorrow for sure. But even in Beckett's professional life, waiting was evidently an experience to be borne with indifference masquerading as patience. Beckett's official stance was that the writing was everything, its reception a matter of no significance; he affected indifference to success and pronounced himself more interested in failure. Bair does not go into the question of his sincerity in this attitude, presumably because she believes that he is sincere in everything. The stance is, on Beckett's part, reasonable enough. The crucial relation was between himself and his work; between his imagination and the mess and mud of things. Still, he wanted to be heard, or at least he wanted to have his books published, if only for the relief of secreting himself in them. We are to believe that success meant little or nothing to him. I recognise the logic of that position, but I see no good reason to think that Beckett's public success, starting with *En Attendant Godot* in 1952 and including the Nobel Prize in 1969, was a matter of indifference to him, even though it also meant that he was pestered by critics and journalists.

The most impressive aspect of Bair's book is that she managed to write it at all. When she approached Beckett in 1971 with a proposal to do his biography, he told her that she could do whatever she liked, he would neither help nor hinder her. In the event, he must have helped. Many details in the book could only have come from him.

The book is well worth having. If nothing else, it will help to take away the mystification surrounding Beckett's life, while leaving the mysteries where they belong, in the works he has written. There is an element of Garbo in Beckett, ostentatiously determined to be let alone. There is no harm in it, I suppose.

Magill, September 1978.

THE YEAR OF THE FRENCH

In Irish history the year of the French is 1798, when the French after several failures succeeded in landing soldiers on the northwest coast of Ireland. On 22 August, a force of 1,099 French officers and men landed at Kilcummin Strand, five miles west of Killala in Mayo. Those men were supposed to be the first troops of a major French invasion. If the winds had been favourable and the French as fully committed to an Irish invasion as the Irish were led to believe, thousands of French soldiers would have joined with Irish rebels and driven the English into the sea.

This did not happen. The rebels were untrained and unarmed. The French under General Humbert knew that they were outnumbered by the English under Lord Cornwallis and General Lake. Still, the English were routed at the first battle in Castlebar. There were skirmishes at Killala, Ballina, Tobercurry, Collooney, and Granard. Lake defeated Humbert at Ballinamuck, and the Irish, led by Ferdy O'Donnell, were broken at Ballina. By 23 September, it was all over. The French who surrendered were sent home, but many of the Irish rebels, guilty of treason, were imprisoned and executed. The year of the French was only a month.

Thomas Flanagan's novel tells the story of that month, so far as it affected the lives of the people of Mayo. But it also recites the events as they bear upon Irish history. The narrative really begins in 1791, when a Dublin barrister, Theobald Wolfe Tone, mindful of American success in revolution and glowing with the fervor of the revolution in France, founded the United Irishmen to free Ireland from England by force of arms.

In 1793, England was at war with France. On December 21, 1796, Tone's attempts to persuade the French to invade Ireland seemed successful: on that day, a French fleet of thirty-five ships and 1,200 men reached Bantry Bay. But a storm prevented the ships from landing, and they were driven back to France. On May 24, 1798, Irish rebels started their own rising in Dublin, Wicklow, and Kildare. Within a few days the fight spread to Carlow and Wexford: by the first week of June, it had broken out in the North, where Tone's colleague Henry Joy McCracken led his men in Antrim and Down. By July, the rising in the South had ended in defeat at Vinegar Hill, and the northern rebels were beaten at Ballynahinch.

When the French landed at Kilcummin, they were joined by Irishmen of two kinds: United Irishmen and Whiteboys. The Whiteboys were not interested in revolution or current events in France, they wanted to destroy the landlords who had evicted their tenants and driven them from reclaimed land. The United Irishmen were true revolutionaries, animated by a vision at once Irish and European. The Whiteboys have been discussed in prose, but the United Irishmen have dominated the popular poetry of Ireland. Nineteenth-century Irish poetry is pervaded by the vision of French and Irish joining to make Ireland free of the English. In *Ulysses,* as in Flanagan's novel, Ireland, personified as the *sean bhean bhocht,* the poor old woman, is recalled in her song:

> *Oh, the French are on the sea,*
> *Says the Shan Van Vocht,*
> *The French are on the sea,*
> *Says the Shan Van Vocht,*
> *Oh, the French are in the Bay,*
> *They'll be here without delay,*
> *And the Orange will decay,*
> *Says the Shan Van Vocht.*

The last stanza asks and answers the only question:

> *And will Ireland then be free?*
> *Says the Shan Van Vocht;*
> *Will Ireland then be free?*
> *Says the Shan Van Vocht.*
> *Yes, Ireland shall be free*
> *From the centre to the sea;*
> *Then hurrah for Liberty,*
> *Says the Shan Van Vocht.*

The folklore of Ireland has never forgotten that song. In *Ulysses*, Mulligan explains to the Englishman Haines how the Martello tower in which they are living came to be built: "Billy Pitt had them built [Buck Milligen said] when the French were on the sea." In the "Cyclops" chapter, when the Citizen exults in the vision of Irish freedom achieved with the aid of "our greater Ireland beyond the sea," Ned Lambert says, "we are a long time waiting for that day, citizen"; "since the poor old woman told us that the French were on the sea and landed at Killala." "The French!" says the Citizen: "Set of dancing masters! They were never worth a roasted fart to Ireland." In *The Year of the French*, the voice of History is not as spirited as the Citizen's in *Ulysses*, but when Flanagan's poet Owen MacCarthy sings the song of the Shan Van Vocht, the rueful United Irishman Malcolm Elliott says that if the French are on the sea, "it's because it suits them."

The Year of the French is the first novel Flanagan has published, but not his first book. In 1959, he published *The Irish Novelists 1800–1850*, a study of the fiction of Maria Edgeworth, Lady Morgan, John Banim, Gerald Griffin, and William Carleton. While working on that book, he evidently read more Irish fiction than any other scholar before or since. He was sustained, I imagine, not only by an interest in Ireland far beyond the call of a scholar's duty but by his feeling that the historical material might be turned to a fictional account; that something good in that way might be done which had scarcely been done since Carleton's *Traits and Stories of the Irish Peasantry* (1830–1834).

One of the many novels Flanagan discussed in *The Irish Novelists* is Banim's *The Croppy*, which deals with the rising in Wexford in 1798. But a more immediate source of Flanagan's novel is probably *The Memoirs of Richard Lovell Edgeworth* (1820), begun by Edgeworth and completed by his daughter Maria. A passage in the *Memoirs* tells how Edgeworth and his daughter rode to Ballinamuck a few days after Cornwallis had defeated the French and the Irish there. The French, as Flanagan mentions in *The Irish Novelists,* had been granted amnesty, "but the Irish had been bayonetted almost to a man, and their bodies lay in heaps upon the ground." The Edgeworths and their journey to Ballinamuck become a splendid chapter in *The Year of the French.* I have a sense, reading the novel, that over the years the passions and confusions of 1798 have become living presences in Flanagan's mind. He shows no sign of entertaining the modern misgivings about history, or doubt about the validity of historical writing. The landing at Kilcummin is deemed an important moment in the story of Ireland, and privileged for that reason.

The first chapters of the novel deal with conditions leading up to the invasion. Wolfe Tone is said to have offered the French "a sullen and discontented island sailing on England's flank, a peasantry armed with pikes and aching for insurrection, a wide-flung revolutionary network controlled by radicals." These chapters are recited by an impersonal narrator, the voice of history uttering its disinterested truth. Most of the later events are conveyed from different points of view and in suitably different styles. In certain chapters we hear the voice of history not in complete impersonality but as it yields itself to a particular character: it may be the historical Wolfe Tone; it may be John Moore (an ancestor of the novelist George Moore), a member of the Catholic gentry who was seen as a traitor to his class when he went over to the United Irishmen; or it may be the wholly fictional poet Owen McCarthy who hovers on the edge of events, the observing, word-mongering poetic soul of Ireland, who is finally executed by the British. Still other chapters narrate the events through fictitious documents, such as *An Impartial Narrative of What Passed at Killala in the Summer of 1798,* by Arthur Vincent Broome, the local Protestant minister in the novel.

These devices make for variety in a long novel: the several points of view keep the reader sensitive to the proportions of ignorance and knowledge in any account of an experience. Another effect is that the characters and events in the novel are held at a certain distance, as if to prevent the reader from having only an immediate relation to them; he is to see them not only as they were but as they have become. I imagine, too, that Flanagan was reluctant to produce his characters when they had nothing to show for themselves but their bewilderment: he chose to let them stay in the shadow until they had come to understand the various forms of darkness in which they had lived.

I assume that this is what it means for Flanagan to be a historical novelist: every event, every character has a dual existence in which past and present are diversely engaged. The reader is not gripped by the events as they occur; his concern is drawn to the events as they have occurred, and to the stain of outrage and desolation they have left upon the people who suffered them. Mostly we come upon the events when their form and consequence have already been assessed. There is a certain loss of immediacy, because our interest is not allowed to fasten upon a character as distinct from his role in the story as a whole.

But there is a gain in the depth and resonance of the characters; when we meet them, they have already been changed by their experience. Broome, for instance, is given to us not when he is in the throes of his suffering but when he has survived it; his tone of bewildered care shows that he has been transformed, driven far beyond the range of qualities he would have produced as the local Protestant minister in a peaceful town. We are interested in him mainly for what he has been through, and for the generosity of his vision, flawed as it is:

> I know myself to be vain and affected when I bring Gibbon to mind as I turn the pages of my own poor narrative. Against the enormous fall of mighty empire, I set a squabble in a remote province, a ragbag army of peasants, files of yeomen and militia, ploughboys hanged from crossroads gallows. And the chronicler is but my poor self, a confused clergyman with an indifferent education, a lover of comfort and civility and buttered toast. How confident and false now sounds to me my opening chapter, where I would be the Gibbon of Mayo, setting forth the contending parties upon the eve of conflict, the several social classes, the topography, the weathers. . . . Yet now my words lie dead upon the page, like blackened hulls upon the sands.

Each event is seen not only in its immediate light but in the light of the idea it embodied or humiliated: the mediations issue from Flanagan's sense of modern Irish history, the shapes it has taken in his mind.

It is my impression that Flanagan organized the novel in this way not chiefly for the pleasure of managing several viewpoints and styles but to ensure that the conflicts of class, religion, tradition, and self-interest would be disclosed and interrogated. Impartiality is achieved by admitting to the narrative several different forms of partiality. If, as Walter Benjamin remarked, history is invariably recited in favour of those who have won, Flanagan is alert to the fact that in Ireland the narrative of history is still indecisive. His rhetoric does not say that we Irish are brothers under the torn skin, or that our differences are the kind that reasonable people could sink. But the many different attitudes in the book at least reveal in the characters motives far more diverse than those proclaimed by our warring ideologies. Given a favourable wind, the book might do something to make the antagonists a little ashamed of themselves, but I do not expect such a wind.

Flanagan's part in the novel deserves a few words. He does not speak in his own person; nor does he identify himself with the voice of history. In one sense, he does not come into the book at all; but in another he is pervasive. Most readers will feel, as I do, that the novel is handsomely written, but the urge to remark upon its prose arises from the fact that the book is very much a written thing. We are made aware of the writing, not because the sentences are histrionic or self-regarding but because a pervasive unity of tone suggests that ultimately the prejudices of each style may be reconciled. Since each viewpoint is acknowledged, it is allowed to speak for itself and given an appropriately positive style: one man, one rhetoric. But the tone of the whole book is also felt as issuing from a certain perspective, and the perspective must be pretty high if it is to accommodate every viewpoint decently. None of the styles is transparent, because none can be given the privilege of appearing to issue directly from the events, undarkened by prejudice. Even the voice of history is allowed to sound troubled.

The organisation of Flanagan's novel is an act of rhetoric: that is the main point. Prejudices can be entertained only by a style which runs to a certain grandeur of implication: decency, like the historical novel, requires a certain latitude of sympathy. But I must admit that Flanagan favours a rather high style even for the daily purposes of scholarship. He likes a rich mixture of tropes. In a sullen mood, you would accuse him of fine writing: even in a genial mood, you would sometimes tremble for the safety of his soul, so ardently given to the webbing of words. At the end of *The Irish Novelists* there is a sentence which incorporates one of Yeats's most flashing phrases, without quotation marks, as if Flanagan thought the poet's rhetoric indistinguishable from his own:

To understand the Ireland which shaped two such different men as Yeats and Joyce, one must move back, as we have done, beyond the thronging murmurs of the Dublin streets, beyond the waste of the empty decades, beyond the fields and valleys swept bare of all life, beyond the final delirium of the brave.

A writer is not under oath in the last few paragraphs of his book. Flanagan takes notable risks and evidently enjoys surviving them. In the novel, he insures himself against a sullen reader by ascribing most of the lush passages to the poet MacCarthy. A poet who comes from the Irish bardic tradition, bringing not only Irish poetry but Ovid and Virgil, can get away with nearly any excess: drink, lechery, high talk. But there are also high passages in which the normally impersonal narrator leans down and gives a helping hand to a character supposedly in need of such assistance. Here is a description of Ellen Treacy, fiancée of the rebel leader John Moore, riding home to Bridge-end House:

> On a rise of ground from which she could see the distant bay, she stopped and sat motionless, the reins slack in her thin, capable hands. The bay was empty, not a sail or a hull in sight, the water lifeless and grey. History had come to them upon those waters, three foreign ships riding at anchor, filled with men, muskets, cannon. History had come ashore at Kilcummin strand, watched by fishermen standing beside their huts. Poetry made actual. Not her mother's, not Goldsmith or *The Seasons* by Mr. Thomson. "Now the soft hour of walking comes for him who lonely loves to seek the distant hills." That other, older poetry inscribed on sheets of parchment in her father's study, the black letters of an alphabet remote from English, with prophecies of ships from France, gold from Spain, the deliverance of the Gael. History, poetry, abstractions, words which had transformed and shattered her world.

I would not want a word changed. But I would find it hard to refute the charge that "poetry made actual" is Flanagan's perception, not Ellen Treacy's, and that the invocation to History is Flanagan or the Voice of History putting notions into Ellen's simple mind. It is ventriloquism, a sullen reader would say. Or it is Flanagan drawing Ellen Treacy toward the high perspective of his narrative style, lest some of her remote possibilities remain undisclosed.

Flanagan's knowledge of Irish history, mythology, religion, and local customs has coloured his narrative, but it would be absurd to ask him to bleach his style or pretend that he knows less than he does. When his poet MacCarthy says, "You were slaves on this land before Christ was crucified," a reader may recall that the last phrase turns up in Yeats, who received it from Frank O'Connor, who translated it from the Irish. The recollection doesn't matter, we are not playing the flat historic scale. Only one passage in the novel seemed wrong to me: a bout of military talk, two soldiers mouthing obscenities in Castlebar in 1798 which I would find convincing if ascribed to soldiers in Belfast today. For the rest, while the styles are rhetorically daring, I find them justified or at least justifiable. And there are hundreds of passages in which the question of risk or justification doesn't arise, they authenticate themselves.

The novel ends with the fictitious diary of the local schoolteacher, Sean MacKenna, in the summer of 1799. The French invasion and the battle of Castlebar are already moving from fact into mythology. The three French ships that landed at Kilcummin are now fancied by a local peasant to have "masts so tall that you could not see the tops of them and on the tallest mast of all was an eagle called King Lewis." The eagle, so they say, went with the soldiers into the midlands, "but on the night before the battle the eagle flew off and the battle was lost." Flanagan implies that we must go back through lore and mythology to find the motives, noble and shoddy, which provided the events and the need to transform them into poetry. But he is not cynical, he lets the reader see how natural it is that events are transformed out of need and desire. The facts are not to be thought away, but they cannot be transfixed, arrested in their nature; the novel recognises the need to transform them from their own nature into ours, so that they become at last indistinguishable from ourselves.

Such facts as these persist, and are invoked at the end of Flanagan's novel. In November 1798, Wolfe Tone committed suicide while waiting to be executed. In the summer of 1800 the English persuaded the Irish Parliament to vote itself out of existence. Catholic Emancipation was not included in the Act of Union between Great Britain and Ireland which became law on January 1, 1801, but it was in the haunted air. Meanwhile, those prisoners who had not been executed were transported to the West Indies and Botany Bay. There was a plan to send some of the United Irishmen to America, but President Adams would not have it, they were too dangerous. Nelson's victory at Trafalgar in 1805 ensured that the French would never again try to invade Ireland. The next phase of Irish history was concentrated upon Catholic Emancipation, with O'Connell its leader. Yeats despised him but "a people sheltered within his voice," as *Ulysses* concedes.

The New York Review of Books, 14 June 1979.

HEANEY'S SWEENEY

Scholars take particular care of a literature when it is on the edge of being lost. In the later years of the nineteenth century, Irish scholars translated the remnants of a literature that only a few Irishmen could read. On the spur of those translations, Yeats wrote *The Wanderings of Oisin*, Lady Gregory published *Cuchulain of Muirthemne*, and a generation of Irish writers resorted, not at all incidentally, to the readiest method of distinguishing themselves from their English rivals. Translations of the Old-Irish sagas, and Standish O'Grady's *History of Ireland*, enabled Yeats to invoke a traditional body of myth, lore, and sentiment which he could represent, with a show of rhetorical force, as essentially Irish. The fact that it was demonstrably different from anything proposed by modern English literature was its first merit.

Recent Irish writers have gone back to the ancient Irish literature, but in a different spirit—partly in the hope of circumventing Yeats and silencing his incorrigible voice. Yeats didn't speak or read Irish, so he couldn't submit himself to its literature as to something different from himself. Inevitably, the stories of Oisin, Cuchulain, and Niamh sound as if they were written by Yeats in moods now heroic, now languid. But suppose these stories could be recited by a writer fully at ease in the Irish language, in a spirit not stridently revisionist but free of Yeatsian necessity. By Frank O'Connor, as a case in point; a writer whose Irish gave him far more direct access to the literature than anything Yeats could manage.

O'Connor showed what might be done and how a writer could, in the same breath, avoid imitating Yeats's idiosyncratic splendour. Thomas Kinsella's translation of the *Táin* and of the poems Sean O'Tuama gathered a few years ago in *An Duanaire* has so commandingly freed itself from the Yeatsian mode that its independence hasn't needed to be declared.

Seamus Heaney has never been in danger of enslaving himself to Yeats, but he has taken care to avoid the occasion of that folly by putting himself under Patrick Kavanagh's protection. I don't share the general admiration with which Irish readers have read Kavanagh's poetry, but I see why Heaney, in his early days, found it inspiring. Kavanagh's poems make the most of their origin in rural Ireland, a few acres of Monaghan as penurious as any in the island. The poems issue in a voice I don't find especially secure, but at least it doesn't sound like anything Lady Gregory heard in her drawing room at Coole Park. I can understand, then, why Heaney feels grateful to Kavanagh and continues to recognise a master by surpassing him. Kavanagh's poems speak to Heaney from the double vantage of rural piety and rural cunning; but Heaney has also put himself to school with greater masters—Shakespeare, Wordsworth, Hardy, Hopkins, Yeats, Frost, and Eliot. In the past few years he has turned to Dante and translated some cantos of the *Divine Comedy*. So he is in no danger of yielding his rhetoric to Kavanagh's.

Sweeney Astray is a version—for the moment call it that, rather than a translation—of *Buile Suibhne* (Sweeney's Frenzy), an Irish poem written sometime between the years 1200 and 1500, in the period between late Middle-Irish and early Modern-Irish. The poem recites the adventures of Suibhne Geilt, son of Colman Cuar, and king—or at least lord—of Dal Araidhe, the northern half of County Antrim. His adventures began when he drove out of his lands one Ronan Finn, a priest, who was marking out a place to build a church. Ronan cursed Suibhne and called upon God to afflict him with many evils. At the battle of Magh Rath— the present Moira—Suibhne went mad, driven wild by the horrors of the battle. By Ronan's curse he was changed into a bird, and forced to live a miserable life in exile from his home, his wife, and every domestic satisfaction. In the end, he is restored to himself and reconciled to Christianity through the ministry of the priest Moling. Killed by the throw of a spear, as Ronan ordained, he receives a Christian burial.

The lore from which the poem arose is as early as the ninth or tenth century. There are three independent manuscripts. The most important one was probably written between 1671 and 1674; another probably in 1721–1722; and the third, the earliest but not the best, in 1629. J. G. O'Keeffe, who edited and translated the poem for the Irish Texts Society in 1913, settled upon the 1671–1674 one for his copy-text. It is a mixture of narrative passages in prose and lyrical sections in verse: the verse mostly Suibhne's lament for his lost greatness, or his rueful sense of the life available to him as a bird. One lyric section of extraordinary power invokes the order of nature which has replaced, for Suibhne, the order of society and fellowship.

Much of the sentiment of the poem arises from the conflict between pagan and Christian values in early Ireland, a theme dear to many writers including Yeats, Austin Clarke, and Frank O'Connor. Heaney makes much of Sweeney's—we can call him that now—association with the North of Ireland, the west of Scotland, and in the end the South of Ireland. Tact prevents him from making anything of the association between Sweeney and himself, two poets beset—in Suibhne's case driven to fury if not to madness—by the horrors of war in the North of Ireland. Heaney emphasises rather the significance of Sweeney as an artist, at odds with a society to the pitch of frenzy.

Sweeney Astray follows O'Keeffe's edition of the poem, but it omits a few transitional or repetitive passages, shortens a few more, and turns two or three prose passages into verse. Heaney has been concerned to remain true to the spirit of *Buile Suibhne* rather than to its letter. He hasn't even tried to reproduce the elaborate metres of the Irish text, or its particular reverberations. Near the beginning, for instance, a passage in prose describes Sweeney going mad at Moira. O'Keeffe's translation reads:

> . . . his weapons fell naked from his hands, so that through Ronan's curse he went, like any bird of the air, in madness and imbecility.

The Irish reads:

> rotuitset a airm urnocht asa lamhuibh co ndeachaidh la breithir Ronain ar gealtacht agus ar geinidecht amail gach n-ethaid n-aeerdha.

Heaney's version doesn't try to retain the internal alliteration of "ar gealtacht agus ar geinidecht"—in madness and imbecility:

> *the weapons fell from his hands*
> *and he levitated in a frantic cumbersome motion*
> *like a bird of the air.*
> *And Ronan's curse was fulfilled.*

I don't see where Heaney has found the frantic cumbersome motion. It is neither in the Irish nor in ornithology: the next line has Sweeneybird skimming over the grasses "so lightly he never unsettled a dewdrop."

Buile Suibhne is a difficult poem. It is my impression that Heaney found it, line by line, hard to deal with. Many of his prose passages are far prosier than the Irish. How do you translate into English a work in prose and verse which developed in some rambling fashion over several centuries of Irish expression, oral and written? Heaney has chosen to stick to the common style of his own lyric poems for his copy-text, but to include archaic words from time to time. The problem is that some crucial words in the English lack the force of the Irish. "Astray" doesn't, even in the North of Ireland, have the force of "ar buile," which means frenzied. In the North, I remember, we said that someone was "astray in the head," meaning daft or simpleminded: not the same ailment. I don't know what readers outside Ireland will make of such words as "rath" and "erenach," though recourse to the O.E.D. will discover "cantreds" and "scuts." Those who know John Crowe Ransom's poems will have no problem with Heaney's "thole." In the passage I've quoted, "levitated" is a respectable seventeenth-century word, though it sounds modern. But I'm not persuaded by Heaney's version of "roclodhadh a chedfadha." O'Keeffe gives "his senses were overcome," which is sound enough, but Heaney gives "his senses were mesmerized," which is too modern, an early-nineteenth-century word coined in reference to Dr. Mesmer (1734–1815).

Heaney comes into his own eloquence when the Irish poem sets him free in ways we have known since *North* and his earlier books. When Sweeney comes back to rebuke his faithless wife, Eorann, she sweet-talks, saying that she'd like to be like him, a bird, and fly away with him. I wish, she says, that we were together, and that feathers would grow on our bodies—"co ttigeadh clumh ar ar ttaobh"—"in light and darkness I would wander with you ever day and night." Heaney's version warms it more:

> *I wish we could fly away together,*
> *be rolling stones, birds of a feather:*

I'd swoop to pleasure you in flight
and huddle close on the roost at night.

It's beautiful, though it's hard to think of rolling stones now without
striking against the other Rolling Stones.

I gather we haven't heard the last of Heaney's Sweeney. He has been
secreting new poems as if in his own voice. I assume that Sweeney will
hold the place in Heaney's poetry that Crazy Jane holds in Yeats's,
speaking out of rage or frenzy against orthodoxies too pious to be borne.

The New Republic, 30 April 1984.

NOTES

WE IRISH

1. William Butler Yeats, *Explorations* (London: Macmillan, 1962), 451.
2. Ibid., 451.
3. Ibid., 423.
4. *The Senate Speeches of W. B. Yeats,* ed. Donald R. Pearce (London: Faber and Faber, 1961), 172.
5. William Butler Yeats, *Essays and Introductions* (London: Macmillan, 1961), 402.
6. Yeats, *Explorations,* 333–4.
7. Alexander Campbell Fraser, *The Life and Letters of George Berkeley* (Oxford: Clarendon Press, 1871), 500–1.
8. J. M. Hone and M. M. Rossi, *Bishop Berkeley.* With an Introduction by William Butler Yeats (London: Faber and Faber, 1931), 29.
9. Yeats, *Essays and Introductions,* 409.
10. Ibid., 405.
11. *Poetry Book Society Bulletin* 85 (Summer 1975).
12. Seamus Deane, "A Noble, Startling Achievement," *The Irish Literary Supplement* (Spring 1985): 34.
13. Seamus Heaney, *Station Island* (New York: Farrar, Straus & Giroux, 1985), 33.

14. Leon Wieseltier, "A Revelation," *The New Republic* (May 20, 1985): 33.
15. Marsh's Library Mss. Z.3.25, 312, No. 79, quoted in Caroline Robbins, *The Eighteenth-Century Commonwealthman* (Cambridge: Harvard University Press, 1959), 146.
16. Berkeley, *Works,* ed. A. A. Luce and T. E. Jessop (London: Nelson, 1953), 6:112.

YEATS: THE QUESTION OF SYMBOLISM

1. William Butler Yeats, *Memoirs,* ed. Denis Donoghue (London: Macmillan, 1972), 36; cf. 87.
2. William Butler Yeats, *Autobiographies* (London: Macmillan, 1961), 193.
3. Yeats, *Memoirs,* 36.
4. Arthur Symons, *The Symbolist Movement in Literature* (London: Constable, 1911), v.
5. Ibid., 4.
6. Ibid., 8.
7. Ibid., 128.
8. Ibid., 129.
9. William Butler Yeats, *Essays and Introductions* (London: Macmillan, 1961), 163.

10. Hugh Kenner, "Some Post-Symbolist Structures," in *Literary Theory and Structure,* eds. Frank Brady, John Palmer, and Martin Price (New Haven: Yale University Press, 1973), 388.

11. Alfred North Whitehead, *Symbolism, Its Meaning and Effect* (Cambridge: Cambridge University Press, 1928), 9.

12. Yeats, *Essays and Introductions,* 156–7. Some of the following paragraphs draw upon material published in another form in my *Yeats* (London and New York: Macmillan, 1972).

13. Ibid., 79.

14. Ibid., 114.

15. Ibid., 50.

16. Ibid., 87.

17. Ernst Cassirer, *The Philosophy of Symbolic Forms,* trans. Ralph Manheim (New Haven: Yale University Press, 1953), 1:118.

18. William Butler Yeats, *Mythologies* (London: Macmillan, 1962), 359.

19. William Blake, *Complete Writings,* ed. Geoffrey Keynes (London: Oxford University Press, 1966), 526.

20. William Butler Yeats, *Uncollected Prose,* ed. John P. Frayne (London: Macmillan, 1970), 1:394.

21. Yeats, *Autobiographies,* 321.

22. William Butler Yeats, *A Vision,* 2d rev. ed. (London: Macmillan, 1962), 135–6.

23. Stéphane Mallarmé, *Poems,* trans. Anthony Hartley (Harmondsworth: Penguin Books, 1965), 165.

24. Yeats, *Autobiographies,* 193–4.

25. Ibid., 254.

26. William Butler Yeats, *Collected Poems* (reprint, London: Macmillan, 1952), 391.

27. Yeats, *Essays and Introductions,* 28.

28. Edmund Wilson, *Axel's Castle* (New York: Scribner's, 1936), 48.

29. Walter Pater, *Studies in the History of the Renaissance* (New York: Macmillan, 1919), 194.

30. Yeats, *Collected Poems,* 392.

31. Ezra Pound, *The Cantos* (London: Faber and Faber, 1954), 563.

32. D. H. Lawrence, *Collected Letters,* ed. Harry T. Moore (London: Heinemann, 1962), 1:302.

33. D. H. Lawrence, *Women in Love* (Harmondsworth: Penguin Books, 1960), 485.

34. James Joyce, *Ulysses* (reprint, London: Bodley Head, 1947), 34.

35. Charles Tomlinson, *Seeing Is Believing* (New York: McDowell, Obolensky, 1958), 49.

36. William Butler Yeats, *Letters on Poetry from W. B. Yeats to Dorothy Wellesley* (London: Oxford University Press, 1940), 135, letter of 4 May 1937.

37. William Butler Yeats, *Explorations* (London: Macmillan, 1962), 336.

YEATS, ANCESTRAL HOUSES, AND ANGLO-IRELAND

1. William Butler Yeats, *Memoirs,* ed. Denis Donoghue (London: Macmillan, 1972), 225–6.

2. Ibid., 230.

3. William Butler Yeats, *Explorations* (London: Macmillan, 1962), 345.

4. Ibid., 337.

5. J. B. Yeats, *Letters to His Son W. B. Yeats and Others,* ed. Joseph Hone (London: Faber and Faber, 1944), 189, letter of 30 August 1914.

6. Donald T. Torchiana, *W. B. Yeats and Georgian Ireland* (Evanston: Northwestern University Press, 1966), 312.

7. William Butler Yeats, *A Vision,* 2d rev. ed. (London: Macmillan, 1962), 268.

8. William Butler Yeats, *Collected Plays* (London: Macmillan, 1953), 683.

9. Yeats, *Explorations,* 441.

10. Arthur Young, *A Tour in Ireland* (Dublin, 1780), 2:40.

11. Ibid., 2:48.

12. Ibid., 2:30.

13. Ibid., 2:35.

14. Thomas Carlyle, *Reminiscences of My Irish Journey in 1849* (London, 1882), 223.

15. J. A. Froude, *The English in Ireland in the Eighteenth Century* (London, 1881), 584.

16. Standish O'Grady, *Selected Essays and Passages* (Dublin, 1918), 181. Quoted in Torchiana, 14.

17. R. P. Blackmur, *Form and Value in Modern Poetry* (New York: Doubleday, 1957), 52, 58.

18. John Crowe Ransom, *Poems and Essays* (New York: Vintage Books, 1955), 104–5.

19. Hugh Kenner, *A Colder Eye* (New York: Alfred A. Knopf, 1983), 45.

BAKHTIN AND *FINNEGANS WAKE*

1. Hugh Kenner, "Notes toward an Anatomy of 'Modernism,'" in *A Starchamber Quiry*, E. L. Epstein, ed. (New York and London: Methuen, 1982), 3–42.

2. Mikhail Bakhtin and V. N. Voloshinov, *Freudianism: A Marxist Critique,* trans. I. R. Titunik (New York: Academic Press, 1976), 38.

3. Tzvetan Todorov, *Mikhail Bakhtin: The Dialogical Principle,* trans. Wlad Godzich (Minneapolis: University of Minnesota Press, 1984), 60.

4. Julia Kristeva, *Desire in Language,* ed. Leon S. Roudiez (Oxford: Basil Blackwell, 1980), 14.

5. *Problems of Dostoevsky's Poetics,* trans. Caryl Emerson (Minneapolis: University of Minnesota Press, 1984), 229.

6. *The Dialogic Imagination: Four Essays by M. M. Bakhtin,* trans. Caryl Emerson and Michael Holquist (Austin, Texas: University of Texas Press, 1981), 27.

7. Ibid., 370.

8. *Problems of Dostoevsky's Poetics,* 129.

9. Katerina Clark and Michael Holquist, *Mikhail Bakhtin* (Cambridge: Harvard University Press, 1984).

10. James Joyce, *Finnegans Wake* (London: Faber and Faber, 1939), 432–3.

11. *Letters of James Joyce,* ed. Stuart Gilbert (London: Faber and Faber, 1957), 216.

12. John Crowe Ransom, "The Aesthetic of *Finnegans Wake,*" *Kenyon Review* 1 (Autumn 1939): 425–8.

13. Arthur Power, *Conversations with James Joyce,* ed. Clive Hart (London: Millington, 1974), 48.

14. Wallace Stevens, *Collected Poems* (London: Faber and Faber, 1955), 397.

15. R. P. Blackmur, *Form and Value in Modern Poetry* (New York: Doubleday, 1957), 216.

PERMISSIONS ACKNOWLEDGMENTS .

The following essays have been previously published:

"The Literature of Trouble" in *Hibernia*; "Bair's Beckett" in *Magill*; "Heaney's Sweeney" and "O'Casey in His Letters" in *The New Republic*; "Austin Clarke" in *The New Review*; "James Stephens," "Drums under the Window," and "*The Year of the French*" (originally titled "The Stains of Ireland") in *The New York Review of Books*; "Frank O'Connor" (originally titled "I've Another Little Story for You") in *The New York Times*; and "De Valera's Day" and "George Moore" in *The Spectator*.

Grateful acknowledgment is made to the following for permission to reprint previously published material:

Edward Arnold Ltd.: "On *The Winding Stair*" from *An Honored Guest: New Essays on W. B. Yeats*, edited by Denis Donoghue and J. R. Mulryne, 1965. Reprinted with permission of Edward Arnold Ltd.

Farrar, Straus & Giroux, Inc.: Excerpts from "Traditions," "Belderg," "Bone Dreams," "Kinship," and "Aisling" from *Poems 1965-1975* by Seamus Heaney. Copyright © 1966, 1969, 1972, 1975, 1980 by Seamus Heaney. Reprinted by permission of Farrar, Straus & Giroux, Inc.

John Hewitt: "Bogside Derry" from *Out of My Time: Poems by John Hewitt* (Blackstaff Press, Belfast, 1974). Reprinted by permission of the author.

Wilfred Laurier University Press: "Yeats: The Question of Symbolism" from *Myth and Reality in Irish Literature*, edited by Joseph Ronsley, 1977. Reprinted by permission of Wilfred Laurier University Press, Waterloo, Ontario.

The London Review of Books: "Synge in His Letters" (originally titled "Rembrandt and Synge and Molly"), "On the Text of Ulysses," "T. C. D.," "At Swim," and "Sean O'Faolain" were originally published in *The London Review of Books*.

Macmillan Publishing Company: "An Acre of Grass," excerpt from "The Circus Animals' Desertion," and an excerpt from "A Bronze Head" by William Butler Yeats. Copyright 1940 by Georgie Yeats, renewed 1968 by Bertha Georgie Yeats, Michael Butler Yeats and Anne Yeats. Excerpt from "Parnell's Funeral" by William Butler Yeats. Copyright 1934 by Macmillan Publishing Company, renewed 1962 by Bertha Georgie Yeats. Excerpts from "Coole Parke and Ballylee, 1931," "Vacillation," "Chosen," "Tom the Lunatic," "Quarrel in Old Age," "Crazy Jane on the Day of Judgment," "Stream and Sun at Glendalough," "A Last Confession," "Blood and the Moon," and "A Dialogue of Self and Soul" by William Butler Yeats. Copyright 1933 by Macmillan Publishing Company, renewed 1961 by Bertha Georgie Yeats. Excerpts from "Two Songs from a Play, II," and "Meditation in Time of Civil War" by William Butler Yeats. Copyright 1928 by Macmillan Publishing Company, renewed 1956 by Georgie Yeats. Excerpt from "The Second Coming" by William Butler Yeats. Copyright 1924 by Macmillan Publishing Company, renewed 1952 by Bertha Georgie Yeats. All poems reprinted with permission of Macmillan Publishing Company from *Collected Poems* by William Butler Yeats. Open market rights administered by A. P. Watt Ltd, London.

Sewanee Review: "Together" (originally titled "Being Irish Together") by Denis Donoghue from *Sewanee Review* 84, 1 (Winter 1976). Copyright 1976 by The University of the South. Reprinted with permission of the editor of *Sewanee Review*.

Colin Smythe, Ltd: "Romantic Ireland" from *Yeats, Sligo and Ireland*, edited by J. Norman Jeffares, 1980. Reprinted with the permission of Colin Smythe, Ltd.

Times Literary Supplement: "Pound/Joyce," "Another Complex Fate," "Castle Catholic," and "AE" were originally published in the *Times Literary Supplement*.